Anton Chekhov: A Life in Four Acts

Carol Rocamora

Books by Carol Rocamora:

Acts of Courage: Vaclav Havel's Life in the Theatre

Chekhov: The Early Plays

Chekhov: Four Plays

Chekhov: The Vaudevilles

"I take your hand in mine..." A new play suggested by the love letters of Anton Chekhov and Olga Knipper

Anton Chekhov: A Life in Four Acts

Carol Rocamora

Smith and Kraus Publishers 2013

ISBN: 978-1-57525-787-7
ISBN:1-57525-787-4
Library of Congress Control Number: 2012946605

Typesetting, layout, and cover design by Elizabeth E. Monteleone

A Smith and Kraus book

Printed in the United States of America

Acknowledgments

In the 1990s, while researching my translations of Chekhov's plays, I made several trips to Moscow. There, Anatoly Smeliansky, my host at the Moscow Art Theatre, introduced me to the photo archives of the Moscow Art Theatre, where I discovered many exciting photos of Chekhov. My thanks to Anatoly, and to the State Museum of Literature, for permission to include these photos in this book.

My thanks, too, to the Rockefeller Foundation, for supporting my residency at their study center in Bellagio in 2007, where I began work on this book.

My very special thanks to Janet Neipris and Richard Wesley in the Department of Dramatic Writing at NYU's Tisch School for the Arts, and Arnold Aronson at Columbia's MFA Theatre program, for providing me with a home where I can teach Chekhov. Thanks also to Zelda Fichandler, Larry Maslon and Mark Wing-Davey at NYU's Tisch School of the Arts, Rebecca Guy at the Juilliard School, and Ron Van Lieu at Yale School of Drama for inviting me to talk about Chekhov to their actors. The students' enthusiasm for the story of Chekhov's life in the theatre (told with photos and letters) has been the inspiration for this book.

Thanks also the many theatres that have produced my translations, including Arena Stage in Washington, DC, Classic Stage Company and Terry Schreiber Studio in New York, and the Orange Tree Theatre in London.

And, finally, thanks to Marisa Smith and Eric Kraus at Smith & Kraus Publishers for their shared passion for Chekhov and abiding commitment to my work.

for Jim, with all my love and gratitude

Contents

"Do you need my autobiography? All right, here it is. I was born in Taganrog in 1869. I graduated from Taganrog Grammar School in 1879. In 1884 I graduated from medical school at Moscow University. In 1888 I received the Pushkin prize. In 1890 I made a journey to Sakhalin across Siberia and returned by sea. In 1891, I completed a tour of Europe, where I drank excellent wine and ate oysters. In 1892 I had a good time at V. A. Tikhonov's name day party. I began to write for the journal 'The Dragon Fly' in 1879. My collected works are: 'Motley Stories', 'In the Twilight', 'Stories', 'Gloomy People', and a tale, 'The Duel'. I have also sinned in the realm of drama, although in moderation. I have been translated into all languages with the exception of foreign ones. However, I have already been translated into German, a long time ago. The Czechs and Serbs also approve of me, and the French don't think too badly of me, either. I experienced the mysteries of love at the age of thirteen. With my colleagues, both medical and literary, I remain on excellent terms. I am a bachelor. I would like a pension. I still practice medicine, to the extent that, in the summertime, I even perform an autopsy of two, although I haven't done one now in a couple of years. Among writers, my preference is Tolstoy, among doctors—Sakharin. However, all this is nonsense. Write whatever you life. If you have no facts, substitute something lyrical."

(Chekhov, letter to Tikhonov, February 22, 1892)

"AUTOBIOGRAPHY? I HAVE AN ILLNESS: AUTOBIOGRAPHOBIA. TO READ DETAILS ABOUT MYSELF, OR WORSE, TO WRITE ABOUT MYSELF FOR PUBLICATION, IS A TRUE ORDEAL FOR ME."

(Chekhov, letter to Orlov, October 11, 1899)

INTRODUCTION

In the early nineties, I made several trips to Russia to research Chekhov's plays. I was in the process of translating his complete dramatic work, as well as preparing to direct his four later masterpieces. So I wanted to know as much about the author as I could.

On the first trip, I visited his dacha in Melikhovo, about ninety miles southeast of Moscow, where he wrote *The Seagull and Uncle Vanya.* A modest, red-colored wooden building with white trim, it was hardly the estate that Chekhov boasted to have bought in 1892.

But as you wander through the charming rooms, covered with bright wallpaper, filled with family furniture and memorabilia, you sense the intoxicating perfume of Chekhov's plays between those walls. It was a lovely June day, filled with sunshine and sweet country air, and as you stroll around the lush green gardens, past the sparkling pond, into the beckoning woods, you imagine Chekhov's characters of *The Seagull* and *Uncle Vanya* doing just the same.

But that's not the point of my story.

In the study of the dacha, a curator was selling memorabilia, including a small collection of postcards featuring photos of Chekhov over various years of his short life. As I leafed through those postcards captioned with quotes from his correspondence to family and friends, one quote caught my eye, from a letter dated May 28, 1892: "Life is short," he wrote, "and Chekhov, whose reply you await, would like it to flash by brilliantly and brightly."

Standing in that study, surrounded by his personal effects—books, photos, writing desk, inkwell, a stand with walking sticks and straw hats—I was flooded with an impression of Chekhov and his brilliant, bright life. It's an impression that has stayed with me for many years.

Indeed, in his forty-four fleeting years on earth (1860-1904), many of which he spent as an invalid, Chekhov lived many lives. He was a short story writer, authoring over five hundred in his lifetime. He was a dramatist, completing seven full-length plays and eleven one-acts. He was a doctor, a humorist, a humanitarian, a human rights activist, a correspondent, a mentor, a literary theorist, and a Russian. The grandson of a serf, the son of a shopkeeper, the chief provider for his parents and five siblings, he played many roles.

For me, nothing since has told the story of that vibrant life more vividly and more vitally than that modest little series of postcards with the photos and the revealing quotations from his letters.

So when I returned to Moscow, I asked my friend Anatoly Smeliansky at the Moscow Art Theatre for access to the theatre's archives. Thanks to him and to the State Museum of Literature, I left Russia with a series of photos that tell the story of that life that flashed by so brilliantly and brightly.

Next, I went through Chekhov's letters in the original Russian, selected brief quotations that illuminate his life as a writer, and translated them. I then prepared a slide presentation with a photo for each year of his life, to show to the cast members of the productions I was directing, and later, to my students at New York University's Tisch School of the Arts, Columbia and Juilliard.

Each time I would make the presentation, the actors and students would ask for copies of these photos and quotations, saying that more than any literary criticism, these materials illuminated the plays for them. Looking at these photos in tandem with excerpts from his letters, they said, was like hearing Chekhov talk about his life and his plays in his own voice.

Buoyed by their enthusiasm, I kept excerpting more letters and adding more quotes.

And now thanks to Smith & Kraus, I have had the opportunity to expand these quotations and put them and the photos into a book, together with biographical narrative.

As you can imagine, once you start delving deeply into Chekhov's voluminous correspondence, you discover gold. Or, as Stanislavsky once said about Chekhov's words of wisdom about his plays: "diamonds." From the age of seventeen until his death at forty-four, Chekhov wrote over 4,000 letters to family, friends, writers, artists, colleagues in the theatre, and the *literati.* These letters are a literary treasure, and the richest single source available that provides an understanding of his life in the theatre and of the plays.

From the initial series of twenty five or more quotes, I've ended up translating hundreds of letters he wrote to dozens of family members, friends, publishers, editors, critics, fellow writers, actors, actresses, mentors and disciples. These letters contain informative, eloquent, revealing passages about his writing and his life in the theatre, with its frustrations, challenges, obstacles, failures, and triumphs. He wrote letters about being a writer and the process of writing. He wrote letters about the state of the contemporary Russian theatre. He wrote letters about the purpose of literary criticism. He wrote letters to younger writers, giving advice on how to write short stories. He wrote philosophical letters about art and literature. He wrote descriptive letters of his natural surroundings as he worked. Of greatest value, he wrote letters about his plays as he was writing them—about their source of inspiration, about his process, about his struggles and frustrations. When he was involved in a production, he described rehearsals, opening nights, the cast, and the audience and critical response. Later in his life in the theatre, he wrote to his directors and actors with suggestions and advice on how to direct and perform his plays.

Any letter I could find about the aforementioned, any detail, section or passage that would illuminate his life as a playwright and the world of his plays, I translated and included in this book.

Since this is a playwright who had many other identities, I've also included selected letters pertaining to other aspects of his life as well—about his work as a doctor and humanitarian, about his life in the countryside, and about his heroic struggle with a terminal illness. I've also included numerous personal letters to the young actress, Olga Knipper, who became his wife, as well as to other women with whom he was involved.

These letters add color and depth to the portrait of a remarkable and complex man and artist.

In summary, Chekhov's letters were more than communication between himself and others—they were the form wherein he developed his idea of the theatre. As his illness progressed, these letters became his primary mood of artistic and philosophical communication, and, toward the end of his life, his sole occupation. They are, in essence, his voice, his identity.

Together, the selected letters in this book create an autobiographical narrative—one that will provide a human portrait of the man himself and that will express, *in his own words,* the source of the plays in his life and imagination. The letters will shed light on these marvelous, mysterious plays for those who direct them, perform in them, produce them, read them, study them, attend them, and love them.

A note about my translations of Chekhov's letters: they are directly from the original Russian. At first, I only intended to translate and include excerpts from his letters pertaining to his life as a writer and his work in the theatre. Then I came to appreciate that, as in his short stories, there is a beauty and rhythm in the composition of Chekhov's letters. So I've left their structure intact, translating the frame of each letter, from salutation to signature. As for the content, in addition to the passages about writing and the theatre, the letters are overflowing with the rich and colorful detail of his everyday life, including everything from reports on the weather, news of the cholera epidemic, love interests, family problems, health issues, and a myriad of other topics. Discussions of art and literature might be followed by reports of visits to the dentist. Revelations of the gravity of his illness might be followed by shopping lists. The content is lively, engaging, moving, and deeply human. And there are always jokes, always. This rich, colorful content is part of the essential character of the letters and of the man, so I've included as much as I can, selectively.

To supplement these two tracks—photos and letters—I've added a third, namely, my own biographical narrative. For this, I acknowledge the many biographers who have written about Chekhov in the last half century. Ernest Simmons, Daniel Gilles, V. S. Pritchett, David Magarshak, Ronald Hingley, among others, have all offered fine studies of Chekhov's life. Of all of the biographical sources, Henri Troyat's *Chekhov* and Donald Rayfield's *Anton Chekhov: A Life* have been the most helpful resource for this book, along with Chekhov's own letters and the plays themselves. In his distinguished scholarly biography (1997), Mr. Rayfield has provided more detail on Chekhov's life than any other recent biographer in the English language. As for Mr. Troyat's *Chekhov* (1984/86), this lyrical account reveals that Chekhov's life can read like a novel, and a deeply moving one. Both these sources have been invaluable, as well as *Letopis zhizni I tvorchestva A. P. Chekhova* (*The Chronicle of A. P. Chekhov's Life and Work*), which gives a daily account of his activities. The memoirs of his contemporaries (including his brothers Aleksandr and Mikhail, Bunin, Gorky, Stanislavsky, Nemirovich-Danchenko), have also been extremely helpful.

About the format of this book. Chekhov's life divides itself naturally into four "acts", corresponding to the four and a half decades of his life:

Act I: Taganrog (1860-1879), where he spent his childhood and adolescence
Act II: Moscow (1880-1899) where he spent his years as a medical student and young doctor, began writing short stories, achieved recognition as a prose writer, and started writing plays
Act III: Melikhovo (1890 –1899), where he moved after a daring humanitarian trip to the island of Sakhalin, lived in the countryside, practiced medicine, and wrote his two mature plays, *The Seagull* and *Uncle Vanya*
Act IV: Yalta (1900-1904) where he retired as an invalid, wrote his two final plays, *The Three Sisters* and *The Cherry Orchard*, and lived until his death.

Within each of these four parts, or "acts", I've devoted a chapter, or "scene," year by year, of his life.

In addition to the three tracks of this book—photos, translated letters, and biographical narrative—I've included supplementary material, with the names and identities of most of Chekhov's correspondents included in this book.

In summary, I've sought to compress, in one volume, the information I found in dozens and dozens of sources over years of translating, directing, and teaching Chekhov's dramatic work—namely, the details and impressions from his life and letters that illuminate his plays and compose a portrait of a remarkable dramatist and human being.

While this book may not be uncovering any startling new facts about Chekhov's life, hopefully it provides (in one volume) the essential information to illuminate the journey for those who work in the theatre, who love dramatic literature, and who are, like me, *"na puti k Chekhovu"* ... "on the road to Chekhov".

Carol Rocamora
January 2013

Act One: *Taganrog*

"In my childhood, I had no childhood..."

(Chekhov, from Aleksandr's memoirs)[1]

1860—1869

"My father began to educate me, or, to put it more simply, to beat me, before I reached the age of five. He thrashed me with a cane, he boxed my ears, he punched my head. Every morning as I awoke, my first thought was: 'Will I be beaten today'?"
(Chekhov, in "Three Years," 1895)

"Despotism and lies ruined our childhood to the extent that it's sickening and frightening even to think about it. Remember the horror and revulsion we felt in those days when Father threw a fit at the dinner table over too much salt in the soup and called Mother a fool? How can he be forgiven?"
(Chekhov, letter to his brother Aleksandr, January 2, 1889, Moscow)

"What a miserable lot we are! All our friends rest, run around, play, visit one another, and meanwhile we must go to church."
(Chekhov, letter to his brothers, from Aleksandr's memoirs)[2]

"In my childhood, I received a religious education and upbringing—choir singing, reading the apostles and psalms in church, attending matins regularly, plus altar boy and bell-ringing duties. And the result? When I think back on my childhood, it seems quite gloomy to me. I have no religion now. When my two brothers and I would sing the trio 'Let my prayer arise' or 'The Archangel's voice" in church, everyone looked at us and was moved. They envied my parents, while we felt like little convicts...There may have been joy in their souls, but they were a lot happier than my brothers and me. For us, childhood was a misery."
(Chekhov, letter to his friend Leontyev-Shcheglov, March 9, 1892, Melikhovo)

It was cold in the shop—so cold that he couldn't stop shaking, sitting on the upturned end of a soap crate, huddled at the counter. And the lone candle provided no warmth—on the contrary, as it sputtered, it shed light on the grimness of the scene.

Nine-year-old Antosha was doing his father's bidding—toiling after school in his father's general store while he was out on business. "But father, I have my lessons to do," he pleaded, clutching his Latin Grammar. "Never mind," his father threatened, his towering figure looming over him, "You can do your lessons in the shop." Little Antosha didn't dare to disobey him. So there he sat into the night, his pen stuck into the inkstand now frozen like ice, shivering through his flimsy school overcoat and worn-out galoshes, wondering how he could prepare for his Scripture lesson the following day.[3]

The shop, adjacent to the family home, was dank and dark. It sold everything from bread, tea, and coffee to vodka and wine. The shelves were crammed with sugar, soap, candles, face cream, castor oil, perfume, olives, rice, oil, vegetables, household items, and even medicines. His father also employed two errand boys without wages (and taught them to short-change the customers and pass off spoiled goods as fresh). Sometimes, his father even had Antosha stand outside with the shop boys, soliciting customers.

That miserable scene would repeat itself night after night throughout his childhood. Anton Pavlovich Chekhov (his family called him "Antosha") the third child of Pavel and Yevgenia, was born on January 17, 1860. He grew up with his five brothers and sister in the muddy, backward, provincial town of Taganrog in the south of Russia, on the northeast shore of the Azov Sea.

The Chekhov family had its origins in serfdom. Anton's paternal grandfather, Yegor (1798-1879), had been a born a serf in the Voronezh province in Southern Russia, halfway between Moscow and the Black Sea, on the edge of the steppes. Ambitious, determined and hard-working, Yegor became manager of his master's sugar beet refinery, and even learned to read and write. In 1841, he had saved up 3,500 rubles, which he offered to his master in return for the freedom of his family. The price at the time was 700 rubles a head, and Yegor had a wife, three sons, and a daughter—a total of six family members. The 3500 rubles would cover only five. So the master offered to give the little girl her liberty as a bonus.

Upon receiving his freedom, Anton's grandfather took his family three hundred miles south. There Yegor became an estate manager to Count Platov, forty miles north of the town called Taganrog. With high hopes for his three sons to rise in status, he apprenticed them and taught them to work hard. Pavel, the second son, worked in a sugar-beet factory, then for a cattle herder, and then as a shop assistant to a merchant in Taganrog. Yegor was hard on his sons. He flogged them for any small misdemeanor—such as picking apples, or falling off a roof they were mending. He beat his son Pavel so hard that the child developed a hernia. Later, Chekhov would write about Yegor: "I have a hot-tempered, testy nature… After all, my grandfather was a slave-driving serf."[4]

Anton's father Pavel was a stern, severe figure, feared by all. He received no formal schooling, but he could read, and a church cantor taught him to read music and to play the violin. He had artistic abilities, but chose instead to be a pious, observant, religious man.

Anton's mother Yevgenia also came from a serf background, and her family had slowly migrated into the merchant class. She was a shy, withdrawn woman. Pavel and Yevgenia married in 1854. Dominated by her severe husband, she lived in his shadow.

Pavel Chekhov had inherited his serf-father's steely determination to succeed. His passions were to achieve status in the merchant community and at church—and he mercilessly shackled his children to both purposes. Anton and his brothers learned life lessons, growing up in that grocery store. The shop was open from 5 a.m. till 11 p.m. at night, and the children were pressed into service soon after they came home from school, long into the evening. As a youngster, Anton made change, served vodka, stocked supplies and watched his father deceive his customers. Once, when a rat drowned in a barrel of oil, he stood by, dismayed, as his father removed the creature, sent for a priest to bless the barrel, and continued to sell the product. Often, Anton would fall asleep in his clothes, exhausted.

If Anton and his brothers displeased his father in any way, he would not hesitate to beat them. Smacks on the face, cuffs on the neck, and floggings were meted out on a regular basis. "They'll be grateful," said Anton's father, who instructed his sons to kiss his hand after every beating, just as he had been instructed by his own father who beat him. Then he would take the children to church and force them to read a certain number of pages from the book of Psalms. His helpless mother's meek protestations were ignored. "One beaten man is worth two unbeaten ones," he would tell her. Having given birth to six children in ten years (Aleksandr, Nikolai, then Anton in 1860; followed by Maria, Ivan and Mikhail), Yevgenia suffered from chronic exhaustion. Unable to placate her husband's fiery temper or to defend her children, she sank deeper and deeper into depression. She never recovered from the loss of her seventh child, a baby girl, when Anton was eleven. While Masha (Maria), the only daughter, was spared this cruel daily occurrence, the boys were all traumatized for life by these merciless beatings. As for the children's friends who came to visit, as soon as Pavel Chekhov would enter the house they would flee in terror (Once, Pavel was even called before the municipal magistrate for excessive beating).

Pavel's priorities for his children were religion, education, and work. He was pious and fastidious in his observation of family name days, church feasts and holidays, especially Easter. Pavel became active in a Russian orthodox congregation that held its services in a Greek monastery. There he formed a choir, and, determined to maintain an upright image in the community, forced his three eldest sons (Aleksandr, Nikolai and Anton) to sing in the soprano and alto sections. The boys were dragged from their beds for early services before school, and then would rehearse all evening in the shop, under a choirmaster who would thrash them. On Sunday mornings, Pavel might awaken them as early as three in the morning to practice, after which they would march to church for compulsory participation to satisfy their father's need to impress the other congregants. "We felt like little convicts," Anton later wrote.[5] Later, doctors blamed the ill health of these three Chekhov boys on this grueling schedule, not to mention the frequent cruel thrashings at their father's hand. The latter, according to Aleksandr, the eldest son, more than anything, scarred them all for life. "What an unfortunate lot we are!" Aleksandr remembers his brother Anton saying. "All our friends rest, run around, play visit one another, and meanwhile we must go to church."[6]

Taganrog was a rough town, with a market square where convicted criminals were brought and given public sentencing. Anton and his older brothers learned to navigate it, and in their spare time (of which there was precious little) lived a "boys' life," catching fish in the smuggler's bay, trapping and selling finches, and avoiding roving convict gangs.

As for his early education, at the age of eight Chekhov first attended the parish school attached to the Greek Church of King Constantine. It was a one-room schoolhouse with long wooden benches. Anton was at first a mediocre student. He irritated the school-master by telling jokes and distracting his fellow pupils. After one year there, Pavel enrolled the boys in the Taganrog public school system, where Anton spent the next eleven years. Their new school provided a safe haven from home for Anton and his siblings, as physical punishment was strictly forbidden there. The Chekhov brothers soon discovered that hardly any of their classmates suffered beatings at home, and came to understand that their father's practice of physical punishment emanated from his cruel personality, rather than from a societal norm. Moreover, the school was an encouraging environment, providing students from poor or merchant class backgrounds (like the Chekhovs) with an opportunity for upward mobility. The quality of education was conservative and classical, teaching both Greek and Latin (and restricting Russian literature as potentially subversive). Ever ambitious for his sons to excel, Anton's father supplemented their education with music and French lessons at home.

During the first decade of his life, Anton, docile and submissive, learned how to survive. Even as he endured the punishing routine of days in school, evenings in his father's shop, frequent beatings, nights of choir practice, and Sunday mornings of religious services, he dreamed of freedom from the miseries and tedium of daily life.

"If only I would pass my matriculation exams, I'd fly to Moscow on wings."

(Chekhov, letter to cousin Mikhail, November 4, 1877)

1870—1879

"Dearest Brother Misha:

May I make a request...? Could you please kindly continue to comfort my mother? She's physically and morally beaten down. To her, you are more than just a nephew, much more. ... Sounds like a foolish request, doesn't it? But you'll soon understand, especially since I'm asking for 'moral' - meaning spiritual - support. In this cold, cruel world, who can be dearer to us than one's mother, and therefore you'll oblige your humble servant by comforting my poor mother, who is more dead than alive. Let us carry on a good correspondence, then. [...]

Your brother, A. Chekhov"

(Chekhov, letter to cousin Mikhail Mikhailovich, April 10, 1877, Moscow)

"Dear Brother Misha:

Here in Taganrog there is no news—absolutely none! It's deadly dull here! I went to the Taganrog theatre recently, and compared it with your Moscow theatre. What a difference! Just as there is a great difference between Moscow and Taganrog. If only I would pass my matriculation exams, I'd fly to Moscow on wings. I love Moscow so much! Write to me when you have time; I'll be grateful...

Your brother, A. Chekhov"

(Chekhov, letter to cousin Mikhail, November 4, 1877, Taganrog)

"Dear Brother Misha:

I received your letter when my terrible boredom was at its peak....

Get into the habit of reading. In time, you'll come to treasure it. Did Madame Beecher-Stowe bring tears to your eyes? I read the book some months ago for educational purposes and after finishing it I experienced the unpleasant sensation that mortals feel when they stuff themselves with raisins or currants.... Read the following book: 'Don Quixote.' A great work. It's by Cervantes, who is believed to be almost on the same level as Shakespeare. I advise all our brothers to read Turgenev's 'Hamlet and Don Quixote' if they haven't done so yet. You, my boy, will not understand it... Give Masha a special greeting from me. . Don't worry if I come in a while. Time flows fast, no matter how much you brag of boredom.

A. Chekhov"

(Chekhov, letter to his cousin Mikhail, April 5 or later, 1879, Taganrog)

"Gracious readers and listeners:

I am in Taganrog...The town of Taganrog gives the impression of a Herculaneum or a Pompeii...All the houses are flat and haven't been stuccoed in ages; the roofs are unpainted, the shutters are closed...Starting at Police Street the road is filled with mud that, once it has dried, turns into a bumpy bog ...

[...] Continuing across the New Bazaar, I realized how dirty, empty, sluggish, illiterate, and dull Taganrog really is. There isn't one single sign without a spelling error—I even saw one saying "Rahssia Tavern.' The streets are empty except for some smug stevedores and dandies standing around in caps and long coats... There is a pervasive sense of idleness, contentment with a few kopecks and an uncertain future. Clearly it's so repulsive here that in comparison I'd take Moscow any day with its dust and dirt and typhoid fever ... "

(Chekhov, letter to his family, April 7, 1887, Taganrog)

"Dear Nikolai Aleksandrovich:

...Everything here in Taganrog is so Asiatic that I can't believe my eyes. Sixty thousand inhabitants and all they do is eat, drink, and reproduce; they have no other interests whatsoever... Wherever you go, all you see is Easter cake, eggs, Santorini wine, and babies; not a newspaper or a book in sight...no patriots, no businessmen, no poets, not even a decent baker. [...]

Yours, A. Chekhov"

(Chekhov, letter to his publisher Leikin, April 7, 1887, Taganrog)

In face of the miseries of his childhood, the young Anton discovered that he had one antidote—his sense of humor. This attribute was publicly acknowledged by one of his teachers at the public school where Anton's parents had enrolled him at the age of eight. He was soon recognized by his teachers and classmates for his astonishing ability to regale them with humorous stories. And he loved playing practical jokes on friends and family alike.

At the age of thirteen, he made a second discovery to help with his survival—the theatre. The first performance he ever saw at the local municipal Taganrog theatre was Offenbach's operetta *La Belle Helene*—and he was immediately enamored. But students could only attend with permission of the headmaster, who heartily disapproved of the theatre, as did his father. Anton and his friends soon got around this obstacle by dressing themselves in their fathers' overcoats to gain admission. High up in the gallery, thrilled, he looked down on productions of *Hamlet*, the Russian classics (including Griboyedov's *Wit Works Woe* and Gogol's *The Inspector General*), operas and operettas. His delight in the theatre was intensified by the machinations needed to gain admission.

At home, Anton organized parlor theatricals to dissipate the atmosphere of tension and dread. Every evening after supper, he would regale his parents and siblings with impersonations (his rendition of a deacon taking an examination was the family's favorite). He assembled his own theatre company, consisting of his brothers and sister, and together they would perform skits he had authored himself. He was invited to a friend's house where amateur dramatics were performed, and wrote vaudevilles—comedic skits and popular entertainment of the day—for their gatherings. Mikhail, his youngest brother, recalled in his memoirs what an excellent actor Anton was. He used to disguise himself so well that even his family members wouldn't recognize him. Mikhail remembers that once Anton dressed as a beggar and walked through the town of Taganrog to deliver a letter to his Uncle Mitrofan's house. Completely fooled by the disguise, his uncle thanked him for the letter and gave him three kopeks for his efforts.

At fourteen, Anton started composing humorous limericks for the school magazine. At fifteen, he plunged into writing and editing his own humorous journal called *The Stutterer*, which he circulated amongst his friends. These efforts gave him popularity with his classmates, as well as admiration from his brothers.

During the summers, Anton found another escape from the tyranny of his home life—the Russian countryside. Visiting his grandparents on the steppes gave him an indelible impression of primitive Russian country life that he would immortalize in his later short stories. Fishing with his brothers in the nearby rivers, roaming the countryside, swimming on the shores of the Azov Sea, all provided relief and respite.

At fifteen, Anton contracted peritonitis (an inflammation of the abdominal lining). The school doctor treated him with such compassion that Anton vowed to become a doctor himself. That same year, his older brothers Aleksandr and Nikolai escaped paternal tyranny and fled to Moscow—Aleksandr (who had been a star student in Taganrog) to study mathematics, Nikolai to paint. They supported themselves as copyists. Now the oldest child in the Chekhov household, Anton became the brunt of his father's rages.

A dramatic turning point in his young life came at the age of sixteen. His father Pavel had plunged the family further and further into debt; there were weeks when Anton could not attend school, as his father couldn't pay the fees. At last, Pavel was forced to declare bankruptcy. Fearing prison, Pavel stole out of the family home one night by cart, avoiding the local train station, to evade his creditors. The cart took him to the steppe, where the Moscow train made its first stop. There Pavel boarded a train to Moscow, leaving his wife, Anton, and the three younger siblings behind. His destitute wife Yevgenia was forced to forfeit the family home to pay their debts.

So at sixteen Anton became the *de facto* head of the destitute Chekhov household, dealing with debtors, selling off the family furniture, caring for his mother and his younger siblings, Masha, Ivan, and Mikhail. Soon Pavel sent for his mother, Masha, and Mikhail. They paid their way to Moscow with proceeds from selling the household goods and from Anton's tutoring. Meanwhile, Ivan moved to a widowed aunt's house, so Anton was now on his own. But Anton did not despair. Here was newfound freedom and relief from paternal tyranny.

He was given a corner to sleep in the family home, which now belonged to their former boarder. Later he moved to board with a family of a child he had tutored. Hungry, penniless, bootless, he continued to give lessons to support himself and spent hours in the local library, reading voraciously. He devoured works of Turgenev, Belinsky, Victor Hugo, Cervantes, and Schopenhauer. He read

Hamlet and *Macbeth, Faust* and *Crime and Punishment*. Heretofore a mediocre student, his marks at school soared. He excelled in the subject of religion, and was teasingly called "Pious Antosha'. After school, he acted in amateur theatricals. He continued to attend the theatre, and saw a production of *Uncle Tom's Cabin*.

He eagerly read the popular humorous journals of the day from Moscow—with colorful names like the *Dragonfly*, *Alarm Clock*, and *Fragments*. If *The Stutterer*, his own journal, was such a success, why couldn't he write for them, too, he wondered. Soon he began to write comedic sketches with names like "He Met His Match," "Diamond Cut Diamond," "Why the Hen Cackled," "The Clean-shaven Secretary with the Pistol," and "The Nobleman"—which he sent off to Moscow, begging his brothers to submit them to the journals.

On other fronts, he sought the company of young ladies ("I experienced the mysteries of love at the age of thirteen," he later reported.). He tasted freedom as he never had before, and expressed his newfound joy in letters he wrote to his Moscow cousin Mikhail Chekhov.

When he was seventeen, his brother Aleksandr sent a train ticket for Anton to visit the family in Moscow. Anton was unprepared for the destitute conditions in which his family lived—all of them in one room, sleeping on the same mattress together on the floor. His mother wore a threadbare man's coat, and did sewing during the day to earn a few kopeks; his sister Masha stayed at home (there was no money to send her to school) to clean house and care for the family. His older brothers Aleksandr and Nikolai were leading a dissolute lifestyle, drinking and womanizing. Meanwhile, Pavel justified his state of unemployment by continuing to maintain a tyrannical rule over the household and declaring that it was now time for the children to support the parents. Finally, after almost a year and a half of unemployment, Pavel was hired as a store clerk in Moscow, and lived on the warehouse's premises during the week, to his sons' great relief.

Anton returned once again to Taganrog to complete his public school education, convinced that it was now his responsibility to save his family from the depths to which they were sinking. He was enamored with Moscow, and above all with the theatre. Inspired, he dashed off a farce ("The Scythe Strikes the Stone") and a full-length drama, *Fatherlessness* (*Bezotsovshchina*), a title that appropriately reflected his last few years in Taganrog). He sent these manuscripts to his brother Aleksandr in October 1878, who read them and responded to Anton, criticizing the farce as shallow and the full-length play as naïve. None of his early dramatic attempts from this period have survived, so their contents remain unknown. The title of the full-length effort, however, suggests that the specter of paternal tyranny continued to haunt Anton after Pavel Chekhov left Taganrog.

In May 1879, he passed his final examinations, excelling in religion, geography, French and German, attendance and "behavior," and doing only passably in mathematics, physics and natural sciences, the subjects most relevant for medicine. In June, he graduated from public school and received his diploma. He soon received word of his acceptance to medical school in Moscow, supported by a local scholarship. His official change-of-residency permit read as follows: height—six feet, one inch; hair and eyebrows—light brown; eyes—brown; nose/mouth/chin—average; face—elongated; complexion—fair; distinguishing features—scar on forehead under hair; class: petit bourgeois. He was nineteen years old.

On August 6, Anton Chekhov boarded a train to join his family once more, this time for good. "To Moscow!," his dream for the past three years, would become a reality. Years later, looking back on his childhood in Taganrog, he would later write:

> *"Write a story about me: how a young man, the son of a serf, a former shopkeeper, a choir-boy, a school boy, taught to respect rank, to kiss the priests' hands, to worship strange thoughts, to be thankful for his daily bread—a young man who appreciated a frequent beating, went to school without boots, fought with his fists, teased little animals, loved to dine at rich relatives, played the hypocrite before God and his fellow man only to satisfy his sense of worthlessness—write how this young man is squeezing the slave out of himself, drop by drop, and one morning awakens and feels that slave's blood does not flow in his veins, but real human blood . . . "*[2]

Act Two: *Moscow*

"I want to live in Moscow forever!"

(Chekhov, letter to Kramaryov, May 8, 1881)

1880-1881

"Come to Moscow!!! I've fallen madly in love with Moscow! Once you come, you'll never leave! I want to live in Moscow forever. Come, and join the ranks of the literati. In Moscow you can earn 150 rubles a year as a writer, at least. And everything is so cheap! You can buy socks for a less than a kopek! And what patriotic spirit there is here!!! (Sigh....) They take every grain of sand, every pebble, and make it into a monument! Come!!!"
(Chekhov, letter to his friend Kramaryov, May 8, 1881, Moscow)

"Even if I love you a hundred thousand times more than I do, I want you to know that I will not accept any more insults from you, on principle or on any other grounds. And if you want to blame it on your usual excuse of 'not being accountable for your actions', then just remember that I know full well that being drunk doesn't give you the right to [...] on anyone else's head. 'Brother'—the word you used to try to frighten me as I left the battle scene—is one that I shall readily drop from my vocabulary whenever it is necessary, not because I am heartless but rather because one must be prepared for anything in this world. I fear nothing, and I advise my own brothers to follow my example."
(Chekhov, letter to his older brother Aleksandr, March 6 or after, 1881, Moscow)

Arriving in Moscow, Anton was horrified to find his family continuing to live in unspeakable conditions. Having already moved twelve times since their arrival three years previous, they now were installed in a one room basement flat in the middle of the red-light district, ten people (including three lodgers) crammed into one small, dark space living in poverty and hopeless disarray. With their father absent, his older brothers had adopted a bohemian way of life. Aleksandr, his brilliant older brother, an aspiring writer and part-time editor, was involved with a married woman and already showed signs of incipient alcoholism. Nikolai, a gifted painter and musician, also drank and slept till noon, and worked as an art teacher only sporadically. Ivan had failed his exams at school. Taciturn and irritable, he constantly fought with his mother and upset the family. There was not enough money to send Mikhail and Masha to school, so they attended sporadically. Yevgenia, Chekhov's mother, took in washing, and Masha cooked in neighbors' houses.

At nineteen, Anton quickly took a leadership role. Taking the situation in hand, he moved his family to larger quarters, scraped together enough funds to send Mikhail and Masha back to school, and sternly advised his older brothers to mend their ways. He encouraged Ivan to apply himself to his studies, and find work as a teacher. Anton himself plunged into his first year of medical studies.

Meanwhile, to provide income for the household, Anton wrote sketches and anecdotes and submitted them to various humorous magazines. After a number of rejections, in January 1880, he was notified by *The Dragonfly*, one of the publications, that one of his sketches (called "A Don Landowner's Letter to a Learned Neighbor," a parody of his father and grandfather) was to be published. Imagine the elation in the Chekhov household when they heard the news that Anton would be paid 5 kopeks a line! (A kopek was valued at half an American penny at the time). The family celebrated by purchasing an enormous cake (they hadn't been able to afford one to celebrate his mother's birthday weeks before).

Still, his meager earnings as a writer were only one source in the family income. His brother Nikolai earned a little money for painting stage sets and portraits of the Tsar, and they continued to borrow from relatives. Money remained the chief preoccupation of the new *de facto* head of the Chekhov household, while he wasn't in the laboratory studying medicine.

Spurred on by his initial success as a writer, in dire need of the income to support his family, Anton dashed off little comic anecdotes whenever he could and sent them to whatever journal editor would read them. By the end of his first year of medical school, nine had already been published. His writing career had been launched, though at the time, this beleaguered medical student and family caretaker wasn't aware of it. Moreover, since he wrote under the *nom de plume* of "Chekhonte" (a name jokingly given to him by Father Pokrovsky, his religion teacher in Taganrog), his fellow classmates were completely unaware of his literary efforts, as well as the huge economic burden this young medical student shouldered.

Later on, looking back on this chapter of his life, he would write: "I was terribly corrupted by having been born, raised, educated, and then having started writing in an atmosphere in which money played a disgracefully enormous role."[1]

"I'LL IMMERSE MYSELF IN MEDICINE... IT'S MY SALVATION"

(Chekhov, letter to Aleksandr, May 13, 1883)

The study of medicine continued to be Anton's primary focus during 1881. He applied himself diligently, and kept a polite distance from fellow students engaged in protest activities against the government.

Then came the news that Tsar Aleksandr II was assassinated. While his classmates attended rallies protesting the repressive policies of the Tsar's successor, Aleksandr III, Anton would look on occasionally, remaining on the margin of activism and detached from any revolutionary sentiments. Instead, an innate belief in the individual as the instrument of social change—as he would later call it—had begun to develop in him, one which found affirmation in his medical studies.

At the same time, Anton was invited to become a contributor to a new weekly magazine, *The Spectator*. His brothers soon joined him there—Aleksandr as an editorial secretary, Nikolai as an artist, and Mikhail as an office assistant after school. They would soon refer to it as the "brothers' club."

Living in Moscow afforded him the opportunity to indulge in his passion—going to the theatre. In November, Sarah Bernhardt performed Dumas-fils's *La Dame aux Camelias* at the Bolshoi Theatre. He reviewed Sarah Bernhardt's appearance for one of the publications to which he contributed, and was irritated by the praise lavished upon her technique, which he found to be quite artificial. While Anton was critical of her histrionic performance, the celebrated actress nonetheless had a great impression on him. Many years later, she would become one of the sources of inspiration for the character Arkadina in his play *The Seagull*.

Stimulated by his immediate proximity to Moscow cultural life, he managed to dash off his second full-length play during the early winter months of the year, while living in impossibly cramped quarters. It was a huge, sprawling melodrama in five acts, and Anton enlisted his younger brother Mikhail to make a copy by hand. Mikhail remembers it as a cumbersome, overwritten work in the manner of a French melodrama, with everything from a railway train charging across the stage to horse thieving to a lynching scene. (Nonetheless, Mikhail wrote in his memoirs that he found it so exciting that it almost "stopped my heart."[2])

Anton had great ambitions for this rambling effort, according to Mikhail. As soon as the copy was finished, he sent it off sent it to Maria Yermolova, the leading lady of the preeminent Maly Theatre, with high hopes of securing a production and thereby making his dramatic debut in the Moscow Theatre. According to Mikhail, it was eventually returned to Anton with a rejection note. Crushed, Anton tore the manuscript to pieces, but his sister Masha had fortunately saved a second copy. The play was never performed during his lifetime.

There is, however, a dramatic postscript to the story. Masha, who became Chekhov's secretary and archivist in his later life, sequestered the manuscript away along with his other unpublished writings after his death. Years later, on the eve of the Russian revolution, Masha made a perilous journey from Yalta to Moscow—one that took three weeks—in the midst of the unrest and turmoil, to lock it away in a safe deposit box with Chekhov's other unpublished work, thus saving it for posterity.

After the revolution, a literary committee under the newly formed Soviet government broke into the safe deposit box and found a hand-written manuscript of a play, without a title page. So no one knows for certain the title Chekhov gave to this early work. Since its discovery, it has been adapted and performed under a variety of titles, including *That Worthless Fellow Platonov, A Play Without a Title, A Play Without a Name, Don Juan in the Russian Manner, A*

Country Scandal, Wild Honey (Michael Frayn's 1986 adaptation), but scholars often refer to it today as *Platonov*, after its protagonist.

The vastly simplified, distilled plot of the uncut *Platonov* is as follows: The young schoolmaster Platonov and his wife Sasha come to visit Anna Petrovna, a beautiful, impoverished widow, on her country estate, where she still attempts to live in style. Anna Petrovna's estate is about to be sold to pay off family debts. A coterie of friends and neighbors gather there for the summer solstice festivities of dancing and fireworks. The chief activity of the characters—apart from celebrating—is love-intrigue. In addition to his wife, Platonov has at least three women with whom he is involved: Sofya Yegorovna, the lovely young wife of Anna Petrovna's foolish step-son, Sergey; Grekova, a young chemistry student; and Anna Petrovna, his hostess. There are other colorful characters in this menagerie, including the lazy young Dr. Triletsky, his eccentric old father (a retired colonel), and a strange forest demon named Osip (a horse thief with a heart of gold), who is also in love with Anna Petrovna. During these days of summer madness, Platonov promises to run off with all of them, while his wife is barely rescued as she throws herself across the train tracks that pass by their cottage. Ultimately, Platonov meets a melodramatic fate.

In its original, unfinished, 134-page state, *Platonov* would have been, quite simply, unproduceable. With its five overly-long acts (the first act alone is the length of *Uncle Vanya*, one of his later, mature works), it would have played over seven hours, if staged. Its twenty characters and clumsy, immature structure—an interminable sequence of two character scenes, with hardly any ensemble—rendered it unwieldy and awkward. A hodge-podge of genres—romantic comedy, vaudeville, comedy of manners and morals, farce—with a sudden melodramatic shift and tragic ending, it revealed an inexperienced dramaturgical hand.

And yet, in this massive, disorganized, seminal work lay a treasure trove of source material for all Chekhov's later plays—locale, characters, themes, and tonalities. Its setting, a Russian country estate in the present, would serve as the setting for all his full-length plays to come. Its historical perspective—the fading world of the landed gentry, the ineffectiveness of the educated class, the alienation of the peasants, and the intractability of country life—

would provide the backdrop of all Chekhov's full-length dramatic work. Its numerous portrayals would serve as the prototypes of the characters to come—the impoverished lady of the estate, the oblivious landowner, the country doctor, the village schoolmaster, the emerging capitalist, the elderly eccentric, the ancient servant, the knavish lackey.

Of special note is the play's central character. In creating *Platonov*, the young Chekhov reveals both a reverence for literary tradition as well as a remarkable ambition. *Platonov* is a bold composite of numerous classical portraits from the European literature he had devoured in the Taganrog library—part Don Juan in his womanizing, part Hamlet in his brooding and inaction, part Byronic anti-hero—all with a Russian twist. *Platonov* is also a variant of several prototypes in the Russian literary tradition. One prototype is the "superfluous man" found in the literature of Pushkin, Lermontov, and Goncharov—a well educated Russian landowner who realizes that he is ineffectual, who cannot find a meaningful place for himself in society, who cannot effect any change, and who is frustrated that he could have been, as *Platonov* says, a "Christopher Columbus." Another prototype is Chatsky from Griboedov's satire *Wit Works Woe*, the nineteenth century Russian intellectual with a social conscience, railing at society's injustices, knowing he can do nothing to alter them.

Above all, it reveals in its young author a youthful flamboyance, a sense of adventure and a bold appetite for dramatic experimentation. Here are the first articulations of the many voices of Chekhov to come—the farcical, the comedic, and the melodramatic, all in one sprawling draft. Moreover, here is an articulated view of the times, in which the fledgling dramatist reveals a passion for his country, a sense of literary tradition, and a precocious insight into his world and its inexorable changes at the *fin de siecle*. *Platonov* was a flamboyant attempt to paint a large canvas of social and economic evolution in Russia at the end of the nineteenth century—as well as a prophecy for the future. The decay of the old social order, the rise of the new bourgeoisie, the naïve attempts at social reform, the gentry's ineffectiveness and gradual extinction—this was Russia in the 1880s, and this is the huge canvas that the ambitious young Chekhov boldly painted in *Platonov*.

Moreover, with his colorful character portrayals, the young

Dr. Chekhov already showed an intuitive understanding of human nature that would later distinguish him as one of the most astute observers of human behavior in dramatic literature.

But at the time, he had no awareness of what he had accomplished. Indeed, he was frustrated by the attempt to write his first full-length play in Moscow. He knew that he hadn't yet acquired the necessary craft. Smarting from the rejection, he set aside his ambitions, at least for the moment. He returned to writing anecdotes for humorous magazines, and by the end of the year thirteen of his anecdotes were published. He even received a raise—from five to six kopeks a line.

In July, Chekhov, his mother and younger siblings spent the summer in Voskresensk, a small village forty miles west of Moscow. Ivan, his dull, reliable younger brother, now eighteen, had found a teaching position at a local school, which provided him with housing enough to accommodate all the Chekhovs during the summer. Anton was enlisted by local doctors to help with the indigent peasant population suffering from malnourishment and disease.

During his second year of medical school, under the most adverse of circumstances and distractions—both personal and political—Anton had somehow found the time to sit down and write a new full-length play. He was determined to make his mark in the Russian theatre.

“There couldn’t be more vile conditions than these for a writer.”

(Chekhov, letter to his publisher Leikin, August 21-23, 1883)

1882 - 1883

“My customs-inspector brother Aleksandr!

...Nikolka is in Voskresensk with Masha, it’s Mishka’s name day, Father is sleeping, Mother is praying, Auntie is cooking, Anna is washing dishes and fetching the chamber pots, I’m sitting here writing and thinking: how many times tonight will I pay for the fact that I’m trying to write? I’m a student of medicine, after all... There are operations every day...

Farewell and goodbye.

A. Chekhov”

(Chekhov, letter to Aleksandr, November 8, 1882, Moscow)

“Most gracious sir, Nikolai Aleksandrovich:

In response to your kind letter I’m sending you several articles. I received your royalty, and also the journal—and I send you thanks for both. I further thank you for the extremely flattering invitation to continue contributing. I write for ‘Fragments’ with extreme pleasure. The guidelines of your publication, its appearance, and the way in which it is managed, will draw other writers as well, as it already has.

Yes, I, too am in favor of brevity, and if I were the editor of a humorous journal, I too would strike any verbosity.... At the same time, permit me to say that restrictions and cuts cause me great discomfort. At times it’s hard to deal with such restrictions... I have a topic. I sit down and write. The thought of “100 words and no more” gives me writers’ cramp from the onset. As a practice, I always tighten, as much as possible, cut, etc.—sometimes (according to my author’s whim) even to the detriment of the content and above all the form... More often than not I gnaw off the ending and end up submitting what I'd rather not have done...

To make a long story short, please enlarge my allotment to 120 lines. I'm sure that I'll rarely take advantage of this allowance, but the knowledge that I have the option will unblock me.

Accordingly, please receive the assurance of the respect and devotion of your most humble servant,

Ant. Chekhov"

(Chekhov, letter to his publisher Leikin, January 12, 1883, Moscow)

"Good Gavril Pavlovich:

...I'm living tolerably well, but my health is only so-so. I'm working like a lackey, going to sleep at 5 a.m. I write for the papers on assignment, and there's nothing worse than trying to meet the deadlines. I've got money. I eat well, I drink, I don't dress too badly, but there's not too much flesh on these bones! They say I've gotten so thin that you wouldn't recognize me. Now, as for women...[...]

I press your hand and remain your faithful servant, A. Chekhov or A. Chekhonte or M. Kovrov or A Man without a Spleen"

(Chekhov, letter to Kravtsov, January 29, 1883, Moscow)

My dear friend Sashenka:

[...] I'm becoming popular and have already been reading reviews of myself.

My doctoring is coming along. I know how to practice the art of medicine, and at the same time can't believe it myself. You can't name a single illness I couldn't treat. We have exams soon. If I make it into the 5th yr, it means 'finita la commedia'...

A. Chekhov"

(Chekhov, letter to Aleksandr, February 3-6, 1883, Moscow)

"Esteemed Nikolai Aleksandrovich:

[...] A work that is short and light can also have serious undertones and still be easy to read. To tell you the truth, chasing humor by the tail is hard work! At times you try to write something funny, and you end up with something

so stupid that it's sickening. So you naturally start turning more serious....

Ever in your service,

A. Chekhov"

(Chekhov, letter to Leikin, after April 17, 1883, Moscow)

"[...] I'm a journalist because I write a lot, but that's only temporary... I won't die one, believe me. If I go on writing it will be from afar, hidden away somewhere. Don't envy me. Writing gives me nothing, except for a bad case of nerves. The 100 rubles I get every month for it go right down my gullet. I can't even pawn my shabby old coat for something less decrepit. I dole it all out to everyone else, and there's nothing left for me. The family alone squanders more than fifty of it ...If I lived alone, I'd be a rich man...

[...] I'll immerse myself in medicine, it's my salvation... Although I still can't believe I'm a medical student"
(Chekhov, letter to Aleksandr, May 13, 1883, Moscow)

"Esteemed Nikolai Aleksandrovich:

...I'm writing to you under deplorable conditions. My medical books sit on my desk, staring at me reproachfully... In the neighboring room howls the child of a distant relative who is living with us now, in another room Father reads aloud to Mother from 'Angel of My Memory'... Someone has wound up a music box, and I hear 'La Belle Helene.' ... I feel like running away to the country, but it's already one in the morning... There couldn't be more vile conditions then these for a writer. My bed is occupied by a relative who has just arrived and keeps on trying to start a conversation with me about medicine. 'My daughter must be suffering from colic,' he tells me, 'that's why she keeps crying'. As you know, I have the misfortune of being a medical student, and there isn't a man alive who doesn't need to have a 'little chat' with me about medicine. And when they get tired, they change the subject to literature.

The conditions are not to be believed. I keep kicking myself for not having fled to the countryside where I could probably have had a good night's sleep, written a story for you, and above all pursue medicine and literature in peace.

I have the honor of remaining

A. Chekhov"

(Chekhov, letter to his publisher Leikin, August 21-24, 1883, Moscow)

"Esteemed Nikolai Aleksandrovich!

...The night before Christmas I wanted to write something, but couldn't. Instead, as fate would have it, I stayed up all night playing cards with the ladies. I played straight through to Mass, and was so bored I kept drinking vodka, which I do from time to time, though only out of boredom. My head's in a fog. Meanwhile I lost twenty-five rubles, and I'm not happy about it...

I drink to your health, nibble on Christmas ham, and remain your faithful and willing servant,"

(Chekhov, letter to Leikin, December 25, 1883, Moscow)

Now under agreement with *The Spectator*, *Moscow*, and *The Alarm Clock*—all Moscow journals—Anton found himself contributing at least once a week to those publications, as well as a growing number of others. He was even asked to serialize a short novel (his first), *The Unnecessary Victory*, from June until September, bringing in several hundred rubles. With increasing confidence, he experimented with a variety of forms, including non-fiction. He frequented courtrooms, cafes and theatre, eagerly providing anecdotal information to the publications about all aspects of Moscow life from event-reporting to gossip. He even reported on crime, too. His goal was to write a hundred stories or articles a year, in order to support his family. (Pavel, his father, brought in next to nothing, Masha and Mikhail were still students, and Nikolai earned little. Aleksandr lived away with his common law wife, who was expecting a baby.)

But his passion was still for the theatre, and now he could express it as a critic. He attended a production of *Hamlet*, and gave it a stern review, condemning the cast for their mechanical performances, stating that he deeply admired Shakespeare and was irritated that Russian actors did not have the training to do his work justice. A desire to write serious theatre continued to stir in him, but it was too early for it to develop, overwhelmed as he was with his current obligations and activities.

Meanwhile, a bohemian-style literary salon of sorts was forming around Anton's two older brothers Aleksandr and Nikolai, who were working at *The Spectator* too, editing and illustrating respectively. A motley assortment of writers, poets and journalists frequented the family quarters (they had moved yet once again), providing entertainment and diversion and at the same time unwelcome interruption to Anton's precious writing and study time. Often Anton had to remonstrate Aleksandr for his drunken bouts and dissolute lifestyle, and Nikolai for his drinking as well as his use of morphine. In addition, there was the endless ebb and flow of visiting relatives who often stayed the night. Their frequent interruptions (not to mention the constant sound of his mother's sewing machine) made it almost impossible for Anton to study. Frequent calls out into the night to attend to his drunken brother provided him with a haven; he would bring his medical books along and study at Aleksandr's flat.

To celebrate passing his third year medical examinations, Anton passed the summer of 1882 in Voskresensk again. He spent halcyon days of fishing, mushrooming, and prowling around the village, searching for ideas for his anecdotes. He dreamed of owning a country estate one day like Turgenev and Tolstoy, but for now he was content with his brother Ivan's modest dwelling. So continued a lifelong passion for the Russian countryside, which would later become a haven as well as a source of inspiration for his work.

But the highlight of 1882—his third year in medical school—was his encounter with Nikolai Leikin, the editor-in-chief of the prestigious St. Petersburg weekly humorous magazine *Fragments*. Impressed with Anton's writing, Leikin offered him a regular column, "Fragments of Moscow Life," promising him an increase in number of lines over any Moscow publication he'd written heretofore, at a rate of eight kopeks a line—or four-five rubles per story. A fortune!

The weekly correspondence that developed between Anton and his eccentric new publisher would provide valuable outlet for his development as a young writer.

"If I lived alone, I'd be a rich man."

(Chekhov, letter to Aleksandr, May 13, 1883, Moscow)

Anton's popularity as a writer increased with each coming month. By 1883, over 125 of his anecdotes and articles had been published in a variety of publications on a broad range of topics under numerous *noms de plume,* including "Antosha Chekhonte" (the one most frequently used), "A Doctor without Patients," "A Man without a Spleen," "My Brother's Brother," "Ulysses," "Don Antonio," "Mr. Baldastov," and so on. His style was recognized and acclaimed; his writing was reviewed favorably. Leikin proved to be a harsh and exacting editor; he demanded exclusivity, and as a result Anton had to curtail his commitments to other Moscow journals. Soon Anton began to feel the pressure and constraints of writing to provoke easy laughter in his readers. Nevertheless, Leikin provided Anton with an opportunity to develop his style and to begin introducing serious undertones to his comedic stories—a dimension that would deepen with every passing year of writing.

With his weekly submissions to both *The Spectator* and *Fragments* (writing under two *noms de plume* for the latter), he was filling almost half an issue. Most importantly, Anton was making money—although at times he had to chase after editors for his remuneration, and fend off their offers to pay him in theatre tickets instead. With both his older brothers now living away from home and Ivan teaching in the provinces, the Chekhov household had shrunk to more manageable proportions. During that period, Anton's correspondence with his brother Aleksandr would contain his most personal reflections on his life and work.

Meanwhile, Anton excelled in his fourth-year medical exams. Medical school was not without its lighter moments that year. Anton found time to indulge in a practical joke or two with his fellow students, providing relief from the intense pressures. According to one story, Anton, Nikolai, and an art student named Levitan (who would play a crucial role in Chekhov's later life as a playwright) played a prank on an orange peddler by buying his fruit and selling it more cheaply on the street. The peddler had the pranksters arrested.

Once again, he spent the summer with his brother Ivan in Voskresensk. There he continued to help at the local hospital and make rounds with the hospital's chief physician. That summer, Ivan introduced Anton to the genteel officers of the battalion stationed there. One of them, a Lieutenant Yegorov, proposed to Masha. She in turn asked Anton's permission to marry. Anton declined to give any response. By that time, it was clear that Chekhov was de facto head of the Chekhov clan, and this position would have its strongest effect on Masha. (Details of that convivial summer with the battalion would resurface years later in his story, "The Kiss," and, much later, his play *The Three Sisters*.)

As for his personal life, Anton found himself surrounded by admiring young women—a trio of sisters named Anna, Anastasia and Natalia Golden (Masha's friends), and a young lady named Olga Kundasova who worked as astronomer in a Moscow observatory. Olga and Anton became lovers, and their relationship lasted for years. There was also a Jewish student named Dunya Efros. He was also reported to have had liaisons with both a ballerina and an actress during his medical school years, as well as interaction with "women of a certain reputation," whom he met through his brothers' café world and also through medical school health care assignments to brothels.

Otherwise, he revealed little of his personal life. Indeed, he hardly had time for one.

“First, I’d get my patients laughing, and only then would I begin to treat them.”

(Chekhov, letter to Leikin, May 20-21, 1884)

1884

“Esteemed Nikolai Aleksandrovich:

[...] Tomorrow I have my last exam, and the day after I shall be presented with the title of ‘doctor’ (that is, if I pass the exam). I am ordering a ‘doctor’ shingle with a pointing finger, not so much for my medical practice as for putting the fear of God in janitors, mailmen, and the tailor. My parents can’t believe their eyes. They treat me with the kind of respect they’d show a police captain. They imagine that thousands of rubles will pass through my hands in the very first year. Fyodor, my tailor, is of the same opinion. They all have to be disillusioned, poor things.

[...] I would enjoy writing a satirical medical text in 2-3 volumes. First, I’d get my patients laughing, and only then would I begin to treat them. [...]

Your respectful contributor,

A. Chekhov”

(Chekhov, letter to Leikin, May 20-21, 1884, Moscow)

“Esteemed Nikolai Aleksandrovich:

[...] Just returned from an autopsy that took place about 10 miles from Voskresensk. I was traveling out there in a rickety old troika, accompanied by an equally decrepit court inspector...I conducted the examination, together with the local doctor, in a field, under a young oak tree by the side of the road. ...The corpse was a man unknown in those parts, and the peasants, upon whose land the body was found, begged us with tears in their eyes, for Christ’s sake, to perform the autopsy right there and not in their village. ‘The women and children will not sleep for fear his spirit will escape and haunt the village...,’ they explained. At first, the inspector balked, worrying it might rain, but then, deciding that rough notes of the procedure could be made in pencil, and seeing that we were ready to begin right

there out in the open, yielded to the peasants' pleas. The scene: a cluster of frightened villagers, assorted witnesses, the peasant policeman, the old widow wailing loudly about 200 paces from the scene of the autopsy, and two peasants guarding the corpse...Near the silent sentinels, a dying fire sputters...The peasants are obliged to guard the body day and night without pay until the authorities arrive...The corpse, dressed in a red shirt and new trousers, is covered with a sheet....On the sheet there's a towel with an icon on it. We ask the policeman for some water....Yes, there's water from a nearby pond, but no one will offer us a bucket to fetch it, for fear we'll contaminate it. One peasant uses his wiles, and gets the Manekhino villagers to steal a bucket from the Tukhlov villagers... After all, no one minds what happens to a neighbor's bucket... How and where they manage to steal it—no one knows. Meanwhile, they're terribly pleased with their accomplishment, and are grinning broadly... The autopsy reveals twenty fractured ribs, infected lungs, and a stomach reeking of alcohol. The death was a violent one, caused by strangulation. The drunken man's chest must have been crushed, probably by a peasant's huge knee. There were numerous abrasions on the body, caused by attempted efforts of resuscitation. The Manekhino peasants had found the body and for two hours had rocked it so zealously that a future defense attorney would have every right to ask the expert if the broken ribs may caused from the rocking. But I suspect that this question will never get asked...There won't be a defense, and there won't be an accused.... Meanwhile, the inspector is so decrepit that anything from a murderer to an ailing bedbug can escape his feeble eye.... One more detail and then I'll stop. The murdered man was a factory worker. He'd left a tavern in Tukhlov with a barrel full of vodka. A witness, who was the first to notice the corpse by the side of the road, reported that he'd seen the barrel close to the body. Ergo, the Tukhlov tavern-keeper, who is not allowed to sell vodka to be taken off the premises in the first place, stole the barrel from the dead man so as to remove any evidence. [...]

Votre A. Chekhonte"

(Chekhov, letter to Leikin, June 27, 1884, Voskresensk)

"Esteemed Nikolai Aleksandrovich:

For three days now I've had blood coming out of my throat. It keeps me from writing and will prevent from going to St. Petersburg... I must say I never expected it! I've had no clear spittle for three days, and I have no idea when the medicines will take effect that my colleagues are stuffing down my throat. My general state is satisfactory... The whole thing is probably due to a ruptured blood vessel...

[...] Wouldn't you know it—I've got patients now... I ought to go and see them, but I can't... I don't know what to do with them... It would be a shame to hand them over to another doctor. After all, it's money.

Farewell,

Yours, A. Chekhov"

(Chekhov, letter to Leikin, December 10, 1884. Moscow)

1884 was to be a landmark year for the young writer and doctor.

Final exams began early in the winter, and Anton had to take and pass no less than seventy-five of them. At last, after five years of toiling over his studies under the most adverse circumstances (cramped quarters, constant interruptions from boarders and relatives, nocturnal house calls to care for his drunken brother, not to mention financial worries and writers' deadlines), on June 16 he graduated from medical school. He spent the summer working as an attending physician in the Chikino hospital, where he found himself treating patients for a variety of ailments—from the upset stomach of a Moscow actress to a monk's dysentery. "I was so overjoyed by the success in my newfound profession that I gathered together all my earned rubles and headed over to Bannikov's Tavern, where I ordered vodka, beer and other medicines for my doctor's table,"[1] he wrote.

To mark his five years of achievement as a writer, too, Anton assembled a collection of his best works under his *nom de plume* Chekhonte, and with Leikin's support, they were published. The title of the collection was *Tales of Melpomene*, and it earned Anton 500 rubles—ten times the amount his publisher Leikin had paid him that month. Another Moscow publication, *News of the Day*, also agreed to publish "The Shooting Party" (Chekhov's second and last novel) in thirty-two installments. Part murder mystery, part melodrama, part parody, "The Shooting Party" filled 170 pages and was his longest work to date. The novel was written in haste, for money. With its wild garden setting and elements of Russian mysticism, it foreshadowed his later story "The Black Monk." Its length and flamboyant style distinguish it as a unique work in Chekhov's canon (Chekhov hardly saw any of these royalties– instead, once again, he was offered free theatre tickets).

In all, during his medical years from 1880-84, three hundred texts authored by Anton had been published. Among these youthful efforts, dashed off under adverse circumstances, were stories such as "Oysters," "He Understood," "The Death of the Government Clerk," "Fat and Thin," "The Daughter of Albion," "An Equestrian Tale"—some hilarious, some satiric and incisive, others touching and tender with darker overtones. Their variety indicated the promise, range and depth of the stories to come.

That summer, Chekhov returned to the hospital in Voskresensk, this time as an attending physician. He earned his first fees as a doctor by curing a young lady's toothache, treating a monk with a case of dysentery, and tending to the upset stomach of a Moscow actress who was summering in the region. He earned extra money by performing autopsies (an episode in this medical life that he would later include in a short story called "On Official Business" in 1899). He saw over thirty patients a day and performed operations, proud of his newly acquired autonomy and responsibilities.

There were distractions, too. A second trio of sisters entered the Chekhov brothers' lives—Elena, Elizaveta, and Margarita Markova, who were staying at a nearby dacha.

In the fall, he returned to Moscow to throw himself into the practice of medicine in earnest, hoping to make a living from it and throw off the mantle of poverty once and for all. What high expectations he had—after all, a doctor could earn 10,000 rubles a year!

At first, the young Dr. Chekhov found that his patients would beg off paying his fees, offering him gifts instead. But gradually he began to receive payments, and his finances improved. He employed a servant, bought furniture, and for the first time paid cash for his groceries rather than buying on credit. No longer in debt, the family was enjoying its new upwardly mobile status toward gentrification. The Chekhovs began to entertain, and soon a regular Tuesday night salon evolved, when the household bustled with the sound of laughter and music and the flow of young artists, musicians, and writers.

Meanwhile, Anton had not forgotten the theatre. That year, he penned a sketch titled "Impure Tragedians and Leprous Dramatists: A Terribly—Horribly—Scandalously—Desperate Trrrrrragedy," published that year under the name of "The Brother of my Brother." A parody of a German drama recently translated into Russian, this six-page theatrical joke—with its cast of dozens, including little green devils, witches, and the King of Sweden, beginning with an epilogue followed by "six acts"—was written for the amusement of its anonymous author. Clearly, it was not intended for production. It did, however, reveal the author's keen satiric view of the current state of the Russian theatre, one that was dominated by foreign imports.

Leikin, Anton's publisher of *Fragments*, was pleased with the success of *Tales of Melpomene*. When he mentioned his author "Antosha Chekhonte" to Khudekov, the editor of the prestigious daily *Petersburg Gazette*, and revealed his true identity, Khudekov, in turn, commissioned Anton to write for his publication.

Then on December 7, a portentous event occurred. In the midst of his busy schedule—caring for patients, meeting writing deadlines—Anton began coughing blood, an episode that lasted three days. His schedule of seeing patients was temporarily interrupted. He tried to make light of it, dismissing any possibility that it might be something serious. After all, he had patients to cure and a family to support. He told Leikin that his lungs were sound and that it was only a burst blood vessel in his throat. To others, he attributed it to overwork.

These symptoms would return later to haunt him.

"MEDICINE IS MY WIFE AND LITERATURE IS MY MISTRESS. WHEN I TIRE OF ONE, I SPEND THE NIGHT WITH THE OTHER."

(Chekhov, letter to Suvorin, September 11, 1888, Moscow)

1885

"Dear Uncle Mitrofan Yegorovich:

[...] My medical career is coming along, I've busy healing the sick. Every day I spend more than a ruble on cab fare, making my rounds. I've got a lot of friends and therefore quite a number of patients. Half of them I treat for free, the other half pays me three to five rubles...I haven't amassed any savings yet nor shall I in the near future, but I live tolerably well and want for nothing. If my health holds out, then my family will be taken care of...

Mama is alive and well and complains, as always, but even she has started to admit that we live far better in Moscow than we lived in Taganrog. No one begrudges her expenses; there is no illness in the house. It's not luxury, but we get by quite nicely.

Ivan is at the theatre now. He's working in Moscow and is very content. He's one of the most decent, reliable members of the family—hard-working and honest. Kolya is thinking of getting married. Misha finishes school this year...

I kiss your hand, and send greetings to my cousins and everyone.

Don't forget your humble and eternally grateful

A. Chekhov"

(Chekhov, letter to Uncle Mitrofan, January 31, 1885, Moscow)

Esteemed Nikolai Aleksandrovich:

I'm in heaven here, and spend my days doing nothing except eat, drink, sleep, and fish. I've been shooting once. Today we caught a burbot, the day before yesterday my fellow huntsman killed a hare. Levitan the artist is staying with me, and he loves to hunt. He's the one who killed the hare. Poor fellow—he's not in a good way. It looks like the beginnings of a psychosis...He wanted to hang himself.

...I've invited him to stay with us, and we go for walks together ....He seems to be doing better...

...If you come to Moscow this summer and make a pilgrimage out here to New Jerusalem, I promise you something you've never seen anywhere else before. ... Ah, nature! It's so luscious you could scoop it up and eat it...

Farewell and don't be angry with your disreputable

A. Chekhov"

(Chekhov, letter to Leikin, May 9, 1885, Babkino)

"Esteemed Nikolai Aleksandrovich:

... Yes, literature earns an uncertain piece of bread, and you were wise to have been born before me in a time when it was easier to breathe and to write.

...As I'm the chief breadwinner of a big family, I never have a ten ruble note to spare.[...] My literary income is a fixed quantity. It may diminish, but it can't increase.

...Meanwhile, congratulations on your purchase. I passionately love anything that's called an estate in Russia! The word hasn't lost its poetic meaning.

Now you'll spend your summers luxuriating in the lap of Nature...

Yours, A. Chekhov"

(Chekhov, letter to Leikin, October 12 or 13, 1885, Moscow)

The year 1885 found the young doctor Chekhov still preoccupied with the balancing act of practicing medicine and writing for journals. His writing brought in a fixed income. Not only did he continue to write his weekly story for the Tuesday issue of *Fragments*, but also he was contributing on Mondays to the *St. Petersburg Gazette*. In this year alone, therefore, he wrote almost one hundred short stories.

At the same time, he recognized the need to keep his medical practice going. "I mustn't write any more than I do now," he wrote his publisher Leikin. "After all, medicine is not law practice: if you don't work, you fall behind."[1]

Meanwhile, he still dreamed of living the country life of a writer, like Tolstoy and Turgenev, whose families owned grand estates. With Ivan now living in Moscow, a summer dwelling was no longer available to him and his family. So for the very first time, Anton was able to scrape up enough money from his combined earnings as a physician and a writer to rent his own "estate" for the summer from Ivan's friends, the Kiselyovs, whose children had been his pupils, just outside of Voskresensk, in a village called Babkino.

In May, he set out with his mother and his sister Masha (his brothers would follow) to spend another summer filled with delights. The Kiselyovs had refurbished a dacha next door to their house. Chekhov was delighted by its furnishings and appointments. "Matchbox stands, ashtrays, cigarette boxes, two wash basins.... heaven only knows what else our gracious hosts didn't think to supply us," he wrote his brother Mikhail, enthralled. The view from his desk thrilled him: "Before my eye stretches an unusually warm, gentle landscape: the river, beyond it the forests...."[2] The estate was sprawling, with immense gardens, meadows, ponds, and flower-beds. The weather was lovely; the singing of the nightingales enthralled him. Days were spent strolling, fishing, and writing. "Yesterday there was a perch in one of the traps, and this morning we pulled out twenty-nine carp. Not bad, eh?! We're having fish soup, fried fish, and fish in aspic today." Evenings were spent with his landlady, Madame Kiselyova, and her family, gathering in their drawing room to enjoy an evening of card-playing and Chopin waltzes on the piano.

Chekhov and Madame Kiselyova took long walks with his friend Isaak Levitan, the landscape painter, who lived across the river. He had met Levitan during his first year of medical school, when his brother Nikolai brought him home and introduced him to Anton along with his other artist friends. Levitan was high-strung and suffered from mercurial mood swings. Anton, in turn, was fond of him, and gave him medical advice. That summer at Babkino, a budding romance developed between Levitan and Masha, Anton's younger sister, who had blossomed into a lovely young woman and was preparing to teach. A fledgling painter herself, she was attracted to Levitan's Byronic demeanor—his moodiness, talent, and flamboyance. Levitan proposed marriage to Masha, and she came to Chekhov once again for approval. But Chekhov discouraged the liaison in a subtle and indirect manner, saying that she could marry him but alluded to his mental instability. Perturbed at the thought that her brother might disapprove (though he didn't directly say so), she in turn discouraged Levitan. And so continued the pattern of withholding approval for Masha's hand that would repeat itself throughout her life.

During that summer, he got his first taste of genteel estate life, and he was enamored by it. The beautiful countryside, the sublime fishing, the scintillating social life—it all beguiled him. He would conjure up this intoxicating setting again and again in his full-length plays.

Even in the midst of this paradise, he couldn't shirk his medical duties. He worked a few days a week at the local hospital. "My patients keep flowing in," he wrote Leikin, "they won't stop bothering me. I've seen hundreds of them this summer and earned a total of one ruble."[3] Family worries preoccupied him as well. He tried to keep track of his brother Nikolai, who had lost his job, lapsed into debt and alcoholism, and went missing for weeks at a time. Chekhov left Babkino briefly to return to Moscow and visit his brother Aleksandr, who was moving to the south with his common law wife and their baby (their life would sink lower and lower into poverty and dissolution).

There were also a few reoccurrences of his spitting blood that summer; once again, he made light of them.

Still, he managed to write a significant story that summer—titled "The Huntsman." Set on an estate and written in the style of Turgenev, it was an homage to that great Russian short story writer and playwright who had died a few years earlier, whom Chekhov admired and whose country life and love of hunting and fishing he sought to emulate. The story was published in the *St. Petersburg Gazette* in July, and was met with enthusiasm and admiration.

That idyllic summer at Babkino made a lasting impression on Chekhov. "The fact is," he wrote Madame Kiselyov in October, "there is nothing in my poor soul except memories of fishing rods, traps, that long, green line for worms… I'm still so immersed in summer that I awaken every morning with only one question: have we caught anything or not?"[4] Without his being aware of it, Anton was filing away people, impressions, images, and incidents in his nascent dramatist's imagination. Eventually, Levitan would become the basis for his character Kostya in *The Seagull*; Turgenev would provide the inspiration for Trigorin, another character in the play; Madame Kiselyova, with her fading estate, her love of entertaining, and her obliviousness to money, would become one of the models for Lyubov Ranevskaya in *The Cherry Orchard*. Already the stage was being set for his later, great plays.

Chekhov returned to Moscow life and a gathering social whirlwind in the fall. He found himself involved with no less than five women. One, Natasha Golden, was the youngest of three sisters whom Anton had met in his medical school days (he and his older brothers would be involved with at least five trios of sisters during the 1880s). Another, Dunya Efros, was a friend of Masha's; like Natasha, she was Jewish. (While anti-Semitism was rampant in those times, Chekhov's father Pavel claimed to have respect for Jews and had no objections to his family befriending them.) He also had liaisons with a Mrs. Golub (his former landlady), a baroness (the landlady of a friend), as well as a guide at the Hermitage museum. The family had moved once again—to a new flat where Dr. Chekhov mounted his brass plate and saw patients most days. There were recurrent money problems; the *St. Petersburg Gazette* payments were late, and he had to write to the *Alarm Clock* again and collect his royalties personally.

Still, he was determined not to lose sight of the theatre. That year, he penned his first serious short play—*On the High Road*. A dark, melodramatic work sub-titled a "dramatic study" and set in a roadside tavern in the provinces, Anton based it on his exposure to the violent side of peasant life he witnessed as a country doctor during his summers in southern Russia. Adapted from an earlier short story ("In Autumn", 1883), it would be the only one-act play he wrote during the 1880s devoid of comedic elements. In May, it was presented to the censors, who rejected it in September for being too sordid and therefore unsuitable for performance. Mikhail, Chekhov's youngest brother and copyist, reported that on the copy of the rejected play the censor had written the word 'barin" (meaning "master," "gentleman") in blue pencil—referring to the principal character in the play. Mikhail speculated that the censors considered it improper to represent a desperate, drunken "barin" onstage. It was not published during Chekhov's lifetime.

Other stories published that fall also depicted scenes from peasant life, including "The Dead Body," "Sergeant Preshibeev," "Grief," and "Artistry." Clearly, his experiences with poverty and death as a country doctor were coloring his writing. Elements of darkness and religious mysticism were also creeping into his work. These stories, with their economy and objectivity, also showed the influence of Maupassant, whose work was so popular in Russia at the time.

In December, at the invitation of his publisher Leikin, Chekhov boarded a train for St. Petersburg to visit the capital for the very first time, unaware that his literary life was about to change significantly.

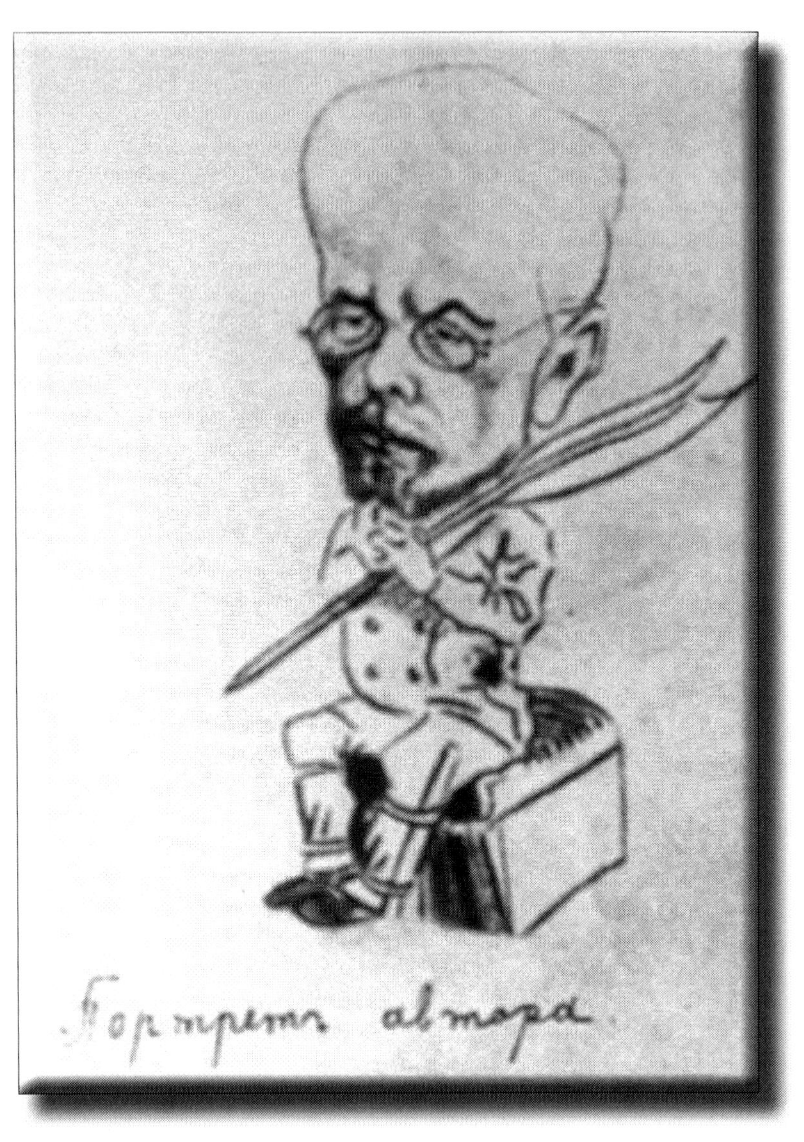

AUTHOR'S SELF-PORTRAIT

"It's not much fun being a famous writer... Money is as scarce as cats' tears."

(Chekhov, letter to Mme. Kiselyova, September 21, 1886)

1886

"Quarantine Customs-House Official Sasha:

[...] I was overwhelmed by the reception given to me by the people of St. Petersburg. Suvorin, Grigorovich, Burenin... They all keep offering me invitations, singing my praises, and I begin to feel badly about having written so carelessly, so offhandedly. If I'd known I was being read like this, I'd never have written 'on assignment'... The moral is: remember that you're being read. Moreover: don't use the names and family names of people you know in your stories...

Write, write! Don't be a dolt and don't forget

Yours, A. Chekhov"

(Chekhov, letter to Aleksandr, January 4, 1886, Moscow)

"Sire!

...I've just finished my dramatic monologue 'On the Harmful Effects of Tobacco' which in my heart of hearts is meant for the comedic actor Gradov-Sokolov. I spoiled it by having only two and a half hours to write it—nonetheless, I sent it, not to hell, but to the 'St. Petersburg Gazette.' My intentions were honorable, but the execution turned out to be 'horriblissimo'!

Write, and I'll conjure up the ashes of Caesar for you.

'Ci devant' [the ex-] A. Chekhov"

(Chekhov, letter to a writer/friend Bilibin, February 14, 1886, Moscow)

"My kind, beloved bearer of good tidings:

Your letter struck me like a thunderbolt. I almost burst into tears, worked myself into a state, and now feel as though your letter has left a deep mark on my soul. As you have blessed my youth, so in turn should God bless your old age. I can find neither word nor deed to thank you. You know with what esteem the ordinary people regard the chosen such as you, so you can imagine how your letter has impacted on my self-esteem. It is higher reward than any diploma, and for a fledgling writer it is a gift for the present and for the future. I'm in a daze. It is beyond my power to judge whether I am worthy of this award... I can only repeat that I'm overwhelmed.

If indeed I have a gift that should be respected, then I confess before the purity of your heart that up until now I myself have not respected it. Hitherto, I felt that I did have a talent, but I was used to thinking it as an insignificant one...

All my nearest and dearest look down on my work with condescension, and never hesitate to offer friendly advice to dissuade me from giving up 'real work' for scribbling. I have hundreds of friends in Moscow, and dozens of writers among them, but I cannot recall a single one who has read my work or who considers me an artist. There is in Moscow a so-called 'literary circle': talents and mediocrities of all ages and varieties who gather once a week in a private room of a restaurant and exercise their tongues. If I were to go there and read them even a sentence of praise from your letter, they would laugh in my face. For the past five years that I've spent hanging around newspaper offices, I've become resigned to this view of my literary insignificance. I've grown accustomed to look down on my own work, and meanwhile I kept right on writing! That's the first thing. Second, I am a physician, and I've become absorbed in my medical work, so that no one has troubled more than I by the proverb about chasing two hares....

I am writing all this for the sole reason of absolving myself in your eyes, at least to some extent. Up until now, I've treated my writing frivolously, thoughtlessly, and indifferently. I cannot recall a single story on which I have worked more than a day. 'The Huntsman', which you liked so much, was written in a bathing house! As reporters dash off their notes about fires, that's how I write my stories –mechanically, thoughtlessly, without the slightest concern for either the reader or myself... And while writing them I'd try every way possible not to waste an image or a scene I liked on them. Instead—God knows why—I'd hide them away for future use... I still have had no faith in my own literary worth...

I'll try to give up writing for a deadline, but not yet...I can't get out of the rut I'm in—not all at once. I'm not afraid of going hungry, as I have in the past, but it's not just a question of me alone... I write at my leisure, say, two-three hours a day and a little at night—time enough to produce only short pieces. In the summer, when I have more free time and less expenses, I'll get down to more serious work.

...All my hopes lie in the future. I am only twenty-six. Perhaps I shall manage to do something, although time flies by so rapidly.

Forgive the length of this letter... If possible, send me your photograph.

I am so moved and inspired by you that I could write—not a sheet—but a whole ream for you. May God grant you health and happiness, and believe in the sincerity of your deeply respectful and grateful

A. Chekhov"

(Chekhov, letter to the writer Grigorovich, March 28, 1886, Moscow)

"Dearest Mr. Aleksandr Pavlovich Chekhov:

... I've just returned from St. Petersburg, where I spent two weeks and had a marvelous time. I've become very close to Grigorovich and Suvorin.

... I think that if you overcome your laziness, you'll be a good writer—but God only knows what a sloth you are!

In my opinion, descriptions of nature should be very brief and have an almost off-handed quality. Clichés such as: 'The setting sun, bathing the waves of the darkening sea, awash with a crimsoned gold' or 'Swallows, flying over the surface of the water, twittered gaily' must be avoided. In describing nature one must seize on the smallest details, arranging them in such a way so that upon reading, you can close your eyes, and a picture is captured. For example, you can evoke a moonlit night if you write that on the mill dam the glass fragment of a broken bottle glimmered like a tiny star, and that the black shadow of a dog or a wolf rolled along like a ball, and so on. Nature becomes animated if you're not afraid to give it human attributes. [...]

Be well and don't forget your

A. Chekhov"

(Chekhov, letter to Aleksandr, May 10, 1886. Moscow)

"...It's not much fun to be a famous writer. To begin with, it's a dreary life. Work from morning till night, and very little to show for it. Money is as scarce as cats' tears...I don't know about Émile Zola, but in my flat, it's cold and

smoky... On the other hand, authorship has its good points. Firstly, sales on my book of short stories are going well. Secondly, soon I'll have some money. Thirdly, little by little I'm beginning to reap the laurels—I'm pointed out in the theatre lobbies, people pay attention to me, and I'm even treated to free sandwiches at the buffet. One artistic director caught sight of me in his lobby and offered me a season's subscription... My tailor has bought my book, and he's reading it aloud at home and prophesizing a great future for me. My fellow physicians sigh when they meet me, talk of literature, and swear they're tired of medicine. And so on.

Farewell and believe the hypocrite, A. Chekhov, when he sends his best to you and your family."

(Chekhov, letter to Mme. Kiselyova, September 21, 1886, Moscow)

"Esteemed Maria Vladimirovna:

[...] With your permission, I'm stealing two descriptions of nature from your latest two letters to my sister. It's amazing—you have a totally masculine style of writing. In every line (except those pertaining to children), you write like a man. Of course, this should raise your self-esteem since, in general, men are 10,000 times superior to women.

...Alas and alack! I've become quite the rage in Petersburg. While Korolenko, a serious writer, is hardly known by the editors, the whole town is reading my dribble... While it may be flattering, nonetheless it offends my literary sensibility... I'm embarrassed to have a public that courts literary lapdogs simply because they can't recognize elephants, and I deeply believe that not one single soul will read me once I start writing serious work.

A. Chekhov"

(Chekhov, letter to Mme. Kiselyova, December 13, 1886, Moscow)

Chekhov arrived in St. Petersburg, unprepared for his welcome as a budding literary celebrity. A regular contributor to the *St. Petersburg Gazette*, he was drawing the attention of serious readers.

A crucial event occurred upon his arrival that would define his literary future—an introduction to Aleksei Suvorin, publisher of the prestigious *New Times*, a Petersburg journal. A powerful magnate in the newspaper world with an imposing stature and a patrician demeanor, Suvorin had read Chekhov's story "The Huntsman" and admired it.

He invited him to submit stories to his publication at twelve kopecks a line—a significant increase over *Fragments*. Moreover, Suvorin wanted Anton to sign his stories "Chekhov" instead of "Chekhonte"—although he still clung to the humorous *nom de plume,* at least for the time being.

Fragments was buckling more and more under censorship. "What is permitted today will demand a visit to the censor's committee tomorrow," Anton had warned its publisher Leikin only months before.[1] So he eagerly accepted Suvorin's invitation. He sent him a new story "The Requiem" immediately, which Suvorin published in February, followed by "The Witch" and "Agafya." Chekhov returned to St. Petersburg again in the spring, and spent all his time in the company of Suvorin, who lavished attention on him and virtually adopted him into his family. He would come to play a towering role in Anton's development as a writer, serving as a father and mentor figure.

Back in Moscow, he toiled as a doctor in face of the threatened typhus epidemic. A new collection of his writings—*Motley Stories*—was published, and once again he was encouraged to attribute his own name to it. Again, he balked, fearing the removal of his mask. After all, Chekhov practiced medicine, whereas Chekhonte wrote stories.

And then he received a letter that would dramatically change his self-image as a writer. Dmitri Grigorovich, the elderly novelist and dean of living Russian writers, whom he had met in St. Petersburg a few months earlier, wrote Chekhov a letter expressing his admiration for his young talent and exhorting him to take himself seriously, stop writing facilely, come out from behind a pseudonym and publish under his own name. Chekhov was overwhelmed. This was a rite of passage—an invitation to evolve from a humorist and peripatetic journalist into the ranks of the serious writers of Russian literature. After all, Grigorovich had identified Dostoevsky's talents decades before and offered him the same encouragement. Chekhov read and reread the letter, sent copies to his parents and friends, and responded with emotion, thanking the elderly writer for his mentorship and expressing his gratitude for the effect it was having on him. He also apologized that *Motley Stories* had already been published under his *nom de plume*, and therefore could not heed his advice. But the letter had worked its power. From that time on, Chekhonte would become Chekhov.

Meanwhile, his life was filled with the usual distractions of funds, family, and friends. He kept a secret engagement to Dunya Efros, delighting in the mischief of it. Ever the practical jokester, he broke it off after a month, telling his friends that she was shrewish and that no doubt he would have divorced her. Otherwise, he was surrounded by admirers, and soon began mentoring young writers himself, both men and women. He continued to be preoccupied with the tribulations of his older brothers, whose lives persisted in being disorganized, dissolute and disreputable. His sister Masha, who by then had graduated from school, tutored part-time and made caring for her brothers—especially Anton—her first priority.

During this year, Chekhov's stories became richer, deeper, and more complex. Shades of his family problems were evident in stories like "Difficult People." There was the moving "Vanka" (about a lost child) and "On the Road," both of which were extremely popular and received praise among St. Petersburg literary circles. As in the year before, his output was prodigious, yielding dozens of stories in 1886.

In September, after more than fifteen moves in seven years, the Chekhov family took up residence in a two-story house on Sadovo-Kundrinskaya Street in Moscow. To them, it was a palace. On the ground floor, there was a parlor, a dining room, and a separate entrance to rooms which served as Anton's surgery where he saw patients daily. On the second floor, there was a study for Anton and a bedroom for every member of the family. Chekhov had to pawn his watch and borrow money from Leikin to pay the rent (650 rubles a year). The stone house was a reddish color; he would describe it affectionately as a "rosy chest of drawers."

Still, he did not forget the theatre. In February, he took refuge in comedy after the serious dramatic attempt of the year before —an alternation that would repeat itself throughout his career. Perhaps it was because of his experience with the censors over *On the High Road*, or perhaps he still had more confidence holding the pen of Antosha Chekhonte. In any event, this time he chose to write in the monologue form. His protagonist—a hen-pecked husband of a headmistress of a girls' school—attempts to give a lecture at his wife's bidding on the topic of her choice, and ends up pouring out his heart over his miserable lot, entreating the unseen audience to protect him from his tyrannical spouse. Chekhov wrote *On the Harmful Effects of Tobacco* on February 14 in a few hours, dismissing it in a joking, trivializing tone that characterized all his commentary about his one-act plays. The first draft was published only two weeks later in the *Petersburg Gazette.*

Over the next sixteen years, Chekhov would return to this

monologue no less than five times to write yet another draft—an act prompted each time not by external influences such as criticism but rather by an internal urge to revisit this remarkable little play and keep refining its tone. And with each rewrite, the portrait of nervous Nyukhin—the persecuted husband of the hellion headmistress who forces him to teach every subject in the school as well as manage the housekeeping, buy the supplies, cook for the pupils, do the bookkeeping, catch the mice—elicits more laughter as well as more pathos. As Chekhov's illness progressed, as his insights into the meaning of life and his understanding of human nature and the human condition matured, as the Russia around him was inexorably moving toward its destiny, the one play he returned to again and again to rewrite and refine was this little monologue. And with each revision, the originally comedic material is overshadowed by the tragic, till he achieved the delicate balance between the two that became the hallmark of his later plays. It is as if this rewriting process were a metaphor for the dramatist's own evolving, darkening tragicomedic *weltanschauung*.

Some time during 1886, Chekhov also wrote a humorous sketch called "The Dramatist."

It began like a joke: "A man walks into a doctor's office…." In it, a physician examines a patient who is complaining of all sorts of maladies. This amusing, wry little one page sketch offered a satirical profile of a day in the life of a playwright, depicting him as a lazy lay-about, a drunk, and a hack, who borrows from foreign playwrights and hasn't an original thought in his head. The piece is extremely revealing on several levels. First, it depicts two characters—a doctor and a dramatist—each of whom represents a side of Chekhov. "'I am a dramatist!' the patient declares, not without pride. 'What an unusual occupation', the doctor mutters."[2] Second, it reveals that Chekhov, the aspiring playwright, already had definite views on contemporary Russian drama and the lack of fresh ideas in new writing. Third, at the same time, he was well aware of difficulties of the theatre and the profession of playwriting.

Despite this detached view, one already gets the sense that, no matter how open Chekhov's eyes may have been about the theatre, the occupation of the dramatist would entice him like a siren throughout his life.

"Yours truly, Schiller Shakespearovich Goethe"

(Chekhov, letter to his brother Aleksandr, November 24, 1887)

"[...] Literature is considered art because it depicts life as it really is. Its aim is the truth, unconditional and honest. Limiting its function to as narrow a field as pearl-fishing, for example, would be dealing art a mortal blow, like requiring the painter Levitan to draw trees without the dirty bark or the yellowing leaves. A pearl is a thing of value, I agree. But the writer is not a confectioner, nor a cosmetician, nor an entertainer. He is a man bound by contract to his sense of duty and his conscience. As such, he must stay the course, and no matter how awful it is for him, he must overcome his squeamishness and besmirch his imagination with the grime of life...

Nothing on earth is impure to a chemist. The writer should be just as objective. He should free himself from everyday subjectivity and realize that manure piles play a highly respectable role in the landscape, and that evil passions are as inherent in life as good ones.

I confess that I rarely consult with my conscience when I write. This is out of habit—as well as the pettiness of my efforts. That is why, when I expound on literature and offer this opinion or that, I don't have myself in mind...

Meanwhile, I have written a four-page play ['Calchas', later renamed 'Swan Song']. It should run about 15-20 minutes long. It's the shortest drama on earth. The famous actor Davydov, who performs at the Korsh Theatre, wants to play the role. It will be published in 'The Season', so it will be shown around. In general, it's much better to write short works than longer ones—less chance of pretension, more chance of success... What more could you want? It took me an hour and five minutes to write my play. I started another one, but haven't finished it. I just don't have the time..."

Devotedly and respectfully,

A. Chekhov"

(Chekhov, letter to Mme. Kiselyova, January 14, 1887, Moscow)

"O Chaste Sir:

Thanks for your efforts... If it weren't for you, the royalty money wouldn't have arrived until next week. I apologize for the inconvenience, and would be glad to give you 1/100% commission...

I'll be glad to give up writing for 'Fragments', I'm fed up with triviality. I want to write something more important, or not write at all. Meanwhile, I'll be broke by the end of January, so to avoid family members and creditors who make me ill, I must once again trouble you for a loan. Help me, and in return I'll send you a prescription.

What a stupid situation! I received a payment of 220 rubles for a translation and the same day I was paid twenty from 'The Alarm Clock,' but now all I have left is thirty rubles and that will be gone by January 22. Tell me, please, my dear, when shall I live like a human being, that is, work and not always be broke? At present, I toil away, and am broke, and as a result I ruin my reputation by having to write trash...

I remain your loving brother and sister

Antonius and Doctor of Medicine Chekhov

P. S. Beside medicine (my wife). I also have literature (my mistress), but I don't talk about her, since they who live in sin will perish in sin."

(Chekhov, letter to Aleksandr, January 17, 1887, Moscow)

"Dear Uncle Mitrofan Yegorovich:

During the holidays I was so overwhelmed with work that on Mother's name day I almost dropped dead from exhaustion...

I must tell you that in Petersburg I am now the most fashionable writer. This is evident in the newspapers and journals, where since the end of 1886 my name has been bandied about every which way and more than I deserve. The result of this growth of my literary reputation is that I get a number of assignments and invitations resulting in high-pressure and exhaustion. My work is nerve-wracking, agitating and straining. ... Every newspaper report about me upsets both my family and me... They read my stories aloud at public gatherings. Wherever I go, people point me out: I'm overwhelmed with acquaintances, and so on. I've had not one day of peace, and feel as though I were on tenterhooks every moment...

That's all. Please accept my sincerest regards...

Yours, A. Chekhov"

(Chekhov, letter to Uncle Mitrofan, January 18, 1887, Moscow)

"[...] I wrote this ['Ivanov'] play off the top of my head, almost, after one conversation with Korsh ...Went to bed, thought up a theme, and wrote it down...and in 10 days time, too. As for the merits of the play, I cannot be the judge. It came out to be suspiciously short in length. Everyone likes it. Korsh hasn't found a single flaw or any mistake in the stage directions, for that matter, which proves how sharp and discerning my critics are. It's the first time I've ever written a play,[1] ergo mistakes are unavoidable. The plot is fairly complicated and not at all crude. I end each act like a short story. All the acts run on peacefully and quietly, but at the end I give the audience a wallop ... No matter how bad the play is, I have created a type of literary significance...

There are fourteen characters in the play, of whom five are women. I fear, however, that my women, with the exception of one, are not well developed.

Regards,

A. Chekhov"

(Chekhov, letter to Aleksandr, October 10-12, 1887)

"Well the play ['Ivanov'] has opened...I'll give you an account, point by point. To begin with: Korsh promised me ten rehearsals and only gave me four, of which only two can be called rehearsals, since the other two were more like tournaments for the actors to display their skill

in argument and verbal abuse. Only the actors Davydov and Glama knew their parts; the rest of them relied on the prompter and inner conviction.

Act One. I'm backstage in a little box that looks like a prisoner's cell. The family is in an orchestra box: they're all trembling....Contrary to all expectations, I feel calm and collected... The actors are deeply agitated and tense; they keep crossing themselves... Curtain up. Enter the leading man, uncertain, unfamiliar with his lines. As a result, from the very first moment I don't even recognize my play. The actor Kiselevsky, on whom I had high hopes, didn't get a single line right. Literally—not a single one. He simply made it all up. All this notwithstanding (including the director's blunders), the first act was a great success. There were many curtain calls.

Act Two: There's a crowd of people onstage. Guests. Not knowing their lines, they get all muddled and talk nonsense. Every word uttered is like a knife in my back. But—O Muse!—this act is a great hit, too. The entire cast gets a curtain call, and they call me out too, twice. Everyone congratulates me on my success.

Act Three: The acting isn't too bad. Again, it's a huge success. I get called out three times. Talent and virtue reign supreme.

Act Four: Scene I. Again, it's not going too badly. There are curtain calls. Then comes an interminable, exhausting intermission. The audience, unaccustomed to a break and a visit to the buffet between scenes, starts complaining. The curtain goes up on scene two. It's a beautiful set—the table is laid for the wedding scene. The orchestra plays a flourish; enter the groomsmen ––they're drunk, you see, and therefore feel obliged to fool around. It's a brawl, a disgrace, and I'm horrified. Whereupon Kiselevsky enters; it's his most poetic passage, he's supposed to be acting his heart out, but since Kiselevsky doesn't know his lines—he's as drunk as a cobbler—the brief poetic dialogue is painfully drawn out and awful. The audience is at a loss. The hero dies at the end of the play from a mortal insult. Meanwhile, the audience is so tired and bored that they couldn't care less; and they can't figure out why he died, anyway. (This ending was the actors' idea, not mine; I have another version.) During one of the curtain calls, I could hear distinct hissing, although it was drowned out by applause and stamping feet.

In general, I'm exhausted and irritated. In fact, I'm disgusted, even though the play was a solid hit... Theatre lovers say they've never seen such a disturbance in a theatre, ever, nor as much general applauding and hissing and brawling as they heard at my play. And there's never been a playwright at the Korsh who took a curtain call after the second act.

The play will be performed for a second time on the 23rd, with the alternate ending and several other changes—and I am getting rid of those groomsmen.

More details when I see you.

Yours, A. Chekhov"

(Chekhov, letter to Aleksandr, November 20, 1887)

"Well, it's over at last. Everything has settled down, the dust has cleared, and once again I'm sitting at my desk, calmly writing a story. You can't imagine what it was like! ... The devil only knows what they saw in an insignificant piece of nonsense such as my little play. I already wrote to you that the premiere caused more excitement in the audience and backstage than the prompter had seen in all his thirty-two years in the theatre. People were screaming and yelling and clapping and hissing, there was almost a brawl in the buffet, some students in the gallery tried to throw someone out, and two people were ejected by the police. It was general pandemonium. Our sister almost fainted. The schoolteacher Dukovsky had heart palpitations and ran out of the theatre, and Anna Kiselyova's husband, for no apparent reason, held his head in his hands and cried out, in dead seriousness: 'Now what am I going to do?'

The actors were in a state of shock. [...]

The day after the premiere a review appeared in the 'Moscow Press' calling my play insolently cynical, immoral rubbish. The 'Moscow Gazette' praised it. [...]

Am I boring you with all this? I've felt like a psychopath all November.

Yours, Schiller Shakespearovich Goethe"

(Chehkov, letter to Aleksandr, November 24, 1887, Moscow)

Chekhov still hadn't given up on serious dramatic work, an ambition he had been nurturing since he reviewed *Hamlet* in 1882. But the rejection of that earlier unfinished effort, now known as *Platonov*, had discouraged him. Moreover, his internal artistic voice told him he wasn't ready. As a writer with serious intentions whose talent and success lay in the comedic, he had not yet found a way to blend these elements in the dramatic form; indeed, he was just beginning to blend those tonalities in his short stories.

So he continued to write for theatre in the short form. In January, with characteristic offhandedness (a tone he used to mask the attempts he cared for most, but felt the least confident in writing), he wrote *Calchas*, his third short play in three years. In a letter to Mme. Kiselyova, he boasted that it took him an hour and five minutes to write. Adapted from a story "Calchas" he had written the year before, the play features a decrepit old actor inspired by a minor character in Shakespeare's *Troilus and Cressida*. Set in a darkened, empty provincial theatre late at night following a performance, Svetlovidov, (meaning "light" and "see"), a veteran spear-carrier from many a Shakespearean production, sits alone on stage. He seizes the moment and, emboldened by drink, breaks out in impassioned speeches from *Hamlet*, *Othello*, and *King Lear*, reciting the roles he has longed to play to an audience of one—an ancient prompter, who has also remained behind. With its alternating vaudevillian and pathetic tones, *Calchas* (*Swan Song*, as he later titled it) would represent a major step in Chekhov's experimentation in blending the comedic with the tragic. It also was, in a way, his valentine to the theatre.

But before he could send it out, he became distracted with his other on-going responsibilities—medicine and the writing of short stories. In the early months of 1887, he received both a raise and a generous advance from Suvorin to write for the *New Times*, as well as a commission to work on a collection of his stories entitled *In the Twilight*, which would include new ones he had written early that year such as "Typhus," "The Weariness of Life," and "The Mystery."

Then a bout of restlessness followed. In March, to avoid a typhoid epidemic and family obligations, he made a trip south to Taganrog. Contrary to his expectations (he was hoping for a nostalgic journey), he was appalled by the backwardness and squalor of his town of origin. "60,000 inhabitants who do nothing other than eat, drink, procreate, and have no other interests whatsoever," he wrote his publisher Leikin. He found the site of the city beautiful and the climate favorable; however, as he wrote, "all this is wasted.... There are no patriots, no businessmen, no poets, not even a decent baker."[2] In contrast, his nostalgic return to the steppe on his way back to Moscow gave him a broad range of pleasurable experiences. He attended a wildly colorful, two-day Cossack wedding, and wrote to his family: "I got so drunk that I mistook the wine bottles for the girls, and the girls for the wine bottles."[3] He next stayed at a monastery near Kharkov. The beautiful, secluded setting, the services, the pilgrims—all made a lasting impression on him. (He would later incorporate that personal pilgrimage into the fantasies of the pious Varya, one of the characters in his final play, *The Cherry Orchard*.)

Chekhov spent the summer once again in Babkino. Pressured with continued financial worries, he increased his output of stories for the *New Times* to pay off Suvorin's advances. One, "Happiness," included the peculiar detail of the "breaking string," a strange sound he had heard while fishing one afternoon on the river. (Upon inquiring, he was told it came from a mineshaft in the area, where a cable had snapped and a cable car tumbled down into the depths.) Almost twenty years later, he would incorporate that apocryphal sound in his final play *The Cherry Orchard*.

In the fall, to his surprise, he received a *carte blanche* invitation from the most reputable commercial theatre in Moscow to write a full–length play. He had made fun of the Korsh Theatre as producing "preposterous drama," to which its owner, Fyodor Korsh, replied: "Why don't you write a play yourself?!"

At first he declined emphatically. "I have already been to the Korsh Theatre twice," he wrote his friend Mme. Kiselyova, "and both times Korsh tried to convince me write a play for him. I replied: 'With pleasure!' And of course I will not write a play…I don't want to have anything to do with theatres, nor with the public, for that matter—to hell with them!"[4]

But it didn't take long to change his mind. After all, as the playwright, he would receive 2% of the box office as well as a commission. Here, at last, was a chance to make his mark as a serious dramatist and to accomplish on the stage what Pushkin, Lermontov and Turgenev had done—namely, to create a type "of literary significance," as Chekhov put it, but in his own fashion. "Among all the successful Russian writers, I am the most light-hearted and least serious," he wrote his friend Korolenko. "To put it poetically, I loved my pure muse but I didn't respect her. I was unfaithful to her, and I took her to places that were unsuitable for her."[5] With this opportunity, he could change his literary image. Moreover, here was a chance to write a serious play under the name of Anton Chekhov, not Chekhonte.

So, having written his friends that he had no intentions of doing so, in a typical turn-about (where the theatre is concerned), Chekhov leapt at the opportunity for a commission to write a full-length play, and joined the Russian Society of Dramatists and Operatic Composers.

In a burst of excitement and inspiration, he sat down at the end of September and within ten days time delivered to Korsh a full-length play entitled *Ivanov*, subtitled "a comedy." Giddy with accomplishment, he wrote to his brother Aleksandr, boasting of the ease with which he had written it, and taking special pride in the Korsh's praise of his stage directions. He was, however, naïve as to the process of working in the theatre, and his euphoria soon evaporated as preparation began for the production. Things went badly from the outset, when Chekhov discovered that there were only to be four days of rehearsal (he'd been promised ten), and only two of the cast members knew their lines. He desperately tried to withdraw the play, but to no avail. Ultimately, he was told to stay away from rehearsals—which only fueled his agitation.

The premiere performance of *Ivanov* on November 17 is legendary in the annals of Russian theatre. Chekhov's account of it in his letter to Aleksandr reads like a tragicomedy in and of itself. Of the cast, he reported misspoken lines and drunken performances. Vladimir Davydov, the actor playing Ivanov, knew his part, as did

Aleksandra Glama, who played Ivanov's wife Sara, but the other actors were oblivious. Of the audience, he reported responses ranging from general incomprehension to a wild mixture of applauding, hissing, booing, fist fights in the buffet during intermission, and the eviction of some rowdy spectators. Chekhov's sister Masha almost fainted from the trauma of it all. At the same time, to Chekhov's amazement, the audience demanded that he take two curtain calls at the end of the second act and three at the end of the third. (According to the theatre convention of the day, actors took bows at the end of each act of a play. Following that, there would be an intermission that could last up to forty-five minutes, during which they would patronize the buffet and drink champagne.)

The playwright himself was in a state of turmoil and anxiety over the wildly divergent critical response to the play. At first, he was euphoric from all the attention he received from audience, critics, and the *literati* not only in Moscow, but also in St. Petersburg, where there were demands for a production. He playfully signed a letter to Aleksandr: "Schiller Shakespearovich Goethe."

At the same time, however, he took the criticism of his play to heart. What frustrated him most was the public and the critics' misunderstanding of his central character, Ivanov. In telling the story of a young, well-educated, refined member of the landed gentry class, suffocating from *ennui* on his country estate, hating himself for not being able to effect change in his backward, provincial, corrupt country, Chekhov had sought to create a tragic hero. Consumed with frustration and self-loathing, Ivanov acts out. Right before the eyes of his saint-like wife, Anna Petrovna, who is dying of tuberculosis, he begins a love affair with Sasha, the young daughter of his decent, well-intending neighbor, Lebedev (who is also his creditor). Anna's physician, the righteous Dr. Lvov, confronts Ivanov for his cruel, irresponsible behavior, but to no avail. After Anna dies, Ivanov agrees to marry Sasha, but, unable to bear the burden of guilt and self-loathing, he shoots himself (onstage) in front of his horrified bride and wedding guests.

Chekhov had high ambitions for his play. With his central character, Ivanov, he sought to create a Russian Hamlet, whose suffering and ultimate downfall would provoke the same cathartic feelings of pity and fear that classical plays in the Aristotelean tradition inspired. And yet, he was told that Ivanov came across either as a scoundrel or as an unsympathetic "superfluous man."

The response bewildered Chekhov. Clearly this interpretation of his intentions must be attributed to his failure as a dramatist, he felt. He was well aware of the tradition of the "superfluous man"—that romantic, Byronic anti-heroic type found in nineteenth century Russian novels. One example is the character of Pechorin in Lermontov's novel *A Hero of Our Times* (1840)—handsome, moody, damned, unstable, aloof, disenchanted, acting out to relieve the tedium of life or to avenge himself on a society he despises. Another example is the character of Oblomov (1859), in Goncharov's eponymous novel—a privileged, educated member of the landed gentry who is incapable of action of any kind and has sunken into sloth and sleep.

With the character of Ivanov, Chekhov wanted to go deeper than his predecessors did with their "superfluous men" and create his own compelling character of "literary significance." In an eight page letter to Suvorin written a year later (December 30, 1888), Chekhov justified his attempt to create a modern-day Russian Hamlet whose inability to change the world around him comes not from a character flaw but rather from the alienating environment and the times. Ivanov is a tragic victim of Russia life, he explains; his *ennui* is a disease afflicting all educated Russians of the landed gentry. Once a young man of promise and privilege, committed to every cause imaginable after graduating university—schools, peasant life, farming, social reform—Ivanov has burned out at thirty-five. Physically and morally depleted, he is filled with an indefinable feeling of guilt—an exclusively "Russian feeling," as Chekhov puts it—guilt for everything that is wrong with the world around him, a world he is unable to transform. To weariness, disappointment, boredom and apathy, he adds loneliness, isolated on his estate in the provinces, numbed by long winter evenings, surrounded by the same dreary people, burdened with responsibilities and problems. He becomes depressed and irritable. (Chekhov even draws a graph in the letter, charting Ivanov's emotional mood swings.) Surrounded by an insipid coterie of narrow-minded, self-absorbed provincial landed gentry and hangers-on, he feels misunderstood, hopeless, and alone.

It is clear from this impassioned letter that Chekhov was deeply invested in this character portrayal. Indeed, he explained Ivanov's behavior in scrupulous detail, as though he were justifying the behavior of a friend or relative for whom he was responsible. As defensive as his tone was in that letter, however, he accepted responsibility for the flaws in his character portrayal. "I failed in my attempt to write a play," he ended his letter to Suvorin. "It's a pity, of course."[6]

There were other controversial issues in the play, too. Additionally problematic was Ivanov's treatment of his first wife, Anna, a young Jewish woman who is afflicted with tuberculosis. Ivanov falls in love with his neighbor's daughter Sasha right before his invalid wife's eyes. Anna confronts him over his cruelty, saying that she gave up everything for him (her family, her home, her religion, even her name, "Sara") and accusing him of trying to deceive Sasha and her father just as Ivanov had deceived her. Ivanov responds by lashing out at her, calling her a "Jew," telling her that her disease is terminal, and revealing Dr. Lvov's prognosis that she will die at any moment. Ivanov's cruel, arbitrary behavior appears to be incomprehensible, and yet Chekhov insisted that he meant to show that Ivanov is "acting out," driven to such degrees of despair and self-loathing that he cannot help himself.[7]

Chekhov was stung by the negative reviews of *Ivanov* (including one from the editor of *The Dragonfly* who sought revenge for Chekhov abandoning his publication). He fled to St. Petersburg in November. "I wanted to be original," he confided ruefully to Aleksandr.[8] Clearly, he felt he had failed in his attempt. He vowed never again to write serious drama—an oath he would take after the opening of every new play he would subsequently write.

Though his attempt may have been flawed, Chekhov had indeed written something original in *Ivanov*. He sensed, correctly, that the Moscow theatre scene of the 1880s was characterized by stagnation, conservatism, and creative torpor. There were two kinds of theatre at the time: the Imperial Theatre, like the Maly in Moscow and the Aleksandrinsky in St. Petersburg, and the privately owned theatres, like the Korsh in Moscow where *Ivanov* had premiered. At the time, the offerings at the Maly, Moscow's preeminent theatre, were stale and conventional. The repertoire was predictable, dominated primarily by Ostrovsky, a prolific

Russian dramatist of the mid-nineteenth century, and established European classics by dramatists like Schiller and Hugo. As far as new plays were concerned, there were several writers-in-residence at the Maly whose task it was to write expressly for the company's leading actors (Yermolova, for example, the actress who had rejected *Platonov*, was one of the Maly company). The positions of these writers were only secure if their work pleased the actors—and in any event, these were not distinguished dramatists of the day. Moreover, there was no artistic leadership—the theatre was run by an administrator appointed by the government, not an artist. The stage directors had no creative function or power.

In short, at the time Chekhov wrote *Ivanov*, the Russian theatre was stagnating. There were no visionaries on the horizon to lead it into new artistic territory. And there was no system for identifying, nurturing and developing serious new dramatists. The theatre of Chekhov's day was characterized by mediocre new writing, a low level of production values, and uneducated, ill-prepared actors. "The contemporary theatre is like a rash, a bad urban disease. It is necessary to sweep away this disease with a broom," he wrote Suvorin.[9] Years later, Chekhov would once again voice his view of the Russian theatre of the 1880s—this time, through the words of his character, Treplev, in *The Seagull*:

> *"... if you ask me, our theatre today is dull and narrow minded. Every evening, when the curtain goes up and there, under the bright lights, in a room with three walls, those celebrated artists, those high priests of our sacred art, when they play it all out before us, how we mortals eat, and drink, and love, and go around wearing our clothes and leading our lives; when out of this vulgar scenario we are served up some kind of message or moral, however meager, ready for our daily domestic consumption; when after its one thousandth incarnation all these plays seem to me to be the same, time after time after time the same, then I flee—I flee like Maupassant fled the Eiffel Tower, because it outraged him how enormously trite it was." (Treplev, in 'The Seagull,' Act I.)*[10]

And that's exactly what the author of the controversial *Ivanov* did. He had tried to make his mark on the Russian theatre with "something original"—the Russian *Hamlet*—but his efforts were misunderstood. In his eyes, he had failed.

A week after the opening of his new play, he fled from Moscow in frustration and shame.

"It's too early for me to begin writing plays"

(Chekhov, letter to Suvorin, December 30, 1888, Moscow)

1888

"Esteemed Aleksei Sergeevich:

[...] An artist must not be the judge of his characters or of what they say, but only an impartial witness . . . My only job is to be talented, that is to distinguish the important from the trivial, to place my characters in the proper light and speak their language. I have been reproached by Leontyev-Shcheglov [the writer] for having finished a story with the phrase: 'In this world you just can't make head or tail of anything.' He believes that the artist is a psychologist who must make sense of things. But I don't agree. It's about time that writers—especially genuine literary artists—admit that in this world you can't figure anything out, as Socrates himself discovered, and Voltaire, too. The crowd thinks it knows and understands everything; and the more ignorant it is, the broader its horizon appears to be. If, on the other hand, the artist, in whom the crowd believes, has the confidence to admit that he understands nothing of what he sees, this and this alone is a significant contribution to the advancement of knowledge.

Your devoted servant,

A. Chekhov"

(Chekhov, letter to Suvorin, May 30, 1888, Sumy)

"You advise me not to hunt two hares and stop thinking about giving up the practice of medicine... .I don't know why one shouldn't hunt two hares even in the literal sense... I feel more confident and satisfied with myself when I think that I have two professions and not one. Medicine is my lawful wife and literature is my mistress. When I get tired of one I spend the night with the other. Though it's disorderly, at least it's not dull, and besides, neither of them loses anything from my infidelity. If I didn't practice medicine, I don't

think I could give my leisure time and thought to literature. I lack discipline.

Regards to all,

A. Chekhov"

(Chekhov, letter to Suvorin, September 11, 1888, Moscow)

" [...] I am neither liberal, nor conservative, nor gradualist, nor monk, nor indifferentist. I would like to be a free artist and nothing more, and I regret God has not given me the power to be one. I hate lying and violence in all forms... Pharisaism, stupidity and despotism reign not in merchants' houses and prisons alone. I see them in science, in literature, in the younger generation. That's why I show no partiality either to policemen, or butchers, or scholars, or writers, or young people. My holiest of holies is the human body, health, intelligence, talent, inspiration, love and absolute freedom—freedom from violence and freedom from lying, in whatever forms they may take. This is the program I would follow if I were a great artist.

Never mind, I'm going on and on here. Be well.

Yours, A. Chekhov"

(Chekhov, letter to Pleshcheev, October 4, 1888, Moscow)

"Word of the [Pushkin] prize has had a stunning effect. It swept through my apartment and through Moscow like the terrible thunder of immortal Zeus. I walk around these days like a man in love. Mother and Father spout complete nonsense and are ecstatic beyond words; Sister, guarding our reputation with the fierceness and fussiness of a lady at court, is nervous and exacting; she is visiting friends and spreading the news. Jean Shcheglov gabs on and on about literary Iagos and about the 500 enemies I'm acquiring for the 500 rubles. I ran into the Lenskys, and they make me promise I'd have dinner with them. I met a certain lady whose occupation it is to worship the talented—she also invited me to dinner. The inspector of the local school dropped by to congratulate me and to buy a copy of my story 'Kashtanka' for 200 rubles, hoping to make a profit on the deal... Second and third-rate writers of newspaper fiction should build a monument for me or at least present

me with a silver cigarette case—after all, I've paved the way for them to the prestigious periodicals and the laurels straight to the hearts of the ordinary folk. As it stands, this is my sole contribution; meanwhile, everything I've written, everything I've received the prize for, won't last in men's memories for more than a decade.

[...] Indeed, my luck is going so well, that I'm starting to cast suspicious eyes toward heaven. I'd better hide under the table, where I'll sit quietly, calmly, keeping my voice down. Until I take my next big step—namely, to write a novel—I'll lay low, keep to myself, write unpretentious little stories and little plays. I won't climb mountains or fall off them, I'll just keep plodding along....I'll follow the advice of the Ukrainian who said: 'If I were Tsar, I'd steal 100 rubles and scram.' As long I'm a little Tsar in my own ant-hill, I'll steal that 100 rubles and get out of here. Never mind, I'm starting to write nonsense. Meanwhile, people are talking about me. Strike while the iron is hot. There ought to be an advertisement of both my books [in the journals] when the prize is officially announced. Meanwhile, I'll put the 500 rubles aside to buy a farmhouse. The proceeds from the sales of the books will go to that, too.

Yours, A. Chekhov"

(Chekhov, letter to Suvorin, October 10, 1888, Moscow)

"It's not the job of the artist to solve highly specialized problems. It's bad when an artist addresses something he doesn't understand. We have plenty of specialists around for specialized problems—such as financial issues, the harms of alcoholism, boots, women's illnesses, etc. An artist must judge only what he understands. His sphere is as narrow as the sphere of any other specialist—on this point I am consistent. Those who maintain that there are no questions, only answers—they are the ones who have never written and have no experience with images. An artist observes, selects, guesses, combines...

You confuse two things: answering a question, and posing one. Only the latter is the obligation of the artist. In 'Anna Karenina' or 'Eugene Onegin', for example, not a single question is answered, but nonetheless you find these works satisfying only because the questions in them are posed properly. The court is obligated to pose the questions correctly—it's up to the jurors to answer them, each according to his own taste...

[...] When writing a story, you should concern yourself first and foremost about its framework. From an abundance of characters, heroic and semi-heroic, you pick one—a wife or a husband—you place that persona against a backdrop and draw that persona only, and the rest you scatter in the background, like small change, and from that you produce something like a heavenly firmament—one moon and a mass of tiny stars...

...Subjects for at least five long stories and two novels are already floating around in my brain...It's a veritable army, begging to be let out and awaiting its commands. Everything I've written up until now is nonsense in comparison to what I shall one day be able to write...and with pleasure... I don't relish my success, because these new subjects in my head are jealous of those that have already been written down in my other writings. The nonsense has already been written, while the good stuff is lying around in the warehouse... Everything that's still in my head interests me, touches, and excites me...

Forgive me for taking your time with all this nonsense about myself. It just flowed from my pen...

Thank you for printing my pieces. For the love of God, don't stand on ceremony—cut, lengthen, change, discard, do whatever you want with them. I give you 'carte blanche'. I'll be grateful, if my writing doesn't take up other people's space.

Yours, A. Chekhov"

(Chekhov, letter to Suvorin, October 27, 1888, Moscow)

"Dear Jean-ushka:

Now about 'The Bear'. Solovtsov played the role [of Smirnov] phenomenally. Rybchinskaya [in the role of Popova] did just fine; she was lovely. There was continuous and uproarious laughter throughout; the monologues were interrupted by applause. After the first and second performances, the author and the actors were called out for the curtain call. All the dear critics, except for Vasilyev, praised it.

After the first performance we had an unfortunate accident. The coffee pot killed my 'Bear'. Rybchinskaya was drinking coffee, and the coffee pot burst from too much steam and scalded her face. Glama played her role at the second performance, and she was fine. But then she left for St. Petersburg, and so my furry teddy bear died, unfortunately. It didn't even live to be three days old. Rybchinskaya promises to be well by Sunday. [...]

So now I'm a very popular vaudeville writer, am I? My God, how they grab them! If in all my life I somehow succeed in scribbling a dozen empty trifles, I'll thank God for it... This season, I'll write a vaudeville, and that will keep me happy till the summer. Now, is that what you call work?

Yours, Antoine"

(Chekhov, letter to Leontyev-Shcheglov, November 2, 1888, Moscow)

"Greetings, Aleksei Sergeevich:

...[The critic Merezhkovsky] honors me by calling me a poet, he calls my stories novellas, and he calls my heroes 'failures.' We've heard it all before. It's high time we gave these cliches like 'failures,' 'superfluous men,' and so on, and thought up something original on our own... We've got to do whatever we can to see that the theater passes from the hands of the grocers into the hands of the literary. Otherwise the theatre is doomed.

[...] The coffee pot has scalded my 'Bear'. Rybchinskaya is sick, and there's no one to play her role...

Yours, A. Chekhov.

P. S. It's best to publish one-act vaudevilles in the summer. They don't do well in the winter. I'll write a vaudeville every month in the summer, and shall have to forego the pleasure in the winter."

(Chekhov, letter to Suvorin, November 3, 1888, Moscow)

"Dear Jean-chik:

[...] I've scribbled a worthless little vaudeville especially for the provinces called 'The Proposal' and sent it to the censor. [...] If, my angel, you happen to be at the censor's, then tell [them] that...I humbly beseech the cen-

sorial 'hydra' not to keep the vaudeville in quarantine. It's a wretched, vulgar, boring little skit, but it will be fine for the provinces...I won't put it on in the capitals [Moscow and St. Petersburg], though...

The contemporary theatre is like a rash, a bad urban disease. It is necessary to sweep away this disease with a broom; to like it is not healthy. You'll start arguing with me and repeating the same old saying: the theatre is a school, it educates, and so on and so on... But I'll tell you what I see: the present theatre is not above the crowd—on the contrary, the life of the crowd is above the theatre, more clever than the theatre, even! Therefore, that means the theatre is not a school, but something else...

Yours, Antoine"

(Chekhov, letter to Leontyev-Shcheglov, November 7, 1888, Moscow)

"[...] You say that writers are God's elect. I won't argue... I don't know if I've suffered more than shoemakers, mathematicians, or train conductors; and I do not know who speaks through my lips—God or someone worse. Allow me to bring up just one minor irritation which I've experienced and I'm sure you have two. You and I like ordinary people; they like us because they regard us as out of the ordinary. For example, they invite me out and wine and dine me like a general at a wedding. My sister is indignant that she's invited everywhere simply because she is a writer's sister. Hence it follows that if in the eyes of our friends we should appear tomorrow as ordinary mortals, they will leave off loving us, and will only pity us. And that's vile. Vile, too, because they love us for the very things that we often don't love in ourselves.

Yours, A. Chekhov"

(Chekhov, letter to Suvorin, November 24-25, 1888, Moscow)

"[...] I've just finished revising my 'Bolvanov' [Ivanov] and am sending it to you. I'm sick of it... [...] At least now my Mr. Ivanov is much more intelligible. The ending does not entirely satisfy me (except for the shot, everything pales), but I console myself with the thought that it is not yet in final form. [...] One has to write plays either badly

or impudently... [...] I give you my word that never again shall I write such an intellectual and vile play as 'Ivanov'. If 'Ivanov' does not succeed I shall not be surprised, and shall not blame it on intrigues or dirty tricks...

Yours, A. Chekhov"

(Chekhov, letter to Suvorin, December 19, 1888, Moscow)

"Dear Aleksei Sergeevich:

There are moments when I completely lose heart. For whom and for what do I write? For the public? But I don't have a feeling for the public, and believe in it less than I do in ghosts. The public is ill-bred, ill-educated, and the best are insincere in their attitude towards us. Does the public want me or not? I don't know. Some say not, and that I'm wasting my time. The Academy gave me the prize—and who knows why. Write for money? But I never have any money, and, not being used to it, I am almost indifferent to it. So when I write for money, it's without motivation. For praise? But praise merely irritates me. The literary circles, students, colleagues, clever young ladies and so on praised my story 'The Breakdown', for example, but only one critic noticed the description of the falling snow. And so on and so on.

If we had true critics, then I'd know I was providing material, whether good or bad, no matter. I'd know that—for people who are dedicated to the study of life - I am as necessary as stars are to astronomers. And then I'd throw myself into my work, knowing what I was working for. But, as it stands, you, I, and the rest, like lunatics, are writing books for our own pleasure. To please oneself, of course, is a good thing; you feel pleasure while you're writing, but then afterwards? Countless tribes, religions, languages, cultures have vanished without a trace because there were no historians and scientists. In the same way countless lives and works of art vanish, owing to the complete absence of criticism. They say that criticism would be pointless since modern work is so poor and insignificant. But I think that's a narrow point of view. Not only should life's pluses be studied, but also its minuses. The conviction that the 'eighties' haven't produced a single writer may in itself provide material enough for five volumes. [...]

When I'm all written out, I'll start writing 'vaudevilles' and living on them. I think I could write a hundred a year. Vaudeville plots spout out of me like oil from the depths of the Baku. [...] In general, life is boring, and at times I even hate it—something I've never felt before. Long, stupid conversations, visitors, favor-mongers, handouts of a ruble or two or three, cab fare for patients who don't pay me a kopek—in a word, it's all such a mess that I feel like running away from home. People borrowing money from me who don't pay me back, taking books, wasting my time—the only thing that's lacking is unrequited love. [...]

A. Chekhov"

(Chekhov, letter to Suvorin, December 23, 1888, Moscow)

"[...] You write that one ought to work not for the critics but for the public, that it is too early for me to complain. It's very nice to think that one works for the public, of course, but do I know that for sure? Because of the flimsiness of my work and other qualities too, I'm not wholly satisfied with it. As for the public (I'm not calling it base), its attitude toward us is dismissive and insincere. One will never hear the truth from it, and therefore who knows if it needs me or not. It's too early to be complaining, but it's never too early to ask myself: am I occupying myself with work or with nonsense? Critics keep quiet, the public lies, but my intuition tells me I'm writing nonsense. Am I complaining? I don't remember the tone of my letter, but if it is so, then I'm complaining not for myself alone, but for all our fellow writers for whom I have infinite compassion.

All week long I've been as mean as a son of a bitch. Hemorrhoids with itching and bleeding, visitors, boredom. At the beginning of the holidays I was caring for a patient one evening who died before my very eyes. Nothing very cheery to report, I'm afraid. Spite is the pettiness of the soul. I confess it, and I'm not proud of it. I'm particularly annoyed with myself that I've confided in you of my melancholy, which is very uninteresting and shameful at an age as rich and as rhapsodized by the poets as mine. [...]

Sincerely yours, A. Chekhov"

(Chekhov, letter to Suvorin, December 26, 1888, Moscow)

"[...] If my Ivanov comes across as either a scoundrel or a 'superfluous man,' and the doctor a great one, if it's incomprehensible why Sara [Anna] and Sasha love Ivanov, then clearly my play hasn't come across and putting it on [again] is out of the question.

Here's how I see my main characters. Ivanov is landed gentry, a university graduate, not remarkable in any way. In temperament, he's excitable, passionate, easily infatuated, honest, direct, like the majority of educated gentry. He lived on his country estate and held a post in the local government. In sum, he has an excellent background, like the majority of the Russian intelligentsia. However, once he reaches thirty—thirty five, he begins to suffer from fatigue and boredom.

Although he may be conscious of this physical fatigue and boredom, still he doesn't understand what is happening to him and what to do about it.

This change in him offends his sense of decency. He seeks reasons for it and doesn't find them. Instead, he looks within himself and finds only an indefinable feeling of guilt. This is a Russian feeling. A Russian—whether someone in his household has just died, or he has fallen ill, or he owes someone money, or is lending money himself—always feels guilty. And while Ivanov is atoning for one thing for another, at the same time that guilt keeps growing within him.

To fatigue, boredom and guilt add one more enemy: loneliness. If Ivanov were a government official, an actor, a priest or a professor, he would become accustomed to his circumstances. But he lives on a country estate. He is in the provinces. The people around him are either drunkards or compulsive card players or [self-righteous] like the doctor. None of them cares a bit about his feelings or the changes within him. He is lonely. The long winters, endless evenings, withered gardens, empty rooms, carping count, ailing wife... There is no escape. The same question torments him at every moment: Where can I go?

Now comes the fifth enemy. Ivanov is exhausted, he doesn't understand himself, but life goes on with demands and problems he must solve, whether he wants to or not. The sick wife, the debts, the Sasha who clings to him—all are problems. The Ivanovs of the world don't solve them, rather they collapse under their weight. They're at their wits ends, they give up, they're irritable, do foolish things and in the end, give in to their frazzled nerves, lose their footing, and descend to the ranks of the 'broken' and 'misunderstood.'

[...] About the women. Why do they love? Sara [Anna] loves Ivanov because he's a good man, he's passionate, brilliant, and as articulate and fiery as Dr. Lvov. She loves him as long as he's exciting and interesting. But when he starts acting out, she no longer understands him and by the end of the third she speaks her mind.

Sasha is a young woman of the new age. Educated, intelligent, honest, and so on. She chooses the thirty-five year old Ivanov because he's the only fish in the pond, so to speak. He's the best. She's known him since she was little, at a time when he was in top form, before he burned out. He's a friend of her father's, after all.

It's a case of a female whom the males conquer not by the brightness of their feathers, nor by their versatility, nor by their courage, but rather by their complaints and misfortunes. This is a woman who loves men in decline. No sooner does Ivanov fall into a deep slump than the girl is right there beside him. After all, that's what she's been waiting for. My oh my, what a noble, sacred cause! She will resurrect one who has fallen, put him back on his feet again, make him happy. She doesn't love Ivanov, she loves the cause.

My fingers ache, so I'll finish here. If all the above is not in the play, then a production of it is out of the question. It means that I haven't written what I wanted to. Withdraw the play. If the public leaves the theatre thinking that the Ivanovs of the world are scoundrels and that the Dr. Lvovs are great men, then I'll tender my resignation and throw my pen to the devil.

To be perfectly honest, what tempted me to agree to this production was neither fame nor Savina [the actress]... I was counting on earning a thousand rubles. But better to borrow it than to take such a foolish risk.

Don't tempt me with success! For me, success lies ahead, if I don't die, that is. I wager that sooner or later I'll

> *make a killing of six to seven thousand. Want to bet on it?*
>
> *... I've tired you out with this letter, haven't I? 'Basta'!*
>
> *Forgive me, my dear fellow, for this desperately long, tiresome letter.*
>
> *Yours, A. Chekhov*
>
> *P. S. ... I didn't know how to write a play. It's a pity, of course. Ivanov and Lvov seemed so alive in my imagination. I'm telling you this in all honesty, truly, these people sprang from my head—not of sea foam, not of preconceived ideas, not of intellectualization, not by chance. They are the result of the observation and study of life. They are still there in my mind, I feel I haven't distorted or exaggerated them one iota. And if on paper they came out lifeless and unclear, the fault lies not in them, but in my inability to express myself. Apparently, it's still too early for me to be writing plays."*
> (Chekhov, letter to Suvorin, December 30, 1888, Moscow)

With *Ivanov*, it would appear that Chekhov had accomplished what he wanted—he was now being taken seriously as a dramatist. But the conflicting responses from audience and critics—and his growing conviction that their misinterpretation of the play was a result of his own failings as a dramatist—prevented him from enjoying this new-found recognition.

Arriving in St. Petersburg, he took refuge with his brother Aleksandr and his dysfunctional family, while he nursed his own wounds. There, he gave *Ivanov* to his publisher friend Suvorin to read. Suvorin responded with great enthusiasm, encouraging him to have the play produced in St. Petersburg, but advising him at the same time to do some rewriting and change the subtitle of the play to "drama."

With prospects of another high-stakes production of *Ivanov* now looming, Chekhov faced the onerous task of rewriting the play. Based on suggestions from critics and colleagues like Suvorin, he intended to focus on two issues: 1) clarifying the motivations of the character of Dr. Lvov, whom the audience mistook for the play's hero; and, more importantly, 2) eliciting the audience's sympathy for his main character, Ivanov. The key to this sympathy was Ivanov's suicide at the end—a choice that the audience had not understood. How could he preserve that ending—one he insisted upon—and at the same time make his protagonist's death both convincing and moving to the audiences and critics alike? How could he convey that Ivanov's suicide emanated from despair over his inability to translate his idealism into action? Was this concept of Ivanov as a tragic Russian hero, "a type of literary significance," achievable? Could he translate these intentions into drama, he worried? He agonized over the prospects of having to rewrite his "*Bolvanov*" (as he disparagingly called it), now so repugnant to him. "Everyone in St. Petersburg is waiting for me to put on the play here, they are convinced it will be a hit," he wrote his family, "but after Moscow I find my play so repulsive that I can't even think about it," he wrote his family.[1]

To further compound his anxiety, he was spending time with the St. Petersburg *literati*, whom he found to be a bitter, unhappy and envious lot. They admired his short stories, they even called on him for medical advice and attention. But he wondered how this judgmental, back-biting artistic community would respond to his *Ivanov*.

Chekhov eagerly sought distractions from the dreaded rewriting. In the early months of 1888, he wrote a longer story, "The Steppe," about a child's journey through the Don steppes in Southern Russia. Infused with childhood memories of visits to his grandparents, supplemented with folklore told to him by his mother, it was widely admired by critics and readers alike. His fellow writers, including the fearsome St. Petersburg *literati*, showered it with praise, The critic of the *New Times* compared the story's author to Gogol and Tolstoy.

Still avoiding the *Ivanov* rewrites, Chekhov turned to what came most easily to him—the writing of vaudevilles. By the 1880s, the vaudeville (i.e. Russian adaptations of the French genre) had become one of the most popular forms on the Moscow stage. Imported from France to Russia in the early nineteenth century, the vaudeville was "low comedy" entertainment, a hybrid of burlesque and farce (that once included music and dance, though those elements were eventually discarded). By mid-century, one-act vaudevilles had become immensely popular, and contemporary Russian dramatists started to adapt them because they were the only form likely to get by the stern censorial board that Tsar Aleksandr II had put in place earlier in the century.

By the time Chekhov arrived in Moscow, the Russian vaudeville was a staple in the Russian theatre's classical repertoire, as well as a "star vehicle" for the leading actors of the day.The form was just as his playwright described it in his sketch "The Dramatist"—that is, generally translated from French and German vaudevilles (and not very good ones) with superficial themes, little moral and social content, and no "Russian" flavor other than the characters names which had been substituted for the foreign ones. The content was based on a fairly fixed formula: stock settings (landowners' mansions); stock characters (landowners, damsels-in-distress, the old servant, the suitor, etc.), formulaic plots (a couple in love overcoming obstacles, with a relative or servant as the side-kick or foil), and rapid-paced action, culminating in a happy ending.

By the mid-1880s, the Russian vaudeville, a popular form for almost a century, was in a state of ossification. The timing of Chekhov's arrival on the theatre scene, therefore, was opportune. While he was struggling in his early attempts with the full-length form, the short comedic form came effortlessly to him, and there were neither strong censorial issues nor critical expectations.

Calchas (later to be renamed *Swan Song*), the one-act tragicomedy he had written a year before, opened in February at the Korsh to a positive response. Why not write another short work, he asked himself? Chekhov had recently seen the actor N. N. Solovtsov, a good friend and star at the Korsh Theatre, appearing in a French vaudeville. It featured an elegant lady who offers to marry her boorish but warm-hearted suitor, provided she can control his penchant for uttering profanities. Solovtsov was a huge actor with a booming voice, and Chekhov was so charmed by his performance that he decided to write another vaudeville, with the part of a "Russian boor" for him. "Having nothing better to do, I have written a trivial little farce in the French style called *The Bear,*" he wrote to the poet Polonsky. "When they find out at the *Northern Herald* that I write vaudevilles, I'll become their *bête noir*. No matter how hard I try to be serious, it just doesn't come out that way. I'm always alternating the serious with the trivial."[2]

In *The Bear*, Chekhov parodies the stock types of the brutish bully and the simpering, grieving widow. Furthermore, he adds a surprise twist to the predictable situation comedy that arises from an encounter between the two. Smirnov, a boorish landowner, pays a call on his neighbor Popova, a lovely little widow who is deep in mourning. Rudely disregarding her state, he demands that Popova pay him the 1,200 rubles that her late husband owed him. Though Popova promises to give him his money the day after tomorrow, he refuses to leave until he gets it, shouts at her, and demands vodka from her ancient servant. Insulted by her protestations over his boorish behavior, he launches into a tirade against women. Their mutual insults escalate to the point where Popova fetches her late husband's pistols and challenge Smirnov to a duel. But first, she requests that he teach her how to hold a gun and shoot. In the process, he is smitten, and falls in love with Popova on the spot. "A duel!" she cries, as he envelopes her in his huge arms. A coterie of her staff—including her servant, gardener, coachman, and workman—look on in amazement as the dueling couple lock in a prolonged kiss.

Emboldened by the success of *Swan Song*, Chekhov wrote to the critic Pleshcheev in Moscow who admired his work, asking him to submit *The Bear* to the literary committee of the Imperial Theatres to approve for a Moscow production. "If it's not approved, then you will catch hell from Lucifer and his angels in the other world," he joked. "If I were ever a member of that committee, I'd veto it ruthlessly."[3] *The Bear* was criticized by the censor board, who disdained the trivial subject matter but nonetheless permitted it to be performed as long as certain "rude" language was expunged.

The Bear received its debut on October 28 at the Korsh Theatre in Moscow (the same theatre that had premiered his controversial *Ivanov*), and his "foolish vaudeville, because of its foolishness,"[4] as he described it, was a great success. "At the Korsh, the public is roaring with laughter, [although] my sister and I could play it better," he wrote to Suvorin.[5] "The he-bear and the she-bear are playing their roles rather badly," he wrote to Pleshcheev.[6] *The Bear* would become the most popular play of his dramatic oeuvre during his lifetime, one that would produce a steady income for years. It was also a favorite of Tolstoy's, who allegedly told Chekhov: "As you know, I hate Shakespeare. And your plays are worse than his. However, I do like *The Bear*."

Delighted with its success, Chekhov dashed off another vaudeville, entitled *The Proposal*. In it, he parodied the formulaic plot of a marriage proposal, and the stock characters of the suitor and the intended. Chekhov's suitor, Lomov, is not handsome and dashing—rather, he is shy, awkward, neurotic and hypochondriacal. He is seeking the hand of Natalya Stepanova, his neighbor Chubukov's daughter, who is not the lovely young damsel type either—rather, she is pugnacious, outspoken, and obnoxious. Lomov's feeble, stuttering attempts at proposing result in a fierce argument with Natalya over all sorts of issues, including property boundaries, competitive qualities of their dogs, and so on. As they hurl insults at each other over their respective family members, Chubukov enters, falls into the fray, and they all almost come to blows. (The would-be suitor Lomov, meanwhile, has palpitations, fainting spells and so on.) Despite these outrageous, farcical goings-on, all is somehow resolved at the end, and Chubukov shouts "Champagne!" over the happy couple, who are still fighting fiercely. *The Proposal* would be performed the following summer before the Tsar Aleksandr III at his summer residence (Tsarskoe Selo), and soon became the Imperial favorite.

Though he seemed not to take the short form seriously, Chekhov seemed pleased with the success of writing his one-acts. "Vaudeville plots spout out of me like oil from the depths of the Baku," he wrote Suvorin.[7] In his letters, Chekhov referred to all his short comedies as vaudevilles (he would eventually write eleven), whether he subtitled them "farces," "dramatic studies," "monologues" or "one act plays." His consistent use of the term "vaudeville" seems to indicate his true intention—to set up audience expectations to be entertained according to certain existing theatrical conventions, and to inform the censors, the critics, and the *literati* that the author was presenting a popular, second-rate theatrical form that was not to be taken seriously. This literary subterfuge, or disguise, appealed to the practical joker in Chekhov. On the one hand, he was indeed writing vaudevilles, whose purpose it was to entertain, divert and amuse. This provided a smokescreen, a handy camouflage for the young humorist, to have the freedom and flexibility to experiment with the short theatrical form without serious consequences, as he was finding his dramatist's voice. On the other hand, it also provided him with the opportunity to surprise and delight the public by subverting the conventional form with innovative dramatic techniques and devices.

With *On The Harmful Effects of Tobacco, The Bear, The Proposal,* and the others he would write in the following year, Chekhov elevated a conventional, stale, second-rate form—the vaudeville—into an art form, thereby contributing something new and exciting. For a stagnant Russian theatre that was ready for new forms and new voices, this unanticipated contribution was a breath of fresh air.

Then came the momentous news in October that he had been awarded the prestigious Pushkin Prize, bestowed by the Literary Committee of the Academy of Sciences in St. Petersburg for his collection of stories *In the Twilight*. His family was thrilled by this great honor. Chekhov himself was amazed. "I still lack a political, religious and philosophical world view—it keeps changing every month," he wrote the esteemed critic Grigorovich.[8] To a young writer-friend, Lazarev-Gruzinsky, he wrote: "I am a bourgeois amongst the nobility, and people like me don't last very long, like a taut string which suddenly snaps. All that I write will be forgotten in 5-10 years, but the path paved by me will be free and clear—in this lies my sole merit and contribution."[9]

But his elation was short lived. He still had to face the rewriting of *Ivanov*, and the St. Petersburg production that loomed before him. "You can't dissuade me of my dislike for the scaffold on which the playwright[s] are being executed," he wrote Leontyev-Shcheglov, another young writer who admired his work. "The modern theatre is a world of confusion, nonsense, stupidity and idle talk."[10]

His struggle with the rewriting process, his frustration, and his self-doubt as a playwright found expression in an outpouring of letters to publishers, colleagues, and friends. In these letters, Chekhov reassessed his attitudes toward literature, the role and responsibility of the artist, and what it meant to write for the theatre. This rich correspondence would be, in many ways, the most valuable literary achievement of the year—more significant than the rewriting of *Ivanov* itself. Indeed, the writing of these philosophical and reflective letters was part of the process that would shape him as a dramatist in the years to come.

With *The Bear, The Proposal,* and the letters to his colleagues, this would become one of Chekhov's most busy and productive years in his development as a dramatist. Still, in the midst of all the frantic activity, he endeavored to seek a few moments of rest. He tried to settle into another rented estate in the Ukraine for the summer, but was plagued by restlessness. (Was he running away from facing his health problems, or the rewriting of *Ivanov*?) He spent a few interrupted weeks of summer bliss at the Suvorin's estate, filled with his favorite activities of fishing, hiking, and flirtation, and returned to Moscow—only to suffer another unexpected bout of lung hemorrhaging.

Once again, he dismissed the possibility of consumption. After all, there was too much to be done.

Chekhov's troika (pulled by *The Bear*, *Ivanov*, and *The Wood Demon)* at the crossroads of prose and drama.

"There is a sort of stagnation in my soul..."

(Chekhov, letter to Suvorin, May 4, 1889)

1889

"[...] It would be a great pleasure to read a paper before the Literary Society on how the idea came to me to write 'Ivanov'. It would be like a public confession. I was under the impression that all Russian fiction writers and playwrights felt a need to depict 'the despondent man', and that all of them were writing instinctively, without any definite images in mind and without any point of view. As far as my plan went, I was on the right track, but my execution somehow went wrong. I should have waited! Beyond an abundance of material and talent, something more is needed, something no less important. And that's maturity, first of all; second, a feeling of personal freedom is essential, and that feeling has only recently begun to develop in me. I haven't had it up till now; its place has been filled with my frivolity, carelessness, and lack of respect for my own work...

Write a story about me: how a young man, the son of a serf, a former shopkeeper, a choir-boy, a school boy, taught to respect rank, to kiss the priests' hands, to worship strange thoughts, to be thankful for his daily bread, a young man who appreciated a frequent beating, went to school without boots, fought with his fists, teased little animals, loved to dine at rich relatives, played the hypocrite before God and his fellow man only to satisfy his sense of worthlessness—write how this young man is squeezing the slave out of himself, drop by drop, and one morning awakens and feels that slave's blood does not flow in his veins, but real human blood . . .

So be well, and forgive me for this long letter.

Yours, A. Chekhov"

(Chekhov, letter to Suvorin, January 7, 1889, Moscow)

"Greetings, dear Aleksei Nikolaevich:

What foolish demons inspired Fyodorov [the actor] to perform my play ['Ivanov'] on his benefit night? I am worn out, and no honorarium can make up for the cruel enslavement I've been feeling during the past week. Formerly I didn't give a damn about my play, and even regarded it with condescending irony. I wrote it, and to hell with it. But now all of a sudden when I find it in the works again, I realize what a bad job of writing it actually was. The last act is astonishingly bad. All week I was fussing with the play, scribbling versions, rewrites, corrections, insertions. I rewrote the role of Sasha (for the actress Savina), radically changed Act IV, refined the character of Ivanov himself, wore myself out, and started hating my own play to the point that I am prepared to end with Kean's words: 'Flog Ivanov! Flog him!'

...To write a good play for the theatre one must possess a special talent (one may be an excellent fiction writer and at the same time write a play like a cobbler). But to write a bad play and then try to make something good out of it, attempt all kinds of tricks, cross things out, rewrite, insert monologues, resurrect the dead, bury the living—for that, one must possess a greater talent. That is as difficult as buying a soldier's old trousers and trying at whatever cost to turn them into an evening jacket. Then your protagonist wouldn't burst into tragic laughter, but rather neigh like a horse.

When I'm finished with my 'Bolvanov', I'll start writing for 'The Northern Herald.' Fiction writing is an orderly, sanctified occupation. The narrative form is a lawful wife, whereas the dramatic form is a showy, noisy, impudent and tiring mistress.

[...] Meanwhile, I'm broke. I live on the charity of my 'Bear' and Suvorin, who has bought 100 rubles' worth of my stories for his 'Cheap Library'. Heaven preserve them both.

[...] Regards to all.

Yours, A. Chekhov"

(Chekhov, letter to Pleshcheev, January 15, 1889, Moscow)

"Dear Jean:

In your letter, you console me about 'Ivanov'. I thank you, but I assure you from the bottom of my heart that I'm fine with what I've done and with the results. I did what I could with it—and I think I'm right in saying that eyes don't grow above the forehead, after all, and frankly I got more than I deserved. Really and truly, even Shakespeare didn't have to put up with the kind of remarks that I have had to endure. And yet, what else did I expect? If there are a hundred people in St. Petersburg right now who are walking around shrugging their shoulders, smirking contemptuously, wagging their heads, foaming at the mouth, or lying through their teeth—well, at least I can't see it, so it can't bother me. In Moscow, I can see a hundred people daily and not hear a word about 'Ivanov', as if I never wrote the play. The Petersburg ovations and successes are like a restless dream from which I'm now fully awakened.

And speaking of successes and ovations: they're noisy, ungratifying, and give you nothing but fatigue and a desire to run, to run away... A perch caught on a hook satisfies my feelings much more palpably than reviews and an applauding gallery...

Be well. God bless.

Yours, A. Chekhov"

(Chekhov, letter to Leontyev-Shcheglov, February 18, 1889, Moscow)

"Unlike what Turgenev has said, I believe that none of us will become an 'elephant' or any other beast among our contemporary writers, and that we gather strength from our entire generation, not otherwise. They won't remember us as Chekhov, Tikhonov, Korolenko, Shcheglov, Barantsevich or Bezhetsky,—no, we'll be remembered as "the eighties" or 'the end of the nineteenth century'. A guild, so to speak.

Meanwhile, nothing new to report. I'm planning to write a kind of novel, in fact I've already gotten started. I'm not writing plays and won't be writing any, at least not in the near future, as I have neither the topic nor the will. To write for the theatre one must love the work, and without love nothing truly useful will come from it...

Yours, A. Chekhov"

(Chekhov, letter to Tikhonov, March 7, 1889, Moscow)

"Dear Aleksei Sergeevich:

I'm writing to you, having just returned from the "hunt" (catching crayfish). The weather is wonderful. Everything is singing, blossoming and shimmering with beauty. The garden is a lush green, and even the oak has bloomed. The trunks of the apple, pear, cherry and plum trees have been painted white to ward off the worms. The trees have white blossoms, making them appear like brides at a wedding with white dresses and white flowers. They're so innocent-looking that they seem ashamed to be seen. Millions of creatures are born every day. Nightingales, cuckoos, and other feathered creatures keep up an endless chorus day and night, accompanied by frogs. With it all, I'm in a good mood. Nature is a good tranquilizer. It calms you, meaning that it creates in you a state of balance, detachment. And you need detachment in this world. Only detached people can see things clearly and justly, and work. Of course, this pertains only to intelligent and honorable people; egotists and shallow people are detached enough as it is.

You write that I've become lazy. That doesn't mean that I'm any lazier than I used to be. I'm working as much now, as I did three-five years ago... The fire in me burns with a low, even flame; it never flashes or flares, to the extent that I'd write pages and pages in one night or force myself to stay awake when all I really wanted was to go to sleep. I have little passion. To that state, add the following psychopathic trait: over the past two years, and for no particular reason, I've grown weary of seeing my works in print. I've grown indifferent to reviews, talk about literature, gossip, successes, failures, big royalties—in short, I've turned into an utter fool. There is a sort of stagnation in my soul, the source of which seems to come from my personal life. It's not that I'm disillusioned, disenchanted or dissatisfied, it's simply that everything suddenly seems less interesting, somehow. I'll have to light a fire under myself. [...]

If you can believe it, I've already finished the first act of 'The Wood Demon'. It didn't turn out too badly, although it's a bit long. I feel a lot more confident than I did when I was writing' Ivanov'. The play will be ready by the beginning of June. Look out, theatre management! 5,000 goes to me! It's really quite a strange play, and I'm amazed to see such strange things coming from my pen. I'm only afraid that it won't get past the censors. I'm also writing a novel, which is a lot more appealing and closer to my heart than 'The Wood Demon', where I have to pretend and play the fool. Last night I suddenly remembered I promised Varlamov to write him a vaudeville. I wrote it today and I've already sent it off ['The Tragedian in Spite of Himself']. What a harvesting is going on here! And you write that I've grown lazy! [...]

Everyone judges plays as if it were easy to write them. What they don't know is that it is difficult to write a good play and twice as difficult to write a bad play—and terrifying too. I would like to see the entire public merge into one person and write a play, so that you and I could sit in Box I and hiss it off the stage. [...]

So God grant you good health and all the very best.

Yours, A. Chekhov"

(Chekhov, letter to Suvorin, May 4, 1889, Sumy)

"Greetings, dear Aleksei Nikolaevich:

[...] I haven't heard a word about my play ['Ivanov']. Whether or not it's been eaten by mice, whether the directors sacrificed it at the Public Library, or whether it burned in shame due to the lie perpetrated by Grigorovich [the critic], who of course loves me like his own son—all these things are possible, but meantime I know nothing. I've received no notices, no explanations from anyone, and I'm making no inquiries, lest they be interpreted as a plea or an overwhelming desire to be crowned by the Aleksandrinsky laurels. I'm as vain as a swine, truly.

Meanwhile, as for the stubborn silence of the military court that is to pass judgment on my 'Wood Demon', I can explain it in no way other than by their empathy for me, and their desire to prolong the heavenly bliss that this delightful ignorance affords me. Who knows? Perhaps my play is recognized as a work of genius. Isn't it sweet to be kept guessing?

A Petersburg newspaper reports that my play has been considered a 'wonderfully dramatized novel'. How nice. So now there are two alternatives—either I'm a failure as a dramatist, which I willingly admit, or these gentlemen who pretend to love me as their own sons are hypocrites, imploring me to avoid cliché and present some complicated problem on the stage. [...]

Yours truly,

A. Chekhov"

(Chekhov, letter to Pleshcheev, October 21, 1889, Moscow)

"How I long passionately to hide away somewhere for five years or so and busy myself with painstaking, serious work. I must study, learn everything all over again, since, as a man of letters, I'm a complete ignoramus. I must write conscientiously, with feeling and understanding—not five sheets in one month but one sheet in five months. I must leave home and start living on 700-900 a year, not three to four thousand, as I do know, I have much to renounce, but there is more laziness in me than daring. In January I'll be thirty. Vile. But I feel as if I were twenty-two.

Yours, A. Chekhov"

(Chekhov, letter to Suvorin, December 20 [approx.], 1889, Moscow)

"Dear Fyodor Aleksandrovich:

Now, a request: Don't print my play 'The Wood Demon'! ... The Moscow audiences didn't like it, the actors seemed confused by it, the newspapers tore it to pieces. Send it back to me.

If you honor my request, I'll be eternally grateful and shall write you as many short stories as you like, even up to one million two hundred thousand of them.

I'm asking in all seriousness. Please send me your response of compliance as soon as possible. Your refusal will wound me to the core and will cause me more than a little distress, for it will keep me from reworking 'The Wood Demon'. If you have already begun to set the type, I'll gladly pay for it—or throw myself into the river, hang myself—anything you want...

Yours, A. Chekhov"

(Chekhov, letter to his printer, Kumanin, January 8, 1890, St. Petersburg)

Though he expressed some confidence over the rewrites of

Ivanov, rehearsals for the St. Petersburg production found Chekhov once again in a state of deep anxiety. Despite his continuing insecurity, the Petersburg premiere of *Ivanov* at the Aleksandrinksy on January 31 was a success, bringing Chekhov over 1,000 rubles in royalties. Audiences were enthusiastic, and some critics even proclaimed the play to be on the level of Gogol's or Griboyedov's dramas. Others, like the young playwright Nemirovich-Danchenko, had reservations about the play, at the same time recognizing Chekhov's talent and promise as a dramatist.

But Chekhov couldn't trust any praise of *Ivanov*. He'd become weary of the whole process. Traumatized by the unpredictability of the critics (first they panned *Ivanov*, now they liked it, etc.), mistrustful of their motivations and their judgments, he was becoming bitter. "I'm sick of contemporary criticism," he wrote Pleshcheev. "When I read it, I am overcome with horror: Can there really be such unintelligent people on this earth who are writing this stuff? It's so stupid, petty and biased to the point of banality. It's gotten to the point that we just don't need it any more, just as we don't need literature (contemporary literature, that is, of course)." [1]

Indeed, the harshest critic of all was the playwright himself. As Chekhov wrote his publisher, he had been "on the right track." He had wanted to create a protagonist whose tragedy was not only his own, but the Russian intelligentsia and aristocracy's, too—a protagonist for whom the public would have deep empathy when he took his life in despair over his failures. In short, his ambition was to create a Russian *Hamlet*. But, as he put it, his execution was still lacking. He just didn't have the skill yet to write serious drama, he told his publisher. "I think that I were to live another forty years and do nothing but read, read, read, and study how to become a talented writer, at the end of those forty years I would fire on you all so great a cannon that all the heavens would shake," he wrote Suvorin. "But for now I'm but a Lilliputian, like the rest."[2]

Relieved that the burden of writing a work of "literary significance" had been lifted from his shoulders, at least for the time being, Chekhov turned once again to what came easily to him—comedy. His vaudevilles were highly successful, and this pleased him greatly. He called *The Bear* his "cash cow," bringing in more money than any of his short stories. "A gypsy would not have gotten as much money from a live bear as I got from a dead one. I've received five hundred rubles for my beast," he wrote Suvorin.[3]

Energized by *The Bear*'s success, he dashed off a handful of vaudevilles, including *Tatyana Repina*, a parodic sequel to a play by his publisher Suvorin that was playing in St. Petersburg early that year. "I wrote it in a hurry, in only one sitting, so it's absolutely worthless. As for my using your title, you'd better take me to court. Don't show it to anyone, and throw it in the fire when you've finished it. Or else throw it in the fire unread," he teased Suvorin.[4] Written as a practical joke on Suvorin (who took his effort quite seriously), it was never produced. It was soon followed by two other vaudevilles, *The Tragedian in Spite of Himself* in May and *The Wedding* in October.

Meanwhile, *The Proposal* was also enjoying success. "I give you *carte blanche,*" he wrote Leontyev-Shcheglov. "Make of my notoriously stupid play what you like; roll cigarettes with it for all I care."[5] But Chekhov's characteristic offhandedness belied his pride and pleasure over its reception. He was elated to hear that it had been performed at the Tsar's summer palace, Tsarskoe Selo. It was, in Chekhov's words, "a bad little play, which prompted even the Tsar to pay me a compliment in public. I await the Order of Stanislav and the appointment as a member of the State Council."[6] Indeed, the success of his one-acts would occupy him all that year. "There's a whole revolution going on with my vaudevilles," he wrote to Leontyev-Shcheglov, referring (with sly pleasure) to the series of disputes involving theatres and actors over the performance rights to his short works.[7]

Meanwhile, with Suvorin's encouragement, he had begun a full-length comedy entitled *The Wood Demon* (one of whose characters, Serebryakov, a stuffy St. Petersburg professor, was drawn after Suvorin himself). In fact, they had planned to write it together, and Suvorin had even sent Chekhov a first draft, but withdrew from the project. In May, Chekhov set about to write it himself, calling it a comedy, "lyrical in tone," with a happy ending. Apparently, he had chosen this tone to appease the public and the critics, giving them what he thought they wanted from him after *Ivanov*. He was rather excited by the effort. "If the censor doesn't knock me on the head [for *The Wood Demon*], you are going feel such a thrill in the autumn as you never felt even when you were standing on the top of the Eiffel Tower looking down on Paris," he wrote Suvorin.[8]

The Wood Demon, subtitled "a comedy in four act," is a frivolous comedy with a jarring, dissonant event at its epicenter. Set on three different country estates, it tells the story of Yegor ("Uncle George") Voynitsky, owner of one estate, who is suffering a mid-life crisis. He realizes that he has wasted his life idolizing his brother-in-law, Professor Serebryakov (husband of his late sister), and that at the same time he is in love with the professor's second wife, Yelena. Other characters in this country coterie include the professor's frivolous daughter, Sonya (George's niece), and an idealistic doctor/environmentalist, Khrushchov. When George's mother announces she wants to sell the estate that George has given his life to maintain, he shoots himself out of despair at the end of Act III. In an improbable happy ending, two pairs of lovers—including Sonya and Dr. Khrushchov—are united, and the tragic event of Act III is all but forgotten.

The letters written between May and October 1889, while he was working on the play, fluctuate in tone between elation and depression. Chekhov seemed ambivalent about the play and about playwriting too. He worked on it intermittently that spring, welcoming the distraction of the Ukrainian countryside. At times he seemed wildly confident, at others, disenchanted. During this whole period, he seemed to lack creative focus. There was a self-consciousness in his effort, a feeling of artificiality, as if he were standing outside himself, watching himself writing it in fits and starts. Moreover, he felt uneasy writing a "safe" play to appease his critics, rather than writing from inspiration. How could he feel ownership of it? At the same time, he was so confident about it that he even asked the Society of Russian Dramatists to include it in their catalogue of plays.

A traumatic event occurred in June, causing a major interruption to his writing. His brother Nikolai, the least stable of all the Chekhov offspring, died a harrowing death from consumption. The family was thrown into an emotional turmoil. "Our family has never known death before; it's the first time we've seen a coffin at home," Chekhov wrote Pleshcheev.[9] In July, he fled south from this exhausting experience to Yalta. In August, he returned to the Ukraine to finish work on a serious tale, "A Dreary Story." Restlessness, provoked by anxiety over health-related issues, would become a pattern throughout his life.

In September, he resumed work on *The Wood Demon*. Anticipation for the play's completion ran high, and already two leading Russian actors—Svobodin at the Aleksandrinsky Theatre in St. Petersburg and Lensky at the Maly Theatre in Moscow—were vying with one another to play the leading role. Chekhov completed it by the end of October and submitted it to the Aleksandrinksy's literary committee. It was unanimously rejected as being a dramatized novel unsuitable for the stage. Responses from committee members ranged from general disapproval—that he was getting too spoiled by success—to specific criticism of its absence of action and its tedious dialogue. They objected to his negative and unseemly portrayal of the professor Serebraykov. As for "Uncle George," the main character, his suicide disturbed and mystified the committee. Next came word from Svobodin, declining to appear in it, telling Chekhov he did not know how to write plays, and should stick to short story writing. Lensky, too, declined to perform in it.

As with *Ivanov*, a melodrama was unfolding. At first, Chekhov was horrified by these responses. Then the famous actor Solovstov (who had played the leading role in *The Bear* with great success) convinced another Moscow theatre, the Abramov, to produce *The Wood Demon*. Chekhov accepted the invitation gratefully (as well as the 500 rubles in advance), and feverishly set about revising the play all the way up the final days of rehearsal. Once again, the rehearsals were traumatic—the actors didn't know their lines and performed their roles poorly. Even with all his revisions, he had already lost confidence in the play.

The play opened on November 27; it was an unequivocal failure. There were sounds of catcalls, whistling, and booing in the audience. The critics condemned it unanimously as boring, clumsy flat, trivial and novelistic, citing Chekhov's lack of dramaturgical technique. Crushed, Chekhov withdrew the play and wrote a desperate letter to his printer, pleading with him not to publish it until he had the chance to work on it further. The play that sought to entertain—and at the same time express his deep convictions about natural conservation and the impoverishment of Russian literary criticism—had failed miserably. His attempt to amuse the public, and at the same time infuse his play with serious thought, had not resulted in a successful blending of the comedic and the serious. Furthermore, he had expected to live off the royalties from an extended run of *The Wood Demon*, and now found himself once again in financial straits.

By the end of the year, Chekhov felt the effect of the mercurial plunge from success in January with *Ivanov* to failure in December with *The Wood Demon*. He was profoundly disappointed in his abilities as a dramatist, and disenchanted with the theatre. More than ever, he was confused as to where his talents and abilities really lay. He was increasingly dissatisfied with Moscow, its pace, its pressures, and the hypocrisy of the *literati*. As for his personal life, there were still the multiple entanglements (including a lady with the memorable name of Kleopatra), none of which were satisfying. His creative energies depleted, his inspiration numbed, he felt trapped. He longed for what he called a sense of "personal freedom."

Above all, he was traumatized by the death of his brother Nikolai, and at the same time unable to ignore any longer the similarity of his own symptoms of consumption. This realization—combined with his disillusionment with Moscow, a lack of direction in his writing, and a growing need for a change—prompted him to look for an escape.

Then, a plan occurred to Chekhov the doctor that would set Chekhov the writer free. Since childhood, Chekhov had been an avid reader of explorers' biographies and geographic journals. While casually perusing his brother Mikhail's notes on a course in criminal law, his interest was piqued by a passage about the abusive penal colonies on the wild, remote island of Sakhalin, off the Eastern coast of Siberia. A plan began to take focus in his restless mind. Here was a chance to restore his reputation as a writer not of frivolity and triviality, as the author of *The Wood Demon* was accused, but a writer of deeply humanistic principles and priorities. He would journey to Sakhalin to study the penal colonies, care for the inmates, seek for any violation of human rights, and write about his findings.

Somehow, he thought, this journey would put him on the road to personal freedom, his quest since childhood. As he wrote to Suvorin earlier that year, it would set the record straight on his life and achievements thus far. Although Chekhov may not have been aware of it at the time, he had already begun the process of "squeezing the slave out himself, drop by drop"—as a submissive son of a tyrant, as a writer of successful short stories and short plays that came too easily to produce self-satisfaction, as an ambitious young playwright eager to make his mark before he was ready to do so. The letters of 1888-1889 that he wrote to friends, critics, publishers, fellow authors, and artists—about the theatre, about literary criticism, about writing—express that sense of "personal freedom" that he valued above all else.

Still, he was dissatisfied with himself. "In January I'm turning thirty," he wrote Suvorin at the end of 1889. "Hail, lonely old age; burn, useless life."[10] At the time, he felt burned out as a writer, having tried to be innovative, and feeling that he'd failed. "Skits, feuilletons, foolishness, vaudevilles, dull stories, a great many mistakes and absurdities, tons of paper covered with scribbling, the Academy's prize, and despite all this not one line that has in my view any serious literary value," he wrote Suvorin. "Lots of forced labor, but not a moment of serious work."[11]

In October, a month before the fateful opening of *The Wood Demon*, a humorous cartoon appeared in *Fragments*. The drawing showed Chekhov in a cart, drawn by a troika. The three figures drawing it were not horses; rather they were a man labeled "*Ivanov*," a grisly bear labeled "*The Bear*," and an elfin figure labeled "*The Wood Demon*." The troika is stalled at a crossroads. One sign reads: "Road to Prose," another reads "Road to Drama." Chekhov took the joke well.

Looking back on the decade of the 1880s, the cartoon captures Chekhov's "Moscow period" quite accurately. It was an exciting and vigorous time for Chekhov, the young dramatist, during he explored with intense determination both the short and long forms, and the comedic and the tragic. During this period, he wrote three full-length plays and ten one-act plays—an experimental period crucial to his development. He also wrote almost 500 short stories in that decade of varying length and tone—from humorous three page sketches to 170 page novels. The decade gave him great success and recognition as a short story writer.

At the same time it gave him a taste of theatre life that both attracted and repelled him, that both fascinated and frightened him—a life that he would both covet and shun. This love-hate relationship with the theatre would last for the rest of his life.

Act Three: *Melikhovo*

"I AM GOING TO SAKHALIN."

(Chekhov, letter to Suvorin, March 9, 1890)

1890

"You write, for instance, that Sakhalin is of no use or interest to anyone. Is that really so? Sakhalin is a place of unbearable suffering, the kind that only man is capable of creating. From the books I've been reading, we are leaving millions to rot in our jails, for no purpose, indifferently and barbarously. We have people dragged in chains through the cold for miles, we make them toil, we infect them with syphilis, corrupt them, make them into depraved criminals and blame it all on the red-nosed wardens. The wardens of the prisons are not to blame ... we are ... No, I assure you, Sakhalin is of great interest—it's a shame that I'm the one who's going, not someone else who's more informed, qualified and capable of stimulating public interest. [...]"

Yours, A. Chekhov"

(Chekhov, letter to Suvorin, March 9, 1890, Moscow)

"Greetings, dear Jean-chik:

[...] As for the word 'artistry', I fear it as merchants' wives fear a Sodom rain of brimstone. When people talk to me of the artistic and the anti-artistic, of that which is theatrical and non-theatrical, of tendency, realism, etc., I become confused, nod in agreement and answer in platitudes and half-truths that are not worthy a kopek. I divide all literary works into two classes: those I like and those I do not like. I have no other criteria, and if you were to ask me why I like Shakespeare and dislike Zlatovratsky [a Russian novelist of the day], I wouldn't be able to answer. Perhaps in time, when I become wiser, I shall acquire criteria, but meanwhile, all this talk about 'artistry' only tires me...

If criticism, the authority to whom you allude, knows what you and I know, then why has it kept quiet till now? Why doesn't it reveal the truth and immutable laws? If it had indeed known, then believe me, it would have shown us the way long ago... and you wouldn't have been drawn to the theatre and I to Sakhalin... However, let's spit on all this and sing another aria. Don't have any high literary hopes for my Sakhalin trip... if I have the opportunity and ability to write something, then thank God, and if not, don't be hard on me. [...]

Yours, A. Chekhov"

(Chekhov, letter to Leontyev-Shcheglov, March 22, 1890, Moscow)

"[...] You scold me for objectivity, calling it indifference to good and evil, lack of ideals and ideas and so on. When I portray horse thieves, you would want me to say that stealing horses is an evil. But certainly that's been obvious without my saying so, hasn't it? Let the jury pass judgment on them; it is my business solely to show them as they are. And so let me say, for the record, if you deal with horse thieves, then what you should know is that they're not beggars, that they are fairly well-off, that they are a kind of a cult, and that horse thieving is more than stealing, it's a passion. Yes, of course, it would be fine to combine art and sermonizing but personally I find it extremely difficult, all but impossible, for technical reasons. In order to describe my horse thieves in 700 lines, I must speak and think as they do, even feel as they do. If I were to add even a touch of subjectivity, the images would come apart and the story would lack the compactness that short stories need. When I write, I rely on the reader entirely, assuming he will supply the subjective elements missing in the story.

Be well.

Yours, A. Chekhov"

(Chekhov, letter to Suvorin, April 1, 1890, Moscow)

(Chekhov undertook the journey to Sakhalin on April 21. He arrived on the isle of Sakhalin on July 11, spent three months there, and boarded the boat bound for Odessa on October 13.)

"Greetings!

I'm sailing through the Tatar Strait from North to South Sakhalin. I write, not knowing when this letter will reach you. I am well, although cholera is staring at me from all sides with its green eyes, setting a trap for me. From Vladivostok to Japan, Shanghai, Chefoo, Suez, even on the moon—cholera is everywhere, and with its quarantines and panic. They're waiting for cholera to arrive on Sakhalin, and are planning their quarantine. In brief, things are in a bad way. [...]

When I start to think that I'm separated from the rest of the world by over 6,000 miles, I'm overcome with apathy. It feels as if I won't get home for a hundred years.

God grant you happiness and all good things.

A.Chekhov.

P.S. It's boring"

(Chekhov, letter to Suvorin, September 11, 1890, aboard the'Baikal', in the Tatar Strait)

"Greetings, my esteemed one:

Hooray! Here I am, at last, sitting at my desk, praying to my fading deities, writing to you. I have a good feeling, as if I never left home. I'm well and happy to the marrow of my bones. Here is a brief report: I spent three months plus one day on Sakhalin, not two months, as was published in your paper. My work was pressured, intense: I prepared a complete, detailed census of the entire population of Sakhalin and saw everything, with the exception of an execution. When we see each other again, I'll show you a trunkful of information about convict life that is extremely valuable raw material. I know a lot now, but the feeling I've brought back with me is not a good one... In retrospect, Sakhalin seems to me to be complete hell. For two months I worked under extreme tension, sparing no cost to myself, and by the third month, the bitterness I spoke of started to wear me down, not to mention the thought that cholera was making its way from Vladivostok to Sakhalin and that there was the risk that I might have to spend the winter quarantined there. But thank heavens the cholera abated and on October 13 the steamer carried me away from Sakhalin. [...]

... The first foreign port we docked at was Hong Kong. The bay is marvelous, with sea traffic the likes of which I've never seen, not even in pictures. There are excellent roads, horse-drawn streetcars, a railway going up a mountain, museums, botanical gardens...

When we left Hong Kong, the steamer began to churn. Since it had no cargo, it swung so sharply that we feared it would capsize. I was pleased to discover that I'm not prone to seasickness. En route by sea to Singapore, we had to throw two corpses overboard. When you see a dead man wrapped in sailcloth, flying head over heels into the deep, and when you think that there are several miles to the bottom, then a terror overcomes you and you imagine that you too will die and be thrown into the sea. Our cattle fell ill and were slaughtered and thrown overboard—by doctors' orders, mine included. [...]

God's world is good. It's we ourselves who aren't. How little justice and humility there is in this world, how little we understand patriotism! They say in the newspapers that we love our great country, but how do we show that love? Instead of knowledge, there is boundless arrogance and conceit—instead of work, there is indolence and swinishness. There is no justice, and the idea of honor goes no further than 'the honor of the uniform', the uniform that is the everyday adornment of the prisoners' dock. We must work, and the rest can go to hell. The main thing is to be just, and the rest will come.

I'm desperate to talk to you. My soul is churning. And I'll talk to you and only you. To hell with Pleshcheev. To hell with actors, too. [...]

I firmly embrace you and your entire family, but I'll only bow to Dyakov and Burenin [writers for the 'New Times'], who should have been sent to Sakhalin long ago.

Yours, A. Chekhov"

(Chekhov, letter to Suvorin, December 9, 1890, Moscow)

"Dear Sir, Anatoly Fyodorovich:

...My brief Sakhalin past looms so large that when I want to talk about it, I don't know where to begin, and each time I try, it seems I'm not saying what should be said.

I shall try to describe the situation of the Sakhalin children in detail. It's extraordinary. I've seen starving children, thirteen year old 'kept' girls, fifteen year old pregnant girls. Girls serve as prostitutes beginning at twelve years old, sometimes before the start of menstruation. Churches and schools exist only on paper, so it is the environment and the convict conditions that informs their lives. [...]

On the Amur steamer with me going to Sakhalin was a prisoner in foot shackles who had murdered his wife. With him was his daughter, a little girl of six. I noticed that when the father would climb down from the upper deck to use the water closet, an escort and his little daughter would follow, and a soldier with a rifle would stand guard by the door, along with the girl. Then when the prisoner returned by the stairs, the little girl would climb up after him holding onto his shackles. At night she slept in a heap along with the prisoners and the soldiers. [...]

I've seen blind children, filthy, covered with sores—with all kinds of diseases, all the result of negligence. [...]

Of course I cannot save this situation of the children. But it seems that charity and whatever funding is left over in prison allotments will not solve the problem alone...

[...] Yours sincerely, respectfully, and truly,

A. Chekhov"

(Chekhov, letter to Koni, January 26, 1891, St. Petersburg)

No one could believe it—neither family, nor friends, nor fellow writers, nor his publishers. A precarious 6,000 mile journey across the vastest nation in the world, crossing mountains, steppes, and deserts in extreme weather and dangerous conditions by whatever means of transportation available—a trip to be undertaken by an inexperienced young traveler in ill health? Unthinkable!

But Chekhov was determined. He sent Masha to the library together with Olga Kundasvoa and Lydia Mizinova (a lovely young friend of Masha, who was already developing a passion for Chekhov) to copy research notes for him about Siberia and Sakhalin. He was lavished with attention from friends and female admirers on the eve of his departure, promising them to bring back exotic gifts from Asia.

Before he left, he put the finishing touches on *Gloomy People*, his seventh book of collected short stories. Then, equipped with a trunk filled with gear befitting an explorer, plus a 1,500 ruble advance from his publisher Suvorin for a travelogue for the *New Times*, he set out on April 21, leaving his sister Masha and Lydia (Lika) weeping at the station.

The arduous journey—from Moscow to Yaroslavl by train and then from Yaroslavl to Lake Baikal to the Pacific Coast by a combination of train, boat and horse and springless carriage (the cross-continental railway lines had not yet been completed)—covered 6,600 miles and took over two months. The first part, steaming down the Volga to Nizhni and up the Kama to Perm, was pleasurable. But there, the river journey ended. From Perm he took a train across the Urals to Ekaterinaberg, where he picked up the train to Tiumen. And there the railway ended. There he bought a cart and hired horses and a driver to take him to Tomsk. He passed through heavy rains, mudslides, blizzards, dust storms, across endless stretches of forests, flooding rivers, and Siberian plains. He experienced the exotica of remote Russia (visiting the brothels of Tomsk with the local police chief, marveling at the turquoise waters of Lake Baikal, testing the steam baths of Irkutsk, taking in the intoxicating air along the Manchurian border). There were incidents along the way—a collision with a mail coach (he had to sell his carriage at a loss), bruising bumps of the rough, rutty roads, nights of sleeping on the floor. Too exhausted to write letters home, he kept a diary.

Then, finally, he reached the Pacific Coast and boarded a steamer at Sretensk for Sakhalin. After a two week crossing (changing ships twice), he arrived at his destination on July 9. He was not prepared for what he saw.

The island's length measured six hundred miles (the size of Scotland), with Arctic tundra terrain. The weather was severe—either below freezing half the year, or else a miserable combination of rain, fog and insects. The indigenous population consisted of 1,000 aborigines. Its sole interest to Russia was as a penal colony for hardened criminals. The island's governor greeted Chekhov and informed him that he was the only Russian on the island who was neither a prisoner nor a warden. There were roughly 10,000 prisoners—all hardened criminals—their family members, and the 10,000 men and their families who guarded them. There were also a few thousand released prisoners and exiles who were attempting to farm the Sakhalin bogs.[1]

His humanitarian mission began with a census-taking of the prisoners in the island's five penal colonies. He made rounds, questioned them about their conditions and their health, and took notes on hundreds of interviews. He observed convicts in chains who endured inhumane working conditions and whippings, were denied the right to religious prayer, and were brutalized by guards. The plight of women was worse; mothers and daughters of prisoners were forced into prostitution, while children were uneducated and starving. The hospitals lacked both instruments and medicine (doctors spent the allocated money on liquor for themselves). The work was exhausting. "It feels as if I won't get home for a hundred years," he wrote Suvorin.[2]

After a grueling, exhausting three month stay, Chekhov departed Sakhalin on October 13. Bypassing a visit to Japan (and its cholera epidemic), he boarded a steamer back to Russia that visited Hong Kong, endured a typhoon at sea, then stopped at Singapore and Ceylon, avoiding the typhus epidemic with its "green eyes." He was charmed by Ceylon, and swam in the Indian Ocean. After a long sea journey, he finally arrived in Odessa on December 1. His family met him in the Tula train station. There they found Anton sitting in the waiting room, sun-tanned from the journey, together with an aborigine travel companion and a pair of mongeese he had bought in Ceylon. He immediately wrote to Suvorin telling him they had to meet as soon as possible, to hear about his adventures. "I am passionately eager to have a talk with you—my soul is churning—with you and only with you... To hell with actors..." He added, playfully: "To prove I have been a convict I shall attack [your family] with a knife and yell wildly. I'll set fire to [your wife] Anna's room."[3]

Indeed, it had been a year of extremes. "I was both in hell, i.e. Sakhalin, and in paradise, i. e. the island of Ceylon," he wrote Leontyev-Shcheglov. "What butterflies and insects, what flies, what roaches!"[4] Now he was faced with the task of transcribing the thousands of pages and notes of statistics, and deciding on a genre for writing about his experiences. He wanted the Russian people to know what he had seen—the inhumane and cruel treatment of the prisoners, the lack of medical care and education, the neglect of orphaned children, the rampant teen-age prostitution, the enslavement of women convicts as concubines, and the genocidal policies toward the indigenous population. "Before the journey, 'The Kreutzer Sonata' was an event, but now I find it foolish, " he wrote Suvorin. "Perhaps the trip has matured me, or else I've lost my mind, who knows."[5]

Whatever the true motivation of Chekhov's journey to Sakhalin may have been—to escape the capricious Moscow theatre scene and the suffocating *literati*, to flee from the failure of his most recent full-length play, to avoid facing his own serious health issues, to impress the critics with his humanitarian efforts, or a combination of all the above—the journey was a major event in his life and a crucial transition year. At the age of thirty, he was both exhausted and inspired—and gratified that he had accomplished a worthwhile mission.

That feeling of satisfaction would not last long.

Chekhov with family and friends.

"Ah, freedom, freedom…."

(Chekhov, letter to Suvorin, November 22, 1891)

1891

"I'm exhausted, like a ballerina after five acts and eight scenes. Banquets, letters I'm too lazy to answer, conversations and all kinds of nonsense...

I'm surrounded by an atmosphere of ill-feeling, vague and insidious. They feed me dinners and sing my praises, and at the same time they're ready to eat me alive. Were I to shoot myself, it would afford great pleasure to nine-tenths of my friends and admirers. And in what petty ways they express their pettiness! It's awful and silly and boring. They're not people, they're some kind of mildew...

Yours, A. Chekhov"

(Chekhov, letter to Masha, January 14, 1891, St. Petersburg)

"All I can say is that in my whole life I've never seen a city more remarkable than Venice. Its sheer enchantment, magnificence, and exuberance... Instead of streets and alleys, there are canals, instead of cabs there are gondolas, the architecture is astonishing, there isn't a square foot that doesn't spark historical and artistic fascination. You float along in a gondola and see the doges' palaces, the house where Desdemona lived, the homes of great artists, churches. And the churches have sculpture and paintings, such as you've never dreamed of. In a word, it's magical. All day long from morning till night I ride in gondolas and float through the streets or wander over to the famous St. Mark's Square. It's as smooth and clean as a parquet floor. And the evenings! Good lord! It's all so new, you could simply die from it! You ride in your gondola, it's warm and peaceful, the stars are out. You hear singing and music. You go a little further, a boat passes with singers, and then another, and till midnight there hangs in the air a blend of tenors, violins and all kinds of sounds that goes right to

your soul [...] Should you ever happen to go to Venice, it will be the best thing in your life."
(Chekhov, letter to his brother Ivan, March 24, 1891, Venice)

"Yes, you're right—my soul needs balm. Right now I would read with pleasure, and even joy, something serious—not only about myself but in general. I long for serious reading, and all Russian criticism of late does not nourish me, but merely annoys me. I would be thrilled to read something new about Pushkin or Tolstoy—it would be balm for my idle mind...

I, too, am pining for Venice and Florence and am ready to climb Vesuvius once more.

Why don't I know foreign languages? It seems to me that I could translate literary works splendidly. When I read translations by others, I keep altering and transposing the words in my mind, and I experience a sensation of something light, ethereal, like lacework.

On Monday, Tuesday and Wednesday I'm writing the Sakhalin book; on all other days, except Sunday, I'm writing a novel and on Sundays I write short stories. I'm working eagerly, but alas I have a large family and I, the writer, am like a lobster stuck in a trap with other lobsters, and it's quite crowded. [...]

I have no intentions of getting married. Right now, I wish I were a little bald-headed ancient, seating at a huge desk in a grand study. [...]

Yours, A. Chekhov
(Chekhov, letter to Suvorin, May 10, 1891, Aleksin)

"Golden, mother-of-pearl, lisle-threaded Lika, The mongoose ran away the day before yesterday, never to return. [...]

Ach, lovely Lika! While you wept and wailed and watered my right shoulder with your tears (I've removed the spots with benzine) and nibbled away at your bread and beef, we greedily devoured your face and the back of your head with our eyes. Ach, Lika, Lika, what an infernal beauty you are! Come visit us, and you will be engulfed in embraces.

Your important friend,

Hunyadi-Yanos"[1]
(Chekhov, letter to Lydia Mizinova, May 17, 1891, Aleksin)

"Dear Sir:

As you requested, I'm sending you my biographical information...

I was born in 1869, in the town of Taganrog, on the Azov Sea. My grandfather was a Little Russian [Ukrainian], a serf. Before the Emancipation, he purchased his entire family's freedom, including my father's. My father was a tradesman.

I was educated in the Taganrog high school, and then at Moscow University in the Faculty of Medicine, where I received my medical degree. I started writing in 1879. I've been published in numerous journals specializing in the short story, which serve as the contents for a few collections: 'Motley Stories,' 'In the Twilight,' 'Stories,' 'Gloomy People.' I also have written plays which have been presented in both official and privately owned theatres.

In 1888 the Royal Academy of Sciences awarded me with the Pushkin Prize. In 1890, I undertook a journey across Siberia to the island of Sakhalin to study the convicts and prison colonies. When my book on Sakhlin comes out, I'll send it to you, and perhaps in return you'll send me your translation of my stories.

They call me Anton Pavlovich.

I remain your faithful servant,

A. Chekhov"

(Chekhov, letter to A. Vrzal, August 14, 1891, Bogimovo)

"Death gathers men little by little, he knows what he is doing. One might write a play about an old chemist who invents the elixir of immortality—take fifteen drops and you live life eternal. But he breaks the phial in terror, lest such scum of the earth as himself and his wife live forever. Meanwhile, Tolstoy denies immortality, but my God, how much of that is personal! The other day I read his epilogue [to 'The Kreutzer Sonata']. Go ahead and murder me for saying so, but it's even more stupid and smug than Gogol's 'Letters to a Governor's Lady' which I absolutely despise. To hell with the philosophy of the greats on this earth. All these great wise men are despots, like generals, they're rude and coarse like generals, because they're convinced that they are impervious. Diogenes spat on other people's

beards, knowing that nothing would come of it. Tolstoy calls doctors scoundrels and scoffs at important issues of the day, because he, like Diogenes, knows he won't be dragged off to the police station or vilified in the newspaper. And so, to hell with the philosophy of the greats on this earth!

Meanwhile, send my regards to my schoolmate Aleksei and wish him good health, high spirits, and seductive dreams. May he dream of a naked Spanish girl with a guitar.

...I'm very bored.

Yours, A. Chekhov"

(Chekhov, letter to Suvorin, September 8, 1891, Moscow)

"Greetings again, dear Sir:

[...] Here's what is going on. I'm stuck here in Moscow, yet at the same time my Nizhny Novgorod project is going full steam ahead! A friend of mine and I have undertaken a little venture that we figure will raise somewhere around 100,000... In addition to various famine problems, we're mainly trying to save next year's harvest. Because the peasants are selling their horses for practically nothing, there is a grave threat that the fields won't get plowed in the spring and that the whole famine cycle will repeat itself again. So our plan is to buy up the horses, feed them, and return them to their owners in the spring. So here's why I'm writing you about all this. Just in case you or anyone else, in the course of some sumptuous banquet or other, should collect even half a ruble for the benefit of the famine victims or even if you win a hundred rubles playing cards, then in your prayers will all sinners be remembered and please, in your generosity, set aside a fraction of it for us. Each contributor will receive a detailed accounting of every single kopek, and in January we shall appear in the papers.

Yours truly,

A. Chekhov

(Chekhov, letter to his friend Smagin, December 11, 1891, Moscow)

Arriving back from his extraordinary journey, Chekhov found himself, once again, burdened with responsibilities and plagued by distractions. The personal freedom he had sought in escaping from Moscow seemed farther away than ever.

First, there were the chronic family problems. Once again, his family had plunged into debt. And once again, he had to turn to the task of writing stories to bail them out.

Then there were the issues of his own health. The journey had taken its toll. While he had borne up well during the nine months away, once back in Moscow he suffered from headaches, coughing spells and heart palpitations.

Moreover, there was a general feeling of ill will and envy in the air, coming from his fellow writers. He went to St. Petersburg for a reunion with Suvorin and other friends, and wrote to his sister: "I'm surrounded by an atmosphere of ill-feeling, vague and insidious."[2] Then there were attacks from fellow writers and critics, questioning the sincerity of his Sakhalin visit, calling it a stunt to divert attention from his loss of inspiration. He vowed to set his intentions right in a book about his journey, but there were too many distractions to begin work on it.

To complicate his life, there was a cadre of female admirers in both Moscow and St. Petersburg who continued to pursue him. The names included Lydia Mizinova (Lika, a friend of Masha), the actresses Daria Musina-Pushkina and Maria Zankovetskaya, Olga Kundasova, Yelena Shavrova—the list went on and on. When Chekhov visited the Suvorins in Petersburg, the family telephone reportedly broke down under the strain of their persistent calls and invitations. Chekhov held them all at arms' length, especially the passionate young actress Lydia (Lika). Masha had met her at school and introduced them in late 1889, before Chekhov left for Sakhalin. She was a beautiful blond with green eyes, lovely and shy, and she charmed others with her freshness, naïveté and warmth. By now, she adored Chekhov. He wrote her cruel and teasing letters, ignoring the sincere love she felt for him.

Being in Moscow and St. Petersburg afforded him no pleasure. Nothing could shake his *ennui*—not even attending Shakespeare's *Antony and Cleopatra* in St. Petersburg, starring Eleanora Duse. "I've never seen anything like it," he wrote his sister Masha. "I look at her perform, and I'm overcome with depression from the thought that we have to formulate our taste and standards from those wooden actresses like Y. and her like, whom we call great only because we've never seen anyone better. Watching Duse, I realize why the Russian theatre is so boring."[3]

No wonder, then, that he leapt at an invitation to accompany Suvorin and his son on a European tour—his very first. From March through May, they traveled first class by train in luxury (a stark contrast to his journey to Sakhalin the year before), visiting Vienna, Bologna, Florence, Rome, and Naples. From every city, he sent off ecstatic descriptions to his family, filled with naïve wonder. Awed by Vienna's beauty and refinement, he wrote to Masha of the elegant boulevards, churches that looked as if they were "woven in lace," cathedrals that "look like pastries" and stores that were "dizzying mirages that would make your head turn, with millions of neckties in the windows!"[4] (According to the impressionable Chekhov, the only negative in Vienna was that they charge for bread in restaurants).

The magnificence of Venice enchanted him, dazzled him. "In my whole life I've never seen a city more remarkable than Venice," he wrote Ivan. "There isn't a square foot that doesn't spark historical and artistic fascination… it's magical."[5] He rode the gondolas day and night, thrilled as a child. He strolled by the seaside at Nice, and lost 500 rubles at roulette at Monte Carlo. In Paris, he marveled at the Eiffel Tower. And yet, he signed his letters "Your homesick Antonio." "I left with an empty trunk and shall return with a full one. You'll be rewarded according to your just desserts," he wrote to his family in his last letter before returning to Russia.[6] It was the first Easter he would spend away from home.

Back in Russia, Chekhov rented another summer house in the countryside, in the village of Bogimovo outside of Moscow, for his family entourage. At dawn, before the household would awaken, he would rise and throw himself into the writing of "The Island of Sakhalin," as well as a longer story, "The Duel" (influenced by the ideas of Tolstoy, whose work he alternately admired and criticized). At midday, he'd go mushrooming or fishing. Often the local peasants came to be treated by Dr. Chekhov. Evenings, the house was teeming with visitors, including Lika and Levitan the artist. Chekhov had made a roulette wheel, and served as croupier while everyone played. They put on theatrical performances, and played with the mongoose.

The trip to Sakhalin had provided Chekhov with a humanitarian focus that gratified him. That fall, he found yet another one. A famine raged in Central Russia; crops had failed, the peasants were subsisting on grass alone, starvation was everywhere. Chekhov mobilized his friends and family to contribute to the cause.

Even with the gratification that these efforts provided, however, Chekhov still felt unsettled, unfocused and easily distracted. He resorted to the writing of another vaudeville —*The Jubilee*—but that only provided temporary amusement. (Around this time, he also wrote *The Night Before the Trial*—a strange, dark, unfinished one-act based on an earlier, eponymous short story). He felt himself growing dull and indifferent. The solitude of his writer's life, living in the city, began to suffocate him. "Ah, my friends, how bored I am," he wrote Suvorin in October. "If I am a doctor, I ought to have patients and a hospital; if I am a writer, I ought to live among people and not in a room with a mongoose, I ought to have a little social and political life...but this life between four walls, without nature, without people, without the countryside, without health or appetite—that's not life, but some sort of 'I don't know what'."[7] To compound things, his coughing was increasing.

"Ah freedom, freedom," he wrote longingly to Suvorin toward the end of the year.[8] How he longed for escape from Moscow life, with its social, financial and literary pressures, the hypocrisy of the *literati*, the carping of the critics, the fickleness of the public, and so on. He was tiring of city life where "literary men are swept out of the theatre with brooms, and plays are written by young and old alike with no credentials, while journals and papers are edited by merchants, clerks and young girls," he protested to Leikin. "Never mind, to hell with them all!"[9]

He dreamed of finding a place away from Moscow where he could integrate his life as a doctor with his life as a writer, a place with air and space, rather than in cramped city quarters with the attendant anxieties of meeting the monthly rent. "If I can live on not more than 2,000 a year, which is only possible in the country, I shall be absolutely free from all anxieties over money coming in and going out," he wrote Suvorin. "Then I shall work and read, read...In a word, it will be 'marmalade'..."[10]

In December, he wrote "In Moscow," a strange, *ennui*-filled eulogy in essay/monologue form to the life he longed to leave behind. Its protagonist, calling himself "a Moscow Hamlet," laments the endless boredom of his life, and expresses a self-loathing for what he refers to as his ignorance, lack of culture, and excessive envy of others. The only escape from his ennui that he can think of? "Oh, well, you simply take a piece of telephone cord and you hang yourself on the nearest telegraph pole! That's all that's left for you to do!"[11]

Fortunately, Chekhov had another escape plan in mind. In December, he began his search to purchase his very own "estate" in the countryside.

"The estate has been purchased… Be impressed!"

(Chekhov, letter to Aleksandr, February 23, 1892)

1892

" [....] Do you need my autobiography? All right, here it is. I was born in Taganrog in 1860. I graduated from Taganrog Grammar School in 1879. In 1884 I graduated from medical school at Moscow University. In 1888 I received the Pushkin Prize. In 1890 I made a journey to Sakhalin across Siberia and returned by sea. In 1891, I completed a tour of Europe, where I drank excellent wine and ate oysters... I began to write for the journal 'The Dragonfly' in 1879. My collected works are: 'Motley Stories', 'In the Twilight', 'Stories', 'Gloomy People' and 'The Duel'. I have also sinned in the realm of drama, although in moderation. I have been translated into all languages with the exception of foreign ones. However, I have already been translated into German, a long time ago. The Czechs and Serbs also approve of me, and the French don't think too badly of me, either. I experienced the mysteries of love at the age of thirteen. With my colleagues, both medical and literary, I remain on excellent terms. I am a bachelor. I would like a pension. I still practice medicine, to the extent that, in the summertime, I even perform an autopsy of two, although I haven't done one now in a couple of years. Among writers, my preference is Tolstoy, among doctors—Zakharin.

However, all this is nonsense. Write whatever you life. If you have no facts, substitute something lyrical. [...]

A. Chekhov"

(Chekhov, letter to Tikhonov, February 22, 1892, Moscow)

"My fireman-brother!

[...] Here's the news... The estate has been purchased in the Serpukhov district, a dozen miles from the railroad station. Be impressed: 575 acres, 432 of them wooded, two ponds, a scraggly stream, a new house, an orchard, a piano, three horses, cows, a springless carriage, a drozhky,

carts, a sleigh, hotbeds, two dogs, birdhouses for starlings, and other items too numerous for your fireman's mind to comprehend—all that was purchased for 13,000 rubles, apart of the amount borrowed. I shall pay 490 rubles a year interest on the debt, half of what I previously paid to rent the flat and the summer cottage. Thirty-eight acres have already been sown to rye. In March, I shall sow clover, oats, lentils, peas, and whatever belongs a kitchen garden. If I keel over, I shall leave it to my relatives to pay the interest. [...]

Come to see us, Sasha! You can stay in the hen coop, and for your entertainment I shall arrange a fire alarm. There are minnows in the ponds, mushrooms in the woods, the air is fresh, and inside it's cozy. By the first of March we can move, and it's farewell to Moscow. So I won't have to pay rent on both an apartment and a dacha. I'll try to pay off the debt in four years. [...]

Landowner A. Chekhov"

(Chekhov, letter to Aleksandr, February 23, 1892, Moscow)

"[...] Living in the country is uncomfortable, but meanwhile something amazing and quite moving is going on in nature, and its poetry and novelty compensate for all the discomforts of country life. Every day brings new surprises, each better than the one before. The starlings have arrived; there is the babbling of water everywhere, and patches of green are already peeking through the thawing earth. A day lasts an eternity. You live as if in Australia, somewhere on the edge of the world. The mood is peaceful, contemplative, animal in the sense that you neither regret yesterday nor anticipate tomorrow. As I watch for spring, I'm overcome with longing for a paradise beyond. [...]

Yours, A. Chekhov

(Chekhov, letter to Suvorin, March 17, 1892, Melikhovo)

"Lika: there is a cruel frost outside and in my heart, too, and so I won't write you the long letter you have longed to receive.

So, have you sorted out your summer plans? You're a liar, and I don't believe you: You just don't want to live near us at all... We're nothing to you. We're only the starlings of yesteryear, whose song has long been forgotten. [...]

The thermometer has gone down to ten below. I curse at it with all the words I can think of beginning with the letter "s," and all I get for a response is a cold and gleaming stare... When will it be spring, Lika, when? Do take this question literally and don't look for a hidden meaning.

Alas, I am already an old young man. My love brings neither sunshine nor springtime—not for me, not for the little bird I love. Lika, it's not you whom I love so passionately. In you, I love my past sufferings and my lost youth."
(Chekhov, letter to Lydia Mizinova, March 27, 1892, Melikhovo)

"[...] Levitan the artist is staying with me. Yesterday evening, he and I went out to the woodcock mating area. He fired at a woodcock and the latter, wounded in the wing, fell into a puddle. I picked it up. A long beak, large black eyes, and a glorious plumage. It looked at us, astonished. What could we do with it? Levitan knit his brow, closed his eyes, and begged me in a trembling voice: 'My dear good fellow, please smash its head against the butt of the rifle.' I said I couldn't. He kept shrugging his shoulders nervously, twitching his head and begging me. And the woodcock kept looking at us in astonishment. So I had to obey Levitan and kill it. One beautiful, enamored creature less in the world, while two fools returned home and sat down to supper. [...]

A. Chekhov"

(Chekhov, letter to Suvorin, April 8, 1892, Melikhovo)

"Life is short, and Chekhov, whose reply you await, would like it to flash by brilliantly and brightly. He'd love to travel to the Princess Islands, to Constantinople, to India again and to Sakhalin... But he's not free to do so. Firstly, he has a noble family to protect, and secondly he's got a large dose of cowardice. I'm afraid of getting over-extended, and each trip would complicate things and impact on my pocketbook significantly. No, do not tempt me needlessly! Don't write to me of the sea. [...]

It's hot here. Warm rains, ravishing evenings. A few miles from here there are good spots for bathing and for picnicking, but there is no time to do either. I either write, gnashing my teeth, or solve problems with carpenters and workers that aren't worth a kopek. [...]

It is wonderful in the woods. Landowners are fools to live surrounded by parks and orchards and not by woods. In the woods you sense a divine presence... If I were in your place I'd buy 500-600 acres of good woods, build roads and paths through them and even build a castle. A road cleared through a forest is more majestic than a tree-lined avenue. [...]

God willing that you win or inherit 300,000, so you can buy an estate...

Yours, A. Chekhov"

(Chekhov, letter to Suvorin, May 28, 1892, Melikhovo)

"Noble, upright Lika!

[...] Does Levitan of the dark eyes full of passion still haunt your dreams? There's a great big crocodile in you, Lika, and I know I'm doing right in heeding my head instead of my heart, into which you have already sunk your teeth. Stay away from me! Or don't—and let come what may! Make me dizzy with your perfume and tighten the lasso you've thrown around my neck.

I can only imagine how you're gloating, yes, laughing demonically, as you read these lines. (I'm writing rubbish, aren't I? Tear this letter up. Forgive its illegibility, and don't show it to anyone.)

I hear you've started smoking again. That's vile, Lika. I despise your character.

Goodbye, cornfield of my soul. With abject deference I kiss your powder box and envy your old boots because they see you every day. Write me of your successes. Be well, and don't forget he whom you have conquered.

Signed, Tsar of the Medes"[1]

(Chekhov, letter to Lydia Mizinova, June 28, 1892, Melikhovo)

"I'm not going to write to you any more, not even if you cut my throat. I've written to you in Abazzia, and at least ten

times to St. Moritz. Till now, you haven't sent me one single correct address, and that's the reason why not a single one of my letters has reached you, and my long descriptions of cholera and lectures on the topic have all been in vain. It pains me. But what is most painful is that after a whole series of letters concerning the plight of cholera, you write out of the blue from your gay, turquoise blue Biarritz that you are envious of my leisure! May Allah forgive you!

Meanwhile, sir, I'm alive and well. The summer was superb—dry, warm, with a veritable cornucopia of earthly offerings, but all its delights were spoiled by the news of cholera... I've already become the Serpukhov district doctor, chasing cholera by the tail and whipping the district into shape. There are twenty-five villages, four factories and a monastery under my purview. Mornings I see patients and make rounds the rest of the day. I ride around, lecture the locals, treat patients and all the while my blood's boiling. Since the district council hasn't given me a kopek for the clinics, I have to beg and borrow from the rich. I've turned out to be a terrific beggar, by the way, and thanks to my eloquent groveling the district now has two fully equipped clinics and five so-so ones....

Meanwhile my soul is tired, and I'm bored to the marrow of my bones. Not to belong to yourself, to be awakened every night by barking dogs and knocking at the gate (have they come to fetch me?), to drive miserable nags over unchartered roads, to read only about cholera and wait only for cholera and at the same time to be utterly indifferent to the disease and to the people whom you care for—all this is a mess that would do nobody any good. [...]

Of course, there's not a moment to think of literature. I'm not writing a thing. I refuse any commissions, so as to retain at least some freedom. So as a result I don't have a kopek. I am waiting until the rye is threshed and sold, and until such times I shall live off mushrooms, of which we are in endless supply, as well as my play 'The Bear.' By the way, I've never lived as cheaply as I do now. We even make our own bread... Imagine my cholera-begotten solitude, and enforced literary inactivity, and write me often...

Yours, A. Chekhov"

(Chekhov, letter to Suvorin, August 16, 1892, Melikhovo)

"Trofim![2]

You son of a bitch—if you don't stop fawning all over Lika, I'll drill a corkscrew into you, you swine, right into the place that rhymes with 'brass.' You scum! Don't tell me you don't know that Lika belongs to me and that we already have two children! You pig's snout! You shrimp! Go out into the barnyard and wash yourself in the mud puddle, or else, you son of a bitch. Feed your mother and respect her, but leave the girls alone. You scum!!!

Signed, 'Lika's Lover'"

(Chekhov, letter to Lydia Mizinova, November (no date), 1892, Melikhovo)

"Your response [to my story 'Ward No. 6'] is clear, and you unjustly chastise yourself that it isn't. You are an inveterate drunkard, and I've given you sweet lemonade, and while you've given lemonade its due, you justifiably note that lemonade has no intoxicants. There isn't enough alcohol in our stories to intoxicate and enthrall you, and you've made that perfectly clear... The reasons lie neither in our stupidity, nor in mediocrity or impudence, as Burenin thinks, but rather in an illness that for an artist is worse than syphilis or sexual exhaustion. We don't have that special "something," it's true, and that means that if you lift up our muse's skirts, you'll see a flat place.

Just remember that the writers we call universal or lasting or simply good, the writers who intoxicate us, have one highly important feature in common: they are moving toward something definite and summon you to follow, and you feel with your entire being, not only with your mind, that they have a certain goal, like the ghost of Hamlet's father, who had a reason for coming and stirring Hamlet's imagination. Some writers, depending on their caliber, have tangible goals—the abolition of serfdom, the liberation of one's country, politics, beauty, or simply vodka...while the goals of others are less defined—like God, life after death, the happiness of mankind, etc. The best of them are realistic and describe life as it is—but because each line is saturated with the consciousness of its goal, you feel that they're writing about more than 'life as it is', but 'life as it should be', and you are captivated... And as for us? Us! We write about life as it is, and that's it. We wouldn't lift a hoof even if you lashed us with a whip! We have neither immediate nor far-reaching goals; there's a kind of emptiness in our souls. We have no politics, we don't believe in revolution, or God, we're not afraid of ghosts, and I personally am not even afraid of death or blindness. And yet no one who wants nothing, hopes for nothing and fears nothing can be an artist. [...]

Yours, A. Chekhov"

(Chekhov, letter to Suvorin, November 25, 1892, Melikhovo)

The search for a place in the countryside—his long-cherished dream—was difficult at first. Efforts to purchase an estate in the Ukraine in December 1891 fell through.

Then one winter morning early in 1892, he read in a newspaper advertisement that a small property of 575 acres was for sale about 90 miles southeast of Moscow just outside the tiny village of Melikhovo. He quickly dispatched Masha and Mikhail by train to visit it. Though unable to see the main house and other features in the snow-covered countryside, they were nonetheless impressed and advised their brother to purchase it. And so he did, sight unseen, for 13,000 rubles, with the help of an advance from Suvorin and a five-year mortgage.

Soon, the melting snows revealed a small, wooden, ten-room main house, painted in a deep red with white trim, which he proudly referred to as his "estate" (though in reality it was a modest-sized one-story structure). The house was surrounded by hothouses, sheds, an avenue of linden trees, meadows, two ponds, plenty of beds for flowers and vegetables, woods, and much more. Chekhov moved there in early March, and after the initial euphoria of ownership, saw that Melikhovo fell far short of the grandeur of the estates of Tolstoy and Turgenev, whose estate life was the object of his fantasies during his twenties. In fact, the house and property were in a sorry state.

So he set out to restore his dilapidated new dwelling and its surroundings to working order, enlisting his family to address the task. The entire household was plunged into a frenzy of activity. That spring, he supervised a complete restoration of the house—

installing up-to-date plumbing, repairing of the roof, patching up the floor, installing partitions, wallpapering, moving the kitchen from the house to the servants quarters, demolishing the furnace, installing a tile stove. He hired peasants to till the land, as well as a cook and a maid to serve the family and guests. He personally planted apple orchards, cherry orchards, firs, elms, and rose bushes. He supervised the repair of the carriage and the digging of the pond. He filled the barnyard with geese. He built bird-houses for the starlings. He scrutinized every detail. "How lovely it is to play lord of the manor," he wrote Leontyev-Shcheglov. "Still, it's an easy fall from lord to concierge to porter."[3]

Above all, he loved the out-of-doors, and delighted in strolling through the gardens and fields and woods surrounding the property. He supervised the sowing of forty acres of rye. He planted orchards and raised bees. "There are raspberries and strawberries everywhere you look—and don't look! Currants too. And plenty of plum and apple trees," he wrote one of his admirers, Natalya Lintvaryova.[4] His special pride was the row of linden trees, reminding him of the grander estates he had visited. The spring sounds of nightingales singing and frogs clamoring enchanted him. And whenever he had a free moment from his newly acquired responsibilities, he dashed off letter after letter, describing the delights and novelties of "estate life."

To his list of occupations (doctor, short-story writer, playwright, human rights champion, supporter of a large family) Chekhov could now add a new occupation—landowner, a time-consuming one with added fiscal responsibilities. "My soul longs for breadth and height, but I am forced to lead a narrow life spent over worthless rubles and kopeks," he wrote Suvorin. "My soul languishes from the knowledge that I work for money and that money is the center of my activity. This gnawing feeling, which is justified, makes my writing a contemptible occupation in my own eyes."[5] Still, the novelty of being a landowner and running an "estate" buoyed his spirits that spring. "I haven't a kopek," he wrote Lydia Avilova, "but here's how I see it—it's not the man with lots of money who is rich, but rather the man who lives in the luxuries that early spring offers. I was in Moscow yesterday and almost suffocated from boredom."[6] The new list of activities and responsibilities seemed to energize him even more.

That first summer in Melikhovo, the house was filled to overflowing with guests. His brothers—who by now were all employed—came with friends and family in tow. The ever-hopeful Lika and her friend Tatyana visited; so did Levitan the artist. But that did not stop Chekhov from continuing his landowner activities. "I wanted to enjoy life, to live it fully," he wrote Suvorin. "How many trees I have planted! And we bought a carriage with good springs and a top, we built a new road so that we don't have to drive through the village, we're digging a pond...what more could we want?!"[7]

Several incidents—seemingly inconsequential at the time—occurred during that first year in Melikhovo that would have a lasting impact. The first was a yet another proposal by an attractive young estate owner named Aleksandr Smagin for Masha's hand. When she declared to her brother her intention to marry, Chekhov said nothing. Masha—who had toiled alongside her brother all spring to restore Melikhovo and was now his chief deputy in running the household and maintaining family stability—understood this as an expression of her indispensability and an implicit request to remain by her brother's side.

(The image of the self-sacrificing young woman working on the estate would be an inspiration for transforming an older play—*The Wood Demon*—into a new one yet to be written.)

The second was a hunting expedition that Chekhov and Levitan took together one spring day. Levitan shot and wounded a woodcock; unable to finish the task, he entreated his doctor friend to do so. That event stayed deeply in Chekhov's mind. Later, it would resurface as the pivotal moment of a play that was slowing taking shape in his dramatic imagination during the early Melikhovo years.

That spring and summer, Chekhov set up the practice of a country doctor. Peasants and workers in a twenty-five mile radius surrounding Melikhovo came to see him; indeed, he treated over 1,000 patients in the period of several weeks. "All in all, they are three times easier to put up with than visitors from Moscow with their discussions of literature," he wrote Leontyev-Shcheglov.[8] A flagpole was installed in the garden before the little wooden main house; the hoisted flag announced to the peasants of the surrounding villages that Dr. Chekhov was seeing patients. He treated the local population for typhus, diphtheria, and scarlet fever. He awaited the anticipated cholera epidemic (and even seemed disappointed that he hadn't had a case yet). As a doctor, Chekhov was experiencing another side of country life. "The peasants are crude, unsanitary and untrustworthy, but the thought that our labors will not be in vain makes it possible to overlook it all," he wrote Suvorin, "Of all the doctors in the district I am the most pathetic. My carriage and horses are mangy, I don't know the roads, I can't see anything at night, I have no money, I tire very quickly, but above all—I can't seem to forget that I ought to be writing."[9]

So he found time to write stories, including "The Grasshopper" (about Levitan, who was furious over it), "My Wife," "The Neighbors" and, his longer, serious story entitled "Ward No. 6." And he somehow found time to continue advising his admirers on writing, too.

After the thrill of the first spring and summer as a landowner, the realities of country life set in. That fall, while Chekhov continued with his medical practice, country life grew duller, harder, and increasingly monotonous. As a diversion, he occasionally indulged in a teasing correspondence with the adoring Lika, whom he alternately encouraged and rebuffed. At the same time, he corresponded with yet another Lydia—Lydia Avilova, a young short story writer from St. Petersburg who had sought out Chekhov as a mentor and had also fallen passionately in love with him. Married and a mother of three children, this naïve young woman had met Chekhov three years earlier, and developed such wild fantasies about their relationship that she was convinced Chekhov wished to marry her. She wrote him urgently, persistently; he replied with calm and objectivity, and gave no assurances. He limited the contents of his letters to advising her on her short story writing. "One must be indifferent when writing lugubrious stories," he wrote her. "When working on such stories you may weep and moan, you may suffer right along with your characters, but you must do it in a way that the reader will not notice it. The more objective the telling, the more powerful the effect."[10]

On the other hand, he discouraged neither female correspondent. In fact he seemed to enjoy the exchange of letters, while keeping both Lydias at arms length. "I have no desire to marry, and there's no one around for me to do so, anyway," he wrote Suvorin. "What's the point? Too much trouble. Falling in love, however, is another matter. It's boring to live without love."[11]

By the end of the year, the novelty of his landowner role was wearing off. "Oh, if only you knew how exhausted I am! I'm tired to the breaking point," he wrote Suvorin. "Guests, guests, guests... My estate is located near the highway, and every passing intellectual considers it necessary and in fact his duty to drop in on me to warm up... I left Moscow to get away from visitors..."[12]With the long winter ahead to face for the first time in Melikhovo, Chekhov would begin to develop an ambivalence for country life. In addition to the constant stream of visitors, the rough practice of medicine, and the additional expenses, there were its difficulties, its isolation, its numbing monotony, and above all, its silences. That ambivalence would express itself in his later plays.

But first, he had the long, winter months to live through, while he waited for inspiration to come.

"I don't intend to write any plays. I don't feel like it."

(Chekhov, letter to Suvorin, November 11, 1893)

1893

"Thanks for your efforts, Sashechka. Everything here isn't going so well. Here's a blow-by-blow report:

1) Father is ill. He has terrible pains in his spinal cord plus numbness in his fingers. It isn't continuous, it comes and goes like angina. The symptoms clearly are related to senility. He needs medical care, and yet 'his lordship' dines voraciously, ignoring moderation; he eats blini all day, and for supper has all kinds of nonsense. He says, 'I'm paralyzed,' and meanwhile doesn't listen.

2) Masha is ill. She's been in bed for a week with a high temperature. We thought it was typhus. She's better now.

3) I have influenza. I'm listless and irritable.

4) Our pedigree calf has frostbitten ears.

5) The geese have pecked off the cock's comb.

6) Guests keep coming and staying the night.

7) The local authorities are requesting a medical report from me.

8) The foundation of our house has shifted and some of the doors won't shut.

9) The intensely cold weather continues.

10) The sparrows are already starting to mate." [...]

Be well.

(Chekhov, letter to Aleksandr, February 6, 1893, Melikhovo)

"I'd dash up to Petersburg to see you—that's the mood I'm in right now. But there's cholera fifteen miles from here, I'm a district doctor, and am therefore honor bound to stay in one spot, without taking any trips...

Meanwhile, my life this spring was awful. I've already written you about that. Hemorrhoids and a vile, psychopathic mood. I felt angry and depressed, and the family wouldn't forgive me for it—all this resulting in daily spats and my desperate need for solitude. Spring was abominable, cold. And we didn't have any money. But then the wind picked up, summer blew in—and all our problems were swept away with the wave of a hand. It was a rare and amazing summer, filled with warm clear days and a plenitude of moisture. A happy combination like that happens so rarely, maybe once in a hundred years. The harvest is remarkable. Millet rarely grows in the Moscow provinces, but now it's waist high. If there always were harvests like these, then one could live solely on the bounty of the estate... Last fall I dug a new pond and planted trees around it. Now a whole cloud of minnows is swimming around in it. And it's quite nice to swim in.

I didn't smoke or drink all spring, and now all I have is a cigar or two. It's good for one's health not to smoke... I didn't write a play about life in Siberia; instead, I turned in my 'Sakhalin' for publication.... I spent a lot of time on it and for a while I felt I was not on the right track. Then at last I caught on to what didn't feel true about it—namely, that I was trying to instruct my readers with my 'Sakhalin' and at the same time obscuring something and holding back. So as soon as I started to describe what a fool I felt like in Sakhalin and what swine I found there, it became much easier for me and my work flowed, although it turned out to be somewhat humorous...

I've also written a short tale, 'The Black Monk.' If you come, I'll give it to you to read... Getting here is not too hard. I have fairly decent horses and carriages, the road isn't too bad. Yes, it's crowded and there's no privacy here, but you can escape these ills in the woods. I don't feel like writing a play at all ...

Here's news: I now have two dachshunds, named Bromide and Quinine. They're very ugly. Their paws are crooked and their bodies are long, but they're very intelligent.

Practicing medicine is exhausting and petty to the point of vulgarity. Sometimes I have to go out on calls four or five times a day. No sooner do you return from Kryukovo than a messenger from Vaskino is waiting in the courtyard. And the peasant women with their babies are so demanding. In September, I'm going to give up the practice of medicine altogether...

You say that you feel like going on a spree? I'd like one, terribly. I have a devilish desire to go to the sea. To spend a week in Yalta or Feodosia would be utter bliss. It's all right here at home, but to be on a boat would be a thousand times better. I'd like freedom and money. I'd sit out on the deck, guzzling wine and gabbing about literature—and in the evening, the ladies...

My very best!! Write!!

Yours, A. Chekhov"

(Chekhov, letter to Suvorin, July 28, 1893, Melikhovo)

"Dear Lika,

I haven't written you because I haven't had anything to write about. Life is so empty here that all you feel are the flies biting, and that's all. Come, my sweet little blond, we'll talk, we'll quarrel, we'll make up. Without you, I'm bored, and I'd give five rubles to talk to you even for five minutes. There's no cholera here, but there's dysentery, there's whooping cough, there's bad weather, it's raining, it's humid, and it brings on more coughing. Come to us soon, lovely little Lika, and sing something. The evenings have grown long, and there's no one here to break my boredom.

I'll be going to Petersburg when I'm able, i.e. after the cholera. I should be there by October. I keep dreaming of settling there. But all this is idle talk. It's vulgar, and the only thing that isn't vulgar is poetry, of which I feel the lack.

Money! Money! If I had any, I'd go to South Africa, about which I've been reading some very interesting letters. One has to have an aim in life, and when you travel, you have one...

I'm an old man, too. Life is making fun of me, or so it seems, and that's why I call myself an old man... This is all nonsense, though. Forgive me, Lika, really, there's nothing to write about. What I need is not to write to you, but to sit beside you and talk...

Our apples have ripened. I sleep seventeen out of twenty-four hours a day. Lika, if you have fallen in love with someone else and have forgotten me, at least don't laugh at me.

Keep well, darling Lika, and don't forget me.

Yours, A. Chekhov

(Chekhov, letter to Lydia Mizinova, August 13, 1893, Melikhovo)

"I'm alive and well. I cough more than I used to, but I'm still a long way off from consumption, I think. I've cut down on smoking to one cigar a day. I stayed put all summer, practicing medicine, going out and making rounds, caring for the sick, waiting for cholera... I treated a thousand people, wasted a lot of time, but cholera never came. I didn't write a thing, and when I had any free time, I took walks, I read, and tried to put my unwieldy 'Sakhalin' in order.

The day before yesterday I returned from Moscow, where I spent two weeks in a kind of daze. Because my Moscow life consists of an endless sequence of feasts and new acquaintances, they call me Avelan [the Admiral of the Russian fleet]. Never have I felt so free. First, I don't have an apartment, so I can live wherever I like; second, I don't have a passport; third, girls, girls, girls... All summer I've been working about money, I was exhausted, but now that my expenses are less, I'm more at ease. I feel free from financial worries, meaning that I'm beginning to think that I don't need more than 2,000 a year to live on so I can either write or not write. [...]

Lately, I've been overcome by a certain carefree feeling, and at the same time I feel drawn to people as never before.... I've grown so attached to literature that I'm beginning to dislike medicine... I can read for hours on end stretched out on my sofa. I don't have the passion for writing.

And I don't intend to write any plays. I don't feel like it...

So good-bye for now. When we see each other, we'll talk about the stories...

Yours, A. Chekhov"

(Chekhov, letter to Suvorin, November 11, 1893, Melikhovo)

The year got off to a gloomily start. Chekhov turned 33 on January 17, and wasn't feeling well. "I have about two dozen or more diseases," he complained irritably.[1]

First, he was suffering from hemorrhoids, an indignity which was to plague him to varying degrees for the rest of his life. It hurt to sit, it hurt to stand; there was burning and itching. The pain and tension emanated throughout his body. "Your body gets so irritated that you feel like putting a noose around your neck," he wrote Suvorin.[2] Second, his cough was getting worse. Irritable and depressed, the family got on his nerves, and he in turn was peevish with them. The only treatment for his symptoms, he confided in a letter to a friend, was sexual abstinence and solitude. As he wrote half-jokingly to Lika, he was feeling like an old man. He hid from his female admirers, Lika and Olga Kundasova.

Then there was the constant preoccupation with money. Because of his health, he wasn't getting any writing done, and therefore wasn't receiving any income. On the other hand, country life was cheaper, so supporting his family was easier.

At the same time, he couldn't shirk his medical responsibilities. In addition to running the estate, he went out on numerous daily calls to care for the local peasant population, and mobilized his district in face of a cholera threat. Moreover, he was getting an increasing number of consumptive patients. It was exhausting and increasingly burdensome.

So during those early winter months of 1893, isolated at Melikhovo, he suffered from *ennui* and restlessness, a state he periodically found himself in when his health deteriorated. He longed to travel again—to Europe, to America, South Africa, anywhere. He longed for the sea. Even his brother Aleksandr counseled him to get away from Melikhovo, the family, and especially his father.

But Chekhov remained. Eventually, winter gave way to spring, and the family mobilized to face the seasonal responsibilities of the estate. There were crops to be planted and a new pond to be dug. Masha returned from a visit to Moscow, bringing two lively dachshunds—a present from Leikin, the editor of *Fragments*. Chekhov named them Bromide and Quinine. They cavorted around the house, dug up the seed and dirt in the window flower boxes, and cheered the household considerably. The dogs delighted him with their antics–chasing birds, fussing at each other over food, chewing his patients' trousers, following him on walks through the fields and woods, and insisting on sleeping in his room. Chekhov, who had done hardly any writing that dreary winter, felt his spirits lifting. Every night he performed a routine, pretending they were his patients and advising them on going to the hospital. The entire household rang with laughter.

Then came summer—an especially lively one. In July, his brother Ivan married. In August, visitors flocked to Melikhovo, including Lika Mizinova, and once again the house was teeming with Chekhov's friends and admirers. Lika would entertain the family after dinner on the piano. She had a lovely soprano voice, and was studying opera in her spare time. Lured out to Melikhovo by Chekhov's warm, inviting letters, Lika soon saw that he had once again been misleading her, and had no serious intentions. Frustrated, she began a flirtation with Ignati Potapenko, a new visitor to Melikhovo and a talented young playwright and musician. Chekhov had met him earlier in Moscow, and, with his congenial disposition, he soon won Chekhov's friendship. Evenings after dinner, Potapenko would accompanied Lika on the piano with his warm baritone voice or play Tchaikovsky or Glinka on the violin. During those lovely summer evenings in the parlor, listening to their music, Chekhov would stand to the side, observing, and often would disappear to his study to take notes.

Lika was hoping to provoke Chekhov's jealousy, but, on the contrary, Chekhov was pleased for them both. Frustrated all the more by feelings of rejection, poor Lika intensified her liaison with Potapenko—an unlucky choice for her, as Potapenko already had a ailing wife and two children in Paris plus a previous wife in the Crimea, all of whom he was supporting—although that apparently didn't discourage him from pursuing a relationship with Lika. Meanwhile, Chekhov observed these developments with detachment, filing them away in his writer's memory for future use.

Chekhov was finally able to come to Moscow at the end of October. Greeted as a celebrated author, he spent two weeks there in a whirlwind of social activity so frenzied that he acquired the nickname of "Avelan," after the Russian admiral who had recently been wined and dined lavishly in Paris in recognition of Russia's new alliance with France. He stayed at the Grand Hotel in his favorite room, Room No. 5, which became known as "Chekhov's Room." Once again, he was involved with a number of women simultaneously, including a piano teacher named Aleksandra Pokhlebina, a petite poetess named Tatyana Shchepkina- Kupernik, and her friend Lydia Yavorskaya—soon to become the third Lydia in his entourage of female admirers. A flamboyant and ambitious young actress, she and Chekhov carried on a lively flirtation. The third Lydia soon circulated the rumor that Chekhov was going to marry her. Chekhov, in return, promised to write a play for her, entitled "Daydreams."

Meanwhile, Lydia (Lika) Mizinova was also in Moscow, performing in a play which Chekhov attended. As it happened, all the women in Chekhov's Moscow circle knew one another, and poor Lika soon became aware of her rivals for Chekhov's affection. She wrote him numerous letters, asking him to confirm this new liaison. True to his fashion, he kept the correspondence going, but neither confirmed nor denied the rumors. Heartbroken with rejection, she became Potapenko's mistress.

"Girls, girls, girls" ("djevitsa" in Russian, meaning "maiden"), Chekhov wrote to Suvorin, about his two weeks in Moscow that fall.[3] A photograph taken of Chekhov seated with Tanya and Lydia Yavorskaya (who were also involved in a liaison together) shows Chekhov gazing off, distracted. Clearly, he was enjoying the attention, although, as always, he kept a somewhat detached amused stance. He jokingly referred to the photo as "The Temptation of St. Anthony."

As for his writing during that year of highs and lows, Chekhov produced comparatively little, in contrast to the year before. During the early months, ill and depressed, he was content to lie around reading Zola and Turgenev. Indeed, during that year, his reading was as important to him as his writing. "Turgenev is charming, but a lot thinner than Tolstoy," he wrote Suvorin. "His language may become outdated, but he will remain forever young."[4] (Turgenev's name would begin to crop up in Chekhov's correspondence with more frequency over the next few years, and factor significantly in the conception of Chekhov's next play. But that would be a few years away.)

Meanwhile, Chekhov did write a few stories. The first, "Anonymous Story," about a revolutionary, was set in St. Petersburg, and showed the influences of Turgenev, whose work he had been reading. "The Two Volodyas," another story, depicts a young woman who is caught between two men named Volodya, both of whom exploit her and neither of whom loves her. The plot was reminiscent of poor Lika's plight.

Of special note was a third story he wrote that year, one that represented an unusual departure for Chekhov. One July night, he was awakened by a nightmare, in which he dreamed of a black monk. Later that year, in the dark days of autumn, he wrote the story "The Black Monk," whose nocturnal setting was inspired by an event in his own orchard, where workmen had tried to protect his trees from frost by setting fire to huge piles of straw late at night. The eerie image of black tree trunks illuminated by the blaze haunted Chekhov. His fantastical story—of a writer visited by the persistent apparition of a black monk and eventually driven to madness—is equally haunting. Did it represent personal fears about his own fate? Despite its uncharacteristically fantastical, Hoffmanesque tone, "The Black Monk" would become one of Chekhov's best known stories, and his first to be translated into English.

Otherwise, he spent his time reading the proofs of "The Island of Sakhalin," and signed a new agreement with *Russian Thought*, a Moscow publication, in which the serialized version of his report would appear. (Though Suvorin, the *New Times* editor, was hurt by Chekhov's new association with another publication, they still kept up their friendship and correspondence.)

The disjointed year of 1893 ended on an ironic note. To usher in the New Year, Chekhov invited Lika and Potapenko to Melikhovo together. Lika understood the import of the invitation—she was now being passed over—and wrote to Chekhov, asking if he might send something warm for Potapenko and her to wear on the journey, to withstand the cold.

"'AN IDEA FOR A SHORT STORY'...."

(Trigorin, in '*The Seagull*', Act II)[1]

1894

"You mock my thoroughness, dryness, erudition—and those who come after who will value my work ['The Island of Sakhalin']... My 'Sakhalin' is an academic work for which I've received a prize. So medicine can no longer accuse me of betrayal. I have discharged my obligation to scholarship and to what old-school writers used to call pedantry. And I'm glad that the severe smock of the convict now hangs in my literary wardrobe. Let it hang there! It doesn't make sense to publish 'Sakhalin' in a journal, it's not a journalistic work, it will do much better as a book... In any case, he who laughs last, laughs longest. Don't forget, I'll soon be seeing your new vaudeville.

Sergeenko is writing a tragedy about the life of Socrates... It is much easier to write a play about Socrates than about a young girl or a cook. Which merely shows that I do not consider the writing of vaudevilles a frivolous occupation. Nor do you consider it as such, much as you may pretend that it is nothing but a lot of frivolous nonsense.

Yours, A. Chekhov

(Chekhov, letter to Suvorin, January 2, 1894, Melikhovo)

"I'm in good shape psychologically, at least I think I am. True, I don't have much of a will to live, but that's not a disease, strictly speaking, but rather a passing state and even a natural one. In any event, if a writer depicts a person with a mental illness, that doesn't necessarily mean that he's ill himself. I wrote 'The Black Monk' in a detached state of cold objectivity, without any gloomy thoughts. I simply felt like depicting megalomania. And as for the monk floating across the field, I dreamed about him, and upon awakening, told Masha about him. So tell them that poor Anton Pavlovich hasn't lost his mind yet, he simply ate too much at supper and as a result dreams of monks.

May the angels and archangels bless you, and the cherubim and seraphim, too.

Yours, A. Chekhov"

(Chekhov, letter to Suvorin, January 25, 1894, Melikhovo)

"Greetings!!

... Ever since I've given up smoking I don't suffer from doom and gloom. And maybe it's because I've stopped smoking that Tolstoy's writing no longer moves me. In the depths of my soul I'm hostile to it, and of course that's not fair. But I have peasant blood coursing through my veins, so I'm not one to be impressed by the peasant's virtue. I've believed in progress ever since childhood—I couldn't help it, since the difference between the time when they beat me and the time when they stopped beating me was tremendous. I love intelligent people, sensitivity, good manners, wit, and never paid any more attention to whether people picked their calluses or had smelly foot-bindings than whether young ladies walked around in curlers in the morning. No, Tolstoy's philosophy moved me deeply for about six-seven years. It was not so much his basic beliefs that had an effect on me as much as the way in which he expresses them, his rationality, and his charisma as well, I suppose.

But now something in me protests. My common sense and better judgment tell me that there is more love of man-kind in electricity and steam than in chastity and veganism. War is evil, and so is our justice system, but it doesn't follow that I should walk around in sandals and sleep on a stove alongside my workman and his wife, and so on and so on.

I'm fed up with discussions and debates. I can't read them without revulsion. Patients who have a fever don't feel like eating, but they do have a longing for 'something sour', as they call it. So I too, want something 'sort of sour.' This isn't accidental, since I sense the same mood all around me. It's as if everyone who was once in love has now fallen out of it, and is in search of a new infatuation. It's very possible—indeed probable—that the Russian people will once again become infatuated with natural sciences, and that materialism will once more be in style. However, this all is in God's hands. Once you start philosophizing, your head goes round and round...

Yours, A. Chekhov"

(Chekhov, letter to Suvorin, March 27 1894, Yalta)

"Darling Lika:

Thank you for your letter. Although you frightened me in when you wrote that you will die soon, even though you might be teasing me when you say I've rejected you, nevertheless thank you. I know very well, that a) you won't die and b) no one has rejected you.

I'm in Yalta—it's boring, in fact it's terribly boring. The local so-called aristocracy is presenting 'Faust', and I attended rehearsals, delighting in a veritable flowerbed of brunette, raven, flaxen and blond heads, listening to the songs, eating. At the home of the headmistress of the local girls' high school I dine on meat pies and mutton with grits; when I'm invited to the homes of the wealthy, I have spinach pie... I go to sleep at ten, get up at ten, and after lunch a rest, but still it's boring, darling Lika.

Not for one moment does the thought leave me that I must write, that I must, I must. Write, and write, and write. I am of the opinion that inner happiness is impossible without idleness. My ideal: to be idle and love a fat girl. For me the greatest delight is to walk, or to sit and do nothing: my favorite occupation—to collect what's not needed (papers, bits of straw, etc.) and do useless things. But meanwhile, I am a 'literateur' and must write, even here, in Yalta.

Dear Lika, when you become a great singer and earn a huge salary, then be so good as to marry me and feed me, so that I may do nothing. And if you're really going to die, then let Varya Eberlay do it instead; I like her, as you know. I'm so stressed by the constant thought of unavoidable, compulsory work that I've been tortured by constant palpitations for a week already. It's an awful sensation.

I kiss both your hands.

Yours, A. Chekhov"

(Chekhov, letter to Lydia (Lika) Mizinova, March 27, 1894, Yalta)

"Russian men of letters live in a state of semi-starvation, since every author—even the one who writes 100 pages a year if he's lucky—carries a burden of obligations. And there is nothing more boring and less poetic, so to speak, than a prosaic struggle for existence, draining life of all its joy and bringing on apathy. [...]

Meanwhile I'm starting to dream of taking a trip across the steppes and living under the open sky, even if it's only for twenty-four hours. About ten years ago I was interested in spiritualism and Turgenev's spirit, whom I invoked, said to me: 'Your life is nearing sunset.' Indeed, I'm now craving all kinds of experiences, as though it were the last day before Lent. I could gobble it all up—the steppes, a trip abroad, a good novel... And some nameless force, like a premonition, is urging me on, telling me I'd better hurry. Or maybe it's not a premonition but rather a regret that life is moving by so dully and sluggishly. My soul is in protest, so to speak.

I bow low to you...

Chekhov, Cleric of the Highest Order"

(Chekhov, letter to Suvorin, July 11, 1894, Melikhovo)

"I've been in Sepukhov for a while, serving as a juror. Landed gentry, factory owners and local merchants comprise the jury panel. By accident I ended up on the jury for every trial—this has even provoked laughter. Moreover, I served as the foreman. Here are my observations: 1) Jurors aren't street people, they're people with a social conscience; 2) Good people can wield great authority, whether they be gentry or peasants, educated or uneducated. A rather pleasant impression, in all.

"I've been named trustee of a local village school in Talezh. A teacher earns twenty-three rubles a month. He has a wife, four children, and he's already gray by the age of thirty. So downtrodden is he that no matter what you might be talking to him about, the topic of salary comes up. According to a teacher, poets and prose writers should write only about salary increases...

Write to me with news...

Yours, A. Chekhov

(Chekhov, letter to Suvorin, November 27, 1894, Melikhovo)

"I'll be ecstatic if you would come visit me, but I fear that your delicious cartilages and tiny bones will be dislocated. The road is terrible, the carriage keeps leaping as if in agonizing pain, and keeps losing its wheels. The last time I was driving from the station, the ride was so rough that my heart was torn up from its roots, so now I am incapable of love.

They say that your story will be published in 'The Week'. I'd delighted for you, and congratulate you from the bottom of my heart. 'The Week' is a solid and entertaining publication.

Farewell, my dear little friend.

Yours, A. Chekhov"

(Chekhov, letter to Tanya Shepkina-Kupernik, November 28, 1894, Melikhovo)

It would be a year of restlessness and deepening entanglements.

The year began with an outpouring of publications. First came the launching of the much-anticipated serialized "Sakhalin" in *Russian Thought.* The public, expecting a sensational account, was somewhat let down by the dry, journalistic style of the work. Chekhov, in turn, was disappointed in this muted response. Still, it had a significant impact. A commission was sent to the island to investigate Chekhov's findings, resulting in improved conditions for the convicts. Chekhov had accomplished what he had set out to do.

January also brought the reissuing of "The Black Monk" and the publication of two other stories—"Two Volodyas" in the *Russian Gazette*, and "A Woman's Kingdom" in *Russian Thought.* The latter, a departure for Chekhov in both form and content, is a three-part serialized story of a lower-class woman who inherits an iron foundry, and tells of her struggle for identity. Unable to function either in her world of origin or in her new world of wealth and position, she sinks into depression.

By now, Chekhov's reputation as one of the leading writers in Russia was established. At thirty-four years old, he had a major literary oeuvre of almost 500 short stories with a remarkable scope in length, tone, and thematic content. Meanwhile, his rate of output was changing. Whereas in the first half of the 1880s he had written dozens of stories a year, mostly comedic, his productivity was now down to a handful per year. The short comedic stories of his medical school years had now given way to longer, darker stories with more subtle and ironic content. In these early Melikhovo years, he had time to reflect and experiment and deepen his content, and the results—works as varied as "Ward No. 6," "The Black Monk" and the ones published later in 1894—showed a new scope and depth.

But Chekhov did not have time to reflect on his status. He was deeply embroiled in a love-triangle, and as the months passed, that involvement would grow more and more entangled—with serious consequences to all. It was an evolving saga that would take the most part of the year to play itself out, with its participants shuttling back and forth from Moscow to Melikhovo and eventually to Europe. It would become, as one of Chekhov's characters would later say in the play inspired by these events, "an idea for a short story."

New Year's Day, 1894, had brought Lydia (Lika) Mizinova and Potapenko to Melikhovo to celebrate with its owner. Thrown together by Chekhov's connivance to ward off Lika's advances, the desolate Lika intensified her relationship with the young singer. The couple left, and after a quick visit by Chekhov to Moscow (to participate in his other on-going love triangle with Lydia Yavorskaya and her friend Tania), he returned to Melikhovo, followed again by the newly aligned couple. Chekhov seemed to encourage Potapenko to intensify the affair, knowing full well that Potapenko was married. They left again at the end of January with a gift from Chekhov—two puppies from Quinine. (Was this his consolation gift to Lika for having passed her on to another?)

In February, the plot grew more complex. Once more Chekhov resumed his cat-and-mouse game with Lika, and a flirtatious correspondence ensued between them. "Lika, give me your little hand—the other one you gave me smells of herring," he wrote her. "P. S. When and where are you having lunch today? Can't you drop by and see me, even for a moment?"[2]

Meanwhile, at the end of the month, Lika conceived Potapenko's child.

To make matters even more complicated, Potapenko left Russia for Paris, where his second wife and her children awaited him. Now Masha, Chekhov's sister, became involved, angered by the treatment by both men of her friend Lika, who in March, pregnant and desperate, followed Potapenko to Paris. En route, Lika wrote a tear-stained letter to Chekhov, begging him to come to Paris and visit the woman he had rejected. Meanwhile, Chekhov had slipped away to Yalta, to nurse his aggravating cough. Though distanced from this ever-tightening entanglement, he persisted in teasing Lika in his response to her, indicating that his affections for her might be renewed, and invited her to return to Russia. "Ask Potapenko to buy your ticket and forget to pay him back," he advised her.[3]

It is here that the story of this painful triangle pauses, at least for a few months. While Lika took up residence in Paris for the duration of her pregnancy (only a mile or so from Potapenko, his second wife and children), Chekhov spent April in Yalta, completing a new story called "The Student," a complex tale with a deep, spiritual content about a young student priest who retells the Easter story to two peasant widows. The story was written at a time when he was evaluating the work of Tolstoy and his strong spiritual teachings, just as he wrote "An Anonymous Story" the year after reading Turgenev. Away from all his entanglements, he was able to concentrate on his writing, and had time to reflect. During that period, he also experienced severe heart palpitations, provoking his deepening exploration of themes of mortality.

He returned to Melikhovo in May, and once again was in the thrall of spring and early summer. He supervised the building of a little wooden building adjacent to the main house, where he could retreat from the anticipated overflow of visitors. He called the odd little structure "The Tower of Babel." It would be his writer's refuge. "It's hay-mowing time," he wrote Leontyev-Shcheglov. "The smell of fresh hay is intoxicating, even stupefying. Spend an hour or two sitting in a haystack and you'll imagine yourself in the arms of a naked woman."[4]

Meanwhile, all spring his female correspondents pursued him with their letters, including Aleksandra Pokhlebina, Olga Kundasova, and a new one—Aleksandra Liosova, (his brother Ivan's former fiancée).

Intoxicated as he was by the countryside, in July Chekhov had sudden urge to travel. This restlessness was usually provoked (as before the Sakhalin trip) by increased concern about his health; he mentioned to Suvorin that he had five to ten years to live, whether he sought medical advice or not. He asked, of all people, Potapenko, who had recently returned to Russia without Lika, to join him on a boat trip down the Volga. Reportedly, they enjoyed each other's company without discussing the third person in the triangle. After the boat trip, Chekhov journeyed to Taganrog, where his Uncle Mitrofan was dying. From there, he sailed to Yalta, and thereafter he journeyed to Europe with Suvorin, whom he had convinced to accompany him. From Odessa they went to Vienna, where he resumed his correspondence with Lika, teasing her in the tone of an abandoned lover. Then Chekhov and Suvorin left for Abbazia, a spa on Adriatic, and thereafter Trieste, Venice, Genoa, Milan, and then Nice. Letters from Lika followed him in his journey. In September, awaiting the birth of her child in Switzerland, she opened her heart to him about her pain over his rejection, only to be compounded by Potapenko's rejection (he had returned to his wife). She entreated Chekhov to come to see her. But he begged off with cool responses, and avoided Switzerland. She returned to Paris, to find that he had already been there and left without waiting to see her. He offered his declining health as an excuse. "It appears that I've let my health go, just as I've let you go," he wrote her, persisting in sending her another subtle, misleading double message.[5]

Chekhov returned to Melikhovo in October. Masha was in Moscow, teaching. (Chekhov learned later that she had secretly been seeing Levitan behind his back, and was in a state of agitation over it.) Having temporarily evaded the "furies" (as he called the women who pursued him), he was able to reflect. He turned his attention once again to philanthropic pursuits, entreating Suvorin to donate books to the new library being built in the district for peasants and teachers.

November brought no visitors and no distractions. Chekhov finally got down to writing. He completed the book version of "The Island of Sakhalin" and "Three Years," his longest story since "The Duel." Autobiographical in content, it contains memories of his childhood. Potapenko, Lika, and Olga Kundasova also appear in the story in fictitious incarnations. Cut off from the Moscow literary circles, his concentration was pure. At the same time, he was dissatisfied. "I'm tired of writing the same thing all the time," he wrote one of his admirers, Yelena Shavrova. "I want to write about devils, about terrible, volcanic women, about sorcerers—but alas! They want stories and tales faithful to the life of the Ivan Gavriloviches—that is to say, the ordinary man—and their spouses..."[6]

While Chekhov was writing undisturbed in Melikhovo, Lika gave birth to a baby girl named Christina in Paris, with Potapenko and his second wife and children nearby. Distraught, the second wife threatened to commit suicide and to kill the children. Potapenko, now deep in debt, threatened suicide, too. He wrote to Chekhov, begging him for help. Chekhov, in response, rushed to Moscow and borrowed money from his new editor Goltsev at *Russian Thought* to send to Potapenko. (In a cruel footnote to the affair, Potapenko would never see Lika again after Paris.)

Meanwhile, Chekhov resumed participation in his other love triangle. The notorious duet of Lydia Yavorskaya and Tanya Shepkina-Kupernik had returned from Europe to Moscow. In December, Lydia Yavorskaya performed the role of a courtesan in a play, and delighted in reenacting a scene from it whenever she saw Chekhov, wherein she would sink to her knees before him and throw her arms around his legs, crying: "My darling, you are the last page of my life!" (It was a line that Chekhov filed away in his writer's memory, for future use.) Meanwhile, Lydia's lover Tanya journeyed to Melikhovo to visit Chekhov, where they were named godparents of Chekhov's neighbor's new daughter. Chekhov respected Tanya—a highly intelligent poetess and translator—above all his female involvements, or at least it appeared so. And he was comfortable in her company. Was it because he knew she was also involved with Lydia Yavorskaya and therefore could not be a candidate for a serious relationship?

Duets, triangles, events, images... The details of this intrigue-fraught, love-filled year were filed away in his imagination. Already, an idea for a play was slowly percolating, soon to take shape.

“IMAGINE, I AM WRITING A PLAY...”

(Chekhov, letter to Suvorin, October 21, 1895)

1895

“Dear Viktor Viktorovich,

I am not writing plays, and anyway, I don’t feel like it. I’ve grown old, and the ardor isn’t there anymore. On the other hand, I’d like to write a long novel about sixty miles long...

I live in the country now, I make an appearance in Moscow from time to time, where I eat oysters. I’m growing old. I have no money. No decorations. No rank, either. And a lot of debts. [...]

You and I are great liberals, but for some reasons they called me a conservative. I was glancing through an old edition of ‘Fragments’ not long ago, already forgotten, and was struck by the passion in my writing and in yours, passion that isn’t found today in a single one of the latest geniuses.

Be well.

Yours as ever, A. Chekhov”

(Chekhov, letter to Bilibin, January 18, 1895, Moscow)

“...Kupernik [Tatyana Shchepnika-Kupernik] is a talented girl, but you won’t find her appealing. I feel sorry for her—and annoyed with myself for finding her repulsive three days of the week. She’s a cunning little devil.... Yavorskaya [Lydia] on the other hand is something else. She’s a very kind woman and might have even been a successful actress if her training hadn’t ruined her.... As for Kundasova [Olga], I never thought of using her in a story. [...]

You say that women take away one’s youth? Nonsense! Not mine, at least. ... I have had a few romances, and I resemble Catherine [The Great, with her sexual appetites] as much as a walnut resembles an armadillo. Silk shirts mean nothing to me, except that they’re soft to the touch. I like comfort, but debauchery doesn’t tempt me—I couldn’t appreciate Potapenko’s wife, for example.

For my health's sake, I've got to go far away from here for eight to ten months—to Australia, or the estuaries of the Yenisey River. Otherwise I'll kick the bucket. All right, I'll come to Petersburg, but will there be a room for me to hide away? This is a question of utmost importance, since I'll have to write all February in order to earn enough for my voyage. Ah, how I must go away! My whole chest is wheezing, and the hemorrhoids are enough to make the devil miserable—there will have to be an operation. Anyway, to hell with literature—I should have practiced medicine full-time. On the other hand, I have nothing to complain about. I am indebted to literature for the happiest days of my life. It's what I love above all.

As ever, A. Chekhov

(Chekhov, letter to Suvorin, January 21, 1895, Melikhovo)

You're right: the subject matter [of your story] is risky. I don't have anything definitive to say. I can only advise you to lock the story away for a year, and then reread it. By then, you'll see it clearly. I'm afraid to give you an opinion at this point, lest I be mistaken.

[As it stands], the story is wan—it's tendentious, the details are as cloudy as spilled oil, and the characters are undefined...

I'd like to see you write about something cheerful and life-affirming, in a bright-green color, like a picnic. Leave it to the doctors to write about cripples and black monks. Soon I'll start writing humorous stories, since my psycho-pathological repertoire is now exhausted.

I'm building a bathhouse.

I wish you the best... I enjoy reading your stories. Only allow me to say one thing: no matter how severe my criticism might be, that doesn't mean that a story isn't worthy of publication. My nit-picking is one thing; publication and payment is another.

Yours, A. Chekhov"

(Chekhov, letter to Yelena Shavrova-Youst, February 28, 1895, Melikhovo)

"[...] All right, I'll get married, if you insist. But under

the following conditions: everything must be as it was before, in other words, she must live in Moscow and I in the country, and I'll drop in on her from time to time. As for marital bliss which goes on day after day from one morning to the next—I couldn't bear it. When someone talks on and on about the same thing every day in the same tone of voice, I start feeling violent... I promise to be a splendid husband, but give me a wife who, like the moon, does not appear in my sky every night. N. B. Just because I've gotten married, it doesn't mean that I'll write any better.

I've been living in Melikhovo for four years now. My calves have grown into cows, the woods have grown... My heirs will profit well from the timber—still, they'll call me an ass, since heirs are never satisfied.

Keep writing to me...

As ever, A. Chekhov"

(Chekhov, letter to Suvorin, March 23, 1895, Melikhovo)

"[...] We're having a pathetic spring. The snow is still lying in the fields, and you can't take a ride either in a sleigh or a carriage, and the cattle long for grass and freedom. Yesterday, a drunken old peasant took off all his clothes and was bathing in our pond. His senile old mother was beating him with a stick, and everyone was standing around guffawing with laughter. After he had bathed, the peasant trudged home barefoot in the snow, while his mother followed after. This old woman had come to see me once to be treated for bruises—her son had beaten her, too. How despicable it is to keep postponing the education of the dark masses!

Yours, A. Chekhov"

(Chekhov, letter to Suvorin, April 13, 1895, Melikhovo)

"Thanks for your letter, for your warm words, and for the invitation. I won't come before November, most likely, as I've got so much to do. First, in the spring I'll be building a new school here in the village, where I serve as a trustee. I'll need to draw up plans, estimates, take trips here and there, and so on. Second, imagine—I'm writing a play that I'll also finish, though probably not before the end of November. I can't say I'm not enjoying it, although

I'm flagrantly ignoring the basic dramatic conventions. It's a comedy. There are three female roles, six male roles, four acts, a landscape (with a view of a lake), lots of conversation about literature, little action, and five tons of love. [...]

My visit with the Tolstoys lasted a day and a half. He made a wonderful impression on me. I felt as relaxed as if I had been at home, and my conversations with him were equally relaxing. [...]

Yours, A. Chekhov"

(Chekhov, letter to Suvorin, October 21, 1895, Melikhovo)

"[...] My play is moving ahead, and as of now everything is going swimmingly, but what may happen later, toward the end, I don't know. I shall finish it in November... It must be because of the play that my pulse is irregular; I fall asleep late and don't feel well, in general, although since I returned from Moscow I've been leading an abstemious life in all respects. I should try bathing and getting married, for a change. [...]

I wish you the best.

Yours, A. Chekhov"

(Chekhov, letter to Suvorin, November 10, 1895, Melikhovo)

"Well, sir, I've finished the play. I began it 'forte' and ended it 'pianissimo'—contrary to all the rules of dramaturgical form. It came out more like a novella. I'm more dissatisfied than satisfied with it, and reading over my newborn play, I'm once again convinced that I'm not a dramatist. The acts are very short, and there are four of them. Although it's still only a skeleton of a play, an attempt that will change a million times before the upcoming season, I've nevertheless ordered two copies to be typed on a Remington (the machine makes two copies simultaneously). I'll send one to you. Only don't let anyone else read it. [...]

Be well...

Yours, A. Chekhov"

(Chekhov, letter to Suvorin, November 21, 1895, Melikhovo)

It would be the year when it would all come together in his

imagination—incidents, details, impressions he had been storing up since he had last written a play six years ago. All the elements that had increasingly been in his consciousness during this period—love, art, nature, and the passage of time—were about to meld together in the most unanticipated and magical dramatic form.

Still, the year began with the eclectic mixture of hard work, frivolity, distraction and philanthropy that seemed to have characterized the two years since he moved to Melikhovo.

January saw Chekhov continue his tangled involvement with four women. Lika resumed her correspondence with Chekhov from Paris; she was jealous of Tanya's frequent visits to Melikhovo, and of Lydia Yavorskaya's continued attentions. (In a letter, she asked when he would be marrying Lydia. Lika wrote to Masha, too, alluding to her broken heart over Chekhov, trying to console herself with her baby.) There were letters, too, from Olga Kundasova, whom he had met when she was a young student in Moscow during his medical school years. She suffered from bi-polar disorder, and wrote frantically to Chekhov, who was trying to help with her treatment. Tanya continued her frequent visits to Melikhovo just after New Year's, this time bringing Levitan, who had been angry with Chekhov for portraying him in a recent story, "The Grasshopper." The two reconciled quickly. Chekhov also made a quick visit to Moscow, where he saw Lydia Yavorskaya perform in a play, reciting the declarations of love—"my darling, you are the last page of my life"—the line that she frequently recited for him and others at parties.

During that year, Chekhov would mention marriage several times in various letters to Suvorin. "I should try bathing and getting married, for a change," he wrote Suvorin. "But I'm afraid of a wife and a family routine that would inhibit me and, given my disorderliness, wouldn't work, somehow. Still, I suppose it's better than tossing around in the sea of life and weathering the storm in the flimsy boat of debauchery. The fact is that I no longer love my mistresses. Anyway, little by little I'm becoming impotent with them…"[1]

Despite all these distractions, Chekhov found time make long carriage rides from Melikhovo throughout the countryside, paying calls on sick patients. As a trustee, he participated in fund-raising for the school in the neighboring village. In addition, he faithfully answered letters from young writers, male and female, whom he was mentoring.

One of those literary disciples was Lydia Avilova, whose infatuation for him kept growing and intensifying. He tried to discourage by not writing her at all during 1894. But for some reason, he discreetly sought her Petersburg address, and let her know he was coming to town in February, which only further provoked her feverish fantasies. Her husband was away, and she invited him for an intimate supper, but it was interrupted by some unexpected visitors, to Chekhov's relief.

There are sharply contrasting reports of this evening. According to Lydia Avilova's memoirs, he told her that he'd loved her for years. According to Chekhov, the conversation was quite the contrary. After that evening, he took pains to discourage her passionate letters, restricting his response to comments (not particularly encouraging ones) about her stories. The day after this supper party, he wrote her a detached letter: "In summary, you are talented, but your writing is heavy, or to put it vulgarly, flabby; you belong to the ranks of flabby writers. Your language is as stilted as an old man's... Write a novel. Spend a year writing it, a half-year cutting it—and then publish it...I wish you the very very best."[2]

Dazed by his sudden departure from St. Petersburg, Avilova impulsively ran to a jeweler's two days later and ordered a watch fob as a gift for him, engraved as follows: "Stories and Tales by Chekhov" on one side, and "page 267, lines 6 and 7" on the other. The reference was to a line in Chekhov's short story "The Neighbors": "If ever you have need of my life, come and take it." She sent it to her brother in Moscow, asking him to deliver the gift to the offices of *Russian Thought* in Moscow and request that the editors send it on to Chekhov. Chekhov never acknowledged receipt the gift.

Desperate, Avilova journeyed to Moscow and wrote Chekhov at Melikhovo, asking him if she could see him. Not only did he not respond, he also left word with his editors that he had gone to Taganrog—which of course he had not. He remained at Melikhovo, working on a story, "The Wife," and waiting for spring.

In March, the family reunited at Melikhovo; in April, Chekhov returned to Moscow briefly to see Lydia Yavorskaya perform in a play. That month, the first glimmer that he was thinking of writing a play appears in a letter to Suvorin. "Yes, I shall write a play," he wrote. "I don't feel like writing a drama, but I don't have an idea for a comedy yet. I'll probably sit down and write a play in the fall..."[3]

Then came May, and an unexpected visit to Melikhovo from Lika, whom none of the family had forgotten and whose presence they all missed. She had left her baby with a wet nurse in Paris, and come to Moscow ostensibly to see her grandmother—but her first visit was to Melikhovo to see Chekhov. (Potapenko was still *persona non grata* there; in any event, he was busy writing, earning money to support his two wives, Lika and the baby, as well as pay off his debts to Chekhov and Suvorin.) After that visit came the second mention of his intention to write a play. "I'm going to write something strange," he wrote Suvorin cautiously. "I don't want to write on pain of punishment or for money. I'm quite satisfied with things as they are, and want to write a play just for the sake of writing it..."[4]

In June, Chekhov had Melikhovo to himself briefly, where he began work on "Ariadne," a story that evokes the love triangle he had been involved with the previous year. Lika returned for another visit, as did Olga Kundasova. And in the midst of these interruptions, Chekhov and Masha began archiving all his letters and papers, a task they would continue every summer (and a possible indication that both were aware of his slowly deteriorating health).

At the end of June, however, an event happened which would change the flow of the year and serve as the catalyst for an idea that had been growing in Chekhov's dramatic imagination for several years. Chekhov received an urgent letter from his friend Levitan, who had been summering on an estate between Moscow and St. Petersburg belonging to one of his patronesses. He entreated Chekhov to come, saying that he was suffering from severe depression. At first, Chekhov demurred, but then he received a letter from Anna Turchaninova, Levitan's hostess on the estate, informing Chekhov that Levitan had attempted suicide. She begged him to come, saying Levitan's life depended on his visit. (Evidently, Levitan had been having an affair with at least one of her three daughters, and he had quarreled violently with their mother, who also was attracted to him.)

So Chekhov journeyed north on July 5 to the remote estate. When he arrived, he found Levitan with a bandaged head and a dark countenance. They took long walks together on the estate, a gloomy place situated on a lake filled with seagulls, and Chekhov tried to lift his friend's spirits. The visit made a vivid and lasting impression on him.

In August, following his visit to Levitan, Chekhov journeyed to Yasnaya Polyana, the impressive estate and home of Tolstoy, for a private "audience" with the towering giant of Russian literature. They spent two days together, bathing in the river and bicycling. Tolstoy was charmed by Chekhov—although he later wrote to his son that while Chekhov clearly was talented, he didn't yet have a fully developed *weltanschauung*. Chekhov, in turn, allegedly remarked to friends that Tolstoy was "a perfect man."

With all the traveling, Chekhov wrote few letters that summer in comparison to his usual volume. He had been working on a number of stories though, that would be published later that year, including "Anna on the Neck" (the story of a destitute woman who marries an elderly civil servant to save her family and then in turn becomes a tyrant), "The Murder" (a dark story inspired by his experiences at Sakhalin), and "Ariadne" (inspired by the story of Lika and Potapenko's relationship).

In September, Lika left her baby with her grandmother to visit Melikhovo several times. She craved the company of the Chekhov family, and was welcomed with warmth and acceptance. She professed no bitterness—neither toward Potapenko, nor toward Chekhov. Her daughter was the joy of her life, she claimed, and its consuming focus.

Sometime in October, the people and events swirling around him during these three years at Melikhovo came together in Chekhov's imagination, and poured onto the page in four short weeks. Levitan's visit to Melikhovo in October may have been the catalyst. In any event, to Chekhov's own surprise, the outpouring was in the form of a play, his first after a six-year hiatus. "Imagine—I am writing a play," he wrote Suvorin on October 21. He professed to be flagrantly disregarding classical dramatic structure, and further admitted that he was rather enjoying the process. "It's a comedy," he wrote. "There are three female roles, six male roles, four acts, a landscape (with a view of a lake), lots of conversation about literature, little action, and five tons of love."[5]

Judging from his correspondence to Suvorin, it took him only four weeks to write it, and he seemed both excited and worried. Its four-act form, length, and lack of action did not conform to the conventions of the contemporary theatre, of which Ostrovsky's plays were the model. He begged Suvorin's understanding, saying that he couldn't come to St. Petersburg until he completed it. On November 2, he reported frustration over numerous interruptions, but by November 10, he wrote Suvorin again to say that, "as of now everything is going swimmingly, but what may happen later, toward the end, I don't know. I shall finish it in November... It must be because of the play that my pulse is irregular."[6]

Finally on November 18 he wrote to Yelena Shavrova: "I've finished the play. It's called *The Seagull*. It didn't come out particularly well. All in all, I'm not that good a dramatist."[7]

As soon as he finished the play in late November, he gave it to Potapenko to have it typed out. Despite his apologies and excuses, however, Chekhov was clearly excited. The copying process was too slow for the impatient dramatist who had waited so many years for inspiration, so he gave the manuscript to Suvorin, who had a copy typed out on a Remington.

Suvorin read the play and was shocked—not by the dramaturgy, but by the resemblance of the characters and events to those of Chekhov's intimates. This response was echoed after the second reading of the play in December, held in the drawing room of Lydia Yavorskaya's hotel in Moscow. Korsh (who produced *Ivanov*) found the play decadent and dramaturgically flawed; Lydia Yavorskaya, though polite, was offended by details of her life portrayed in the play. In general, those who attended the reading recognized the characters immediately and shared Suvorin's amazement at the extent to which he had drawn the lives of his friends. They were also mystified by the strangeness of the form and the overall gloominess of the play itself, as one friend put it.

Chekhov was hurt by their response. "My play (*The Seagull*) has flopped even before a production," he wrote Suvorin.[8] He added that if the characters were truly perceived as imitative of people in his life, he would not allow the play to be performed or published.

But objectively speaking, those who read and heard this new play only weeks after it had been written had cause to be shocked. Set on a country estate over a period of three years, *The Seagull* tells the story of a young writer (Treplev) who tries to win the approval of his actress-mother (Arkadina) and her writer-lover (Trigorin) with a new *avant-garde* play he has just written—and the serious consequence of this attempt on all involved. Disgusted with the atrophy of the Russian theatre, Treplev is desperate to make his mark with "new forms," and to impress his mother and the young actress Nina, whom he loves and who stars in his play. Nina, however, is smitten instead with Trigorin. The only ones who appreciate his play are Masha, the daughter of the estate's steward, who is desperately in love with Treplev, and Dorn, a congenial doctor and friend of the family. Enraged by his mother and her lover's ridicule, Treplev acts out. First he shoots a seagull, then he attempts suicide, albeit ineffectively, more likely to provoke sympathy than to succeed at it. The various love triangles of the play become more and more entangled, with dramatic consequences. Arkadina and Trigorin leave the estate for Moscow, and Nina follows after to be with Trigorin.

In Act IV, set three years later (still on the estate), the aftermath of these tumultuous events is revealed. Treplev has become a successful writer, but experiences no pleasure from it. He longs for Nina, who meanwhile has had a baby with Trigorin. He, in turn, has returned to Arkadina. All return to the estate to visit Treplev and his uncle Sorin (Arkadina's brother), whose health is failing. In the play's penultimate scene, Nina reveals to Treplev the tragic events of her life—the death of her baby and her current status as a mediocre actress in the provincial theatre. When Nina hears Trigorin's voice in the next room, she declares that she still loves him "to distraction." After she leaves, Treplev realizes the hopelessness of his love, the loss of inspiration, and the bankruptcy of his soul.

With its absence of Aristotelian elements *The Seagull* has no one central character, no single driving action, and no over-arching theme. Instead, it is about a number of elements—love, art, nature, and the inexorable passage of time. And at the end, there is no moral, no message. All that is left, as Nina says, is to endure.

The sources of inspiration for *The Seagull* spring specifically from the lives, events and details close to Chekhov. First there is the setting, so evocative of the estate by the lake where he had visited Levitan in July, after the latter's suicide attempt. Second, there are the characters, whom Chekhov's friends recognized so readily, who are entangled in various formations—triangles, quartets, and so on—that parallel Chekhov's own personal involvements. Treplev, the young writer, bears a striking resemblance to Levitan—down to the detail of the bandage worn around his head that nurses the wound inflicted by his suicide attempt. Treplev's shooting of the seagull in Act II is reminiscent of Levitan's hunting expedition with Chekhov at Melikhovo a few years earlier. Trigorin, the older writer, is involved in a love triangle with Treplev and Nina very much as Potapenko participated in the love triangle with Lika and Chekhov. What happens to Nina during the play—the transference of her love from one writer to another and her flight to Paris where she become pregnant by Trigorin—parallels Lika's story with Chekhov and Potapenko.

The similarities go on and on. From his actress-friend Lydia Yavorskaya, Chekhov fashioned his flamboyant character Arkadina, who sinks to her knees before her lover Trigorin just as Lydia sank to hers in one of her current roles, reciting the same line: "My darling, you are the last page of my life." From the plodding schoolmaster Mikhailov in a village near Melikhovo, Chekhov fashioned the flat-footed schoolmaster Medvedenko. Especially cruel is the detail of the watch fob that Nina gives Trigorin, mimicking the gift that Lydia Avilova gave Chekhov down to the inscription: "If ever you have need of my life, come and take it." And in another painful touch, Chekhov gave the name "Masha" to the young woman who pines with unrequited love for Treplev—after his own sister who loved Levitan but whom Chekhov never gave consent to marry.

Literary allusions abound in *The Seagull*, ones that were also recognizable to that first private audience—some subtle, others playful and satirical. Chekhov cleverly incorporates two plays he most admired into his new effort. *The Seagull* mirrors, to some extent, Turgenev's *A Month in the Country*, a play written four decades earlier, with its romantic summer setting, portrayals of the landed gentry, and patterns of unfulfilled love. Chekhov deeply admired Turgenev, and had read him extensively in the early winter of 1893. Equally influential is *Hamlet*, the play Chekhov admired above all. The Hamlet/Gertrude/Claudius triangle is mirrored by that of Treplev/Arkadina/Trigorin. Mother and son share deep bonds, while son and mother's new lover compete in their work and for her love. Hamlet's play-within-the-play is also mirrored in Treplev's attempt to win over his mother and unmask her lover for his literary shallowness.

With characteristic playfulness, Chekhov buried other literary "clues" in this play about writers and writing. "Why do you go around wearing black?" "I am in mourning for my life" are quotes from *Bel Ami* by Maupassant, whose work Chekhov was reading at Melikhovo and whose influence he was feeling.[9] (His character Arkadina also reads Maupassant in Act II, and then throws it aside, bored.) Treplev's strange, symbolic play-within-the-play not only invokes *Hamlet*, but also satirizes his admirer Tanya's translation of a French symbolist drama of the day. And the seagull—the play's title and central symbol—might very well be a mocking reference to *The Wild Duck*, Ibsen's play written a little more than a decade earlier.

So on one level, *The Seagull* is a play filled with practical jokes, playful literary illusions, and personal references to others. On another level, it is a play filled with subtle revelations about the author. Treplev, the young writer—who seeks new forms and gets shot down by his severest critics—is one aspect of Chekhov. Trigorin, the successful writer—who carries a notebook, admires Turgenev, invokes Tolstoy, and at the same time is disgusted with the facileness of his work—is another. Some passages in *The Seagull* are lifted directly from Chekhov's own personal letters. For example, lines in Treplev's monologue in Act IV come directly from a letter that Chekhov wrote to his brother Aleksandr (May 10, 1886) advising him on how to capture an image in a story ("the glass fragment of a broken bottle glimmered"). Lines in Trigorin's long speech to Nina in Act II about how he is driven "to write, and write, and write" come directly from a letter that Chekhov wrote to Lydia (Lika) Mizinova only one year before (March 27, 1894).

Treplev's mother laughs at his symbolist play; is Chekhov anticipating that his worst critics will laugh at his? Will *The Seagull* be perceived as symbolic nonsense? Or is Chekhov mocking the symbolist movement, and at the same time exploiting it? If so, what or who is the seagull supposed to represent? The play, or Chekhov, himself?

After the readings, to avert his attention from the unpleasant responses to his play, Chekhov remained in Moscow in his usual room at the Great Moscow Hotel, consumed with work on his story

"The House with the Mezzanine." "As far as my dramaturgy goes, I don't seem destined to be a playwright," he wrote Suvorin. "I have no luck at it. But I don't let it get me down, and I won't stop writing stories. In this field I feel quite at home, whereas when I write a play, I feel anxious, as if someone were looking over my shoulder."[10]

Still, his new play preoccupied his thoughts, as he vacillated between self-doubt and determination to bring his new form to life. He returned to Melikhovo for the new year, but the family commotion bothered him.

He knew he had some rewriting to do.

The Seagull, reviewed in *Fragments*

"It wasn't my play that failed— it was I, myself."

(Chekhov, letter to Suvorin, December 14, 1896)

1896

"Dear Ignatius:

"The play is being sent to you. The censor has marked in blue pencil the passages that he didn't like: namely, that [Arkadina's] brother and son are indifferent to her romantic liaison with the writer. I've cut the phrase "lives openly with that writer" on page four, and on page five I've cut "is capable of loving the young only." If these changes—which I've made on separate pieces of paper—are acceptable, then please fasten them securely to the appropriate places, and blessings to you and your children and your children's children. If the changes are not acceptable, however, then spit on the play—I just don't want to bother with it any more and advise you to do the same.

On page 5, Sorin's line: "So tell me, what kind of a person is her writer"—cross out the word "her." In the same line, instead of the words: "You can't understand him. He never says a word"—you can put: "You know, I don't like him" or whatever you want, even something from the Talmud (or something like: "At her age! Oh, how shameful!")

Her son's disapproval of the liaison is obvious from his tone. On the disgraced page 37, he says to his mother: "Why, oh why has this man come between us?" You can cross out Arkadina's reply: "You don't like the fact that we're intimate, but..." And that's it. See the blue underlinings...

And there's still the committee, you know!! [...]

Should we travel somewhere together? We still have plenty of time. To Batum or Borzhom? We could get drunk."

I embrace you.

Your debtor, Antonio"

(Chekhov, letter to Potapenko, August 11, 1896, Melikhovo)

"[...] Stop the printing of the play. I shall never forget last night, but still I slept well, and am setting off in a reasonable mood...

Write me.

Yours, A. Chekhov

P. S. I am not going to produce the play in Moscow. I shall never write plays again, nor have them produced.
(Chekhov, letter to Suvorin, October 18, 1896, St. Petersburg)

"In your last letter you called me a wimp three times, and said I was a coward. Why such slander? After the performance I had supper at Romanov's, quite properly, and then I went to bed, slept soundly, and the next day left for home without uttering a single self-pitying peep. If I were indeed a coward, I'd have run from editor to editor, and chased down all the actors, nervously begging them for leniency, fussing over needless changes in the script, hanging around Petersburg for two or three weeks, going to see my "Seagull," all angst-ridden, bathed in a cold sweat, complaining... When you came to see me the night after the performance, you yourself said that the best thing for me to do would be to leave, and then the next morning I received a letter from you saying goodbye. So where's the cowardice? I acted as rationally and reasonably as a man who had just proposed, and upon being refused, had no other choice than to leave. Yes, my pride was wounded, but then again all this didn't just drop down from the heavens—I had expected a failure and was prepared for it, indeed, I'd even warned you about it beforehand, and in all sincerity.

Upon arriving home, I took a dose of castor oil, doused myself in cold water—and now I'm ready to write a new play. I no longer feel exhausted or irritable, nor am I afraid that [others] will come see the play and talk about it. I agree with your suggestions for changes, and thank you a thousand times. Only please don't feel badly that you weren't at rehearsals. There was really in fact only one rehearsal, at which no one could understand a thing. And anyway, thanks to the revolting acting no one could see the play at all.

Meanwhile, I received a telegram from Potapenko, saying that the play is a colossal hit. And I received another letter from a lady whom I don't even know, expressing her sympathies in a tone that would indicate that there was a death in my family, which is completely beside the point. Anyway, it's all nonsense. My sister...rushed home from Petersburg, probably thinking that I would hang myself.

I wish you all kinds of blessings, both earthly and heavenly, and thank you from the bottom of my heart.

Yours, A. Chekhov"

(Chekhov, letter to Suvorin, October 22, 1896, Melikhovo)

"Dear Nikolai Ivanovich:

[...] My play opened with a big bang—meaning that some said it made no sense and vilified me till the heavens grew hot, while others were wild about it. I just can't figure it out. Be that as it may, I bolted out of Petersburg like a bomb, and have since received bags of letters and even telegrams. It's playing to full houses.

Be well...

Yours, A. Chekhov"

(Chekhov, letter to Korobov, November 1, 1896, Melikhovo)

"My esteemed Anatoly Fyodorovich:

You can't imagine how happy your letter has made me. I only saw the first two acts of my play from the house; after that I sat backstage, feeling the whole time that my 'Seagull' was a flop. After the performance, all that night and the next day, I was convinced that I'd created nothing but idiots, that my play was clumsy, that it was murky, incomprehensible, nonsensical and so on. You can imagine the situation I was in—thinking it was a flop, the likes of which I'd never dreamed of! I was ashamed and annoyed, and I left Petersburg plagued with all kinds of doubts. I thought that if I had written a play and allowed it to be staged—a play so obviously full of enormous flaws—that my artistic sensibilities had flown out the window and I'd lost it for good. Then, after I'd gotten home, they wrote me from Petersburg that the second and third performances were successful. After that came several letters, some signed, some anonymous, praising the play and scolding the critics. These I read with pleasure, but still I felt ashamed and vexed, and it soon dawned on me that if these kind people went out of their way to console me then my situation must really be bad. But your letter truly had a decisive effect on me. I've known you for a long time, and have the greatest respect for you; moreover, I believe you more than all the other critics put together. You sensed as much, writing your letter, which is why it is so excellent and so convincing. I feel reassured, and already am beginning to think of my play and that opening night performance without disgust.

Komissarzhevskaya is a marvelous actress. At one of the rehearsals many people wept as they watched her and said that she is Russia's greatest actress today. But on opening night she gave way to the general hostile atmosphere toward my 'Seagull', she was frightened and her voice was barely audible. The critics were cold toward her, undeservedly so, and I feel sorry for her.

So allow me to thank you for your letter with all my heart. Believe me, the sentiments that prompted you to write it mean more to me than words can say...

Yours sincerely and truly,

A. Chekhov"

(Chekhov, letter to the critic Koni, November 11, 1896, Melikhovo)

"Dear Vladimir Ivanovich:

Yes, the premiere of my 'Seagull' in St. Petersburg was a huge flop. The theatre was filled with malice, and the atmosphere was bristling with contempt. And—according to the laws of physics—I bolted from Petersburg like a bomb. You're to blame for this—it was you who provoked me to write a play.

I empathize with your growing antipathy towards St. Petersburg. At the same time, there's a lot of good—for example, the Nevsky on a sunny day, or Kommisarzhevskaya, whom I consider to be a great actress...

Regards to your wife, and be well.

Yours, A. Chekhov"

(Chekhov, letter to Nemirovich-Danchenko, November 20, 1896, Melikhovo)

"Dear Friend,

I'm responding to the main point of your letter—namely, why we so rarely have serious conversations. When people are quiet, it means that either they have nothing to talk about or feel inhibited. What is there to talk about? We have no politics, no society, no salons, no street life, even—our urban existence is poor, boring, sluggish, and lacklustre... You say that we are men of letters and that this, in and of itself, makes our lives rich. Is that so? We're buried in our profession up to our ears, and bit by bit it has isolated us from the rest of the world. As a result, we have little free time, or money, or books, we read very little and do so unwillingly, we don't hear much, don't get around much...

Talk about literature? But we've done that already... Every year the same thing, over and over and over, and everything we say about literature usually comes down to who wrote better and who wrote worse. As for conversations on more general and broader themes, they never go anywhere, because when you're surrounded by Tundra and Eskimos, ideas that don't pertain to the present quickly evaporate into thin air, like thoughts of eternal bliss. Talk about our personal lives? Yes, that can be interesting from time to time, and we could talk about it if you like, but even there we are inhibited, we're secretive, insincere, we're held back by the instinct of self-preservation, and we're afraid. We're afraid that while we're talking, our conversation will be overheard by some uncultured Eskimo who bears no love for us and we don't like much in return... I fear our morality, I fear our ladies.

In short, don't hold either of us accountable for our silence or for our superficial conversations—rather, blame it, as the critics say, on 'the epoch,' blame it on the climate, the stretches of space, or whatever you like, and let things take their own fated, inexorable course, putting your hopes in a better future...

I thank you for your letter... Write if you feel like it. I shall answer with great pleasure.

Yours, A. Chekhov"

(Chekhov, letter to Nemirovich-Danchencko, November 26, 1896. Melikhovo)

"If there is going to be a war this spring, I'm going. In the last one and a half to two years so much has been going on in my personal life (a few days ago there was a fire in my house) that there is nothing left for me but to go to war, like Vronsky[1]—only not to fight, of course, but rather to heal. The only bright moment in the last one and a half to two years has been my stay with you at Feodosia, and the rest you can forget about, that's how bad it's been...

My plays are being printed with amazing slowness, slower than my stories... Up until now, I have proof-read only 'Ivanov' and the vaudevilles. Two long plays are not yet published: 'The Seagull', known to you, and 'Uncle Vanya,' unknown to anyone on earth...

Yours, A. Chekhov"

(Chekhov, letter to Suvorin, December 2, 1896, Melikhovo)

"I received your two letters about 'Uncle Vanya'—one in Moscow, the other at home. And not long ago I received another from Koni about 'The Seagull.' You and Koni have given me a few good moments with your letters, but nonetheless my soul is as tough as metal now, and I feel nothing but revulsion for my plays—I even have to force myself to read the proofs. I know, you'll say once again that I'm being silly and foolish, that it's my ego and my pride and so on and so on. Well, I know, but what can I do, tell me? I'd be glad to get rid of this foolish feeling, but I cannot, really, I simply cannot. The problem isn't that my play failed; indeed, the majority of my earlier plays failed, too, and every time it was like water off a duck's back.

No—it wasn't my play that failed on October 17—it was I, myself.

What struck me at the time during the first act was this—the people with whom I'd been friendly and sociable up until October 17, with whom I'd dined in comfort and ease...they all had these strange expressions on their faces, really strange... In short, what happened gave Leikin cause to write me what amounted to a condolence note for having so few friends, and allowed 'The Weekly' to inquire: 'What did Chekhov ever do to them?', and 'The Theatregoer' to publish a whole article about how my fellow writers had humiliated me at the theatre. I'm over it now, my mood is normal. But I still can't forget it, any more than I could have forgotten if they had struck me. [...]

Yours, A. Chekhov"

(Chekhov, letter to Suvorin, December 14, 1896, Melikhovo).

"Dear Franz Osipovich:

It appears that you have a marriageable young lady whom you'd like to get off your hands as soon as possible. Forgive me please, but I can't get married at the present time. First of all, I am infested with bacilli, and they're very undesirable tenants. Second of all, I don't have a kopek, and third, it seems to me that I'm still very young. Give me a few years—two or three—and then we'll see. Maybe I really will get married after all. Only why would you want my wife to 'stir me up'? Life itself stirs me up, and does a good job of it too, thank you.

Yours, A. Chekhov"

(Chekhov, letter to his architect/friend F. O. Shekhtel), December 18, 1896, Melikhovo)

It was to be a tumultuous year—and a momentous one for the determined dramatist. It would be the year that his new play, *The Seagull*, would take its traumatic first flight.

As he did at the beginning of the previous year, Chekhov sought city nightlife for diversion—this time, from anxiety over the response of the first readings of his new play. January in St. Petersburg found him in the midst of a social whirlwind. He made the literary rounds, and was seen at the theatre with a different actress every other night.

At a masquerade party at Suvorin's theatre on January 27, a scene of drama and intrigue unfolded that could have been written by Chekhov himself. Lydia Avilova, his adoring and persistent young protégée, had learned that Chekhov would be present and was determined to attend. The timing was fortuitous—her husband was away, so she enlisted her brother to escort her to the event. At first, Chekhov pretended not to recognize her (they were both masked). Then, according to her romanticized account of the evening in her memoir *Chekhov In My Life*, they sat alone together in an empty private box in the theatre, engaging in a flirtatious, intimate conversation, drinking champagne and talking about the upcoming production of *The Seagull*. She inquired if he had received the gift she had sent him months before—the locket with its loving inscription—and asked why he hadn't responded. He answered elusively that he would reply to her "from the stage," where *The Seagull* would be soon be performed in St. Petersburg. He asked her to come on opening night. Filled with the fantasy that he would be declaring his undying love to her through the play, she agreed.

While some biographers dismiss her accounts as the feverish imaginations of a self-deluded woman in love, her memoirs (which she forbade to be published until after her death) reveal a deep, abiding, single-minded passion for Chekhov that would last all her life.

Like the characters in *The Seagull*, more and more women surrounded the writer as the winter passed. In Moscow, Chekhov visited Tolstoy, to find that his daughter Tatiana was infatuated with him. The playwright Yelena Shavrova, now married, continued to pursue him. Moreover, Lika (Lydia Mizinova) had reappeared, leaving her baby behind with her grandmother as she followed Chekhov to Melikhovo, where she would rent a cottage that spring just to be near him. Their rekindled flirtation would last deep into the summer. Of his personal life that spring, Chekhov wrote: "Everything's gotten so tangled up. I can't tie and untie my affairs any more readily than I can tie my bowtie," he wrote Lika.[2]

Amidst these personal distractions, as well as philanthropic activities at Melikhovo—including road repairs, the building of a new school and library, the installation of a church bell tower—Chekhov kept his focus on rewriting the play. In mid-March, he sent the rewrites to Potapenko, who offered to help get it past the St. Petersburg censors.

Early spring at Melikhovo found Chekhov suffering from a coughing spell that lasted several days. Still, he doggedly minimized his health issues (which were now compounded by headaches and eye problems), and would not admit to the long-term illness he knew that he had. To distract himself with anxiety over his play, he wrote "My Life," a long story and companion to his "House with a Mezzanine." The new work was rich in autobiographical memories of Tagonrog, and served as a vehicle for rejecting some of Tolstoy's social philosophies, such as the idealization of the masses and provincial life.

May 18 brought the coronation of the new Tsar, Nicolas II, and a day of infamy, when almost 2,000 were crushed by a stampeding crowd. Deeply moved by the news, Chekhov visited the graves of the victims in June.

Summer brought new developments for *The Seagull.* While the ads in the Moscow paper ran: "Chekhov's *Seagull* flies toward us," word came from the censors in St. Petersburg. Offended by some of the play's contents, they returned the blue-pencilled draft of *The Seagull* to the go-between Potapenko, who in turn passed it on to Chekhov. The censors were asking for revisions; for example, Treplev needed to be more disapproving of his mother's liaison with Trigorin, Dr. Dorn couldn't be Masha's father, and so on. Chekhov made them, reluctantly, and on August 20 Imperial Theatre Committee begrudgingly approved the play, despite its distaste for the play's so-called "symbolism" or "Ibsenism," its objectionable content (e.g. Masha's taking snuff and drinking vodka), and its unorthodox, plotless structure. This early censorial reaction would be a harbinger of the critical and audience response to come.

Restless and anxious over *The Seagull*, Chekhov escaped from Melikhovo to spend time on the Black Sea with Suvorin, leaving Lika feeling rejected, abandoned, and disappointed. She still harbored hopes that Chekhov would commit to her, and started yet another new love affair to make him jealous, as she had attempted before.

Some time at the end of that summer and into the early fall, before the theatrical storm-clouds gathered, Chekhov accomplished one of his most dazzling literary feats—the transformation of his failed 1889 comedy *The Wood Demon* into a new play called *Uncle Vanya*. Clearly, the intent must have been brewing in him for a while, ever since its embarrassing failure seven years ago. The reason for his secretiveness is open for speculation (he dropped off the manuscript at the printer's in October, and told no one until he mentioned it to Suvorin in a letter to December.) Nonetheless, it was a *tour de force* transformation of a flawed romantic comedy into a tragicomedic masterpiece, accomplished with skill and dexterity. Despite his complaints that he was a "poor dramatist," clearly he had gained insight into the process through the writing of *The Seagull* and felt ready to apply his idea of "new forms" to this older, failed play.

September brought the news that the Aleksandrinsky Theatre in St. Petersburg would be producing *The Seagull* the following month. Known for its productions of French farce and its melodramatic acting style, the theatre could not have been a more unlikely choice for his new play. The direction was assigned to Yevtikhy Karpov, the theatre's administrator, an undistinguished dramatist and director. To make matters even worse, the opening night was set for October 17, a benefit performance for E. I. Levkeeva, a noted comedic actress of the day. *The Seagull* would be followed on the program by a vaudeville, and the latter is what the audience would be expecting. When Levkeeva had heard that there was a new play by Chekhov subtitled "a comedy," she reportedly accepted it without having even read it, assuming it would be a vaudeville like the ones that had made him famous in the 1880s.

Chekhov had delegated the casting to Karpov, but after corresponding with him, realized that he had better go to Petersburg before opening night to confer with the director and cast. He arrived in town, dropped off the manuscripts of *The Seagull* and the unknown *Uncle Vanya* at the printers, and proceeded to what turned out to be the fourth rehearsal. He was appalled by what he saw. Karpov didn't understand the play, the acting style was stilted, the set was meant for a bourgeois farce, and the costumes were awful. Chekhov kept interrupting the rehearsals, attempting to give the actors line readings or to help them understand the simplicity and truthfulness of their characters. Dismayed, he left the theatre and sought refuge at Suvorin's house, where he began to cough blood again. Prospects for the play's success seemed grim.

Then, unexpectedly, there came a surge of hope. Only days before opening night, Savina, the forty-two year old actress who was playing Nina, left the company, refusing to act a role less than half her age. Her replacement, Vera Komissarzhevskaya, was a luminous young actress who breathed life into the role. The cast seemed to be ignited by her freshness, and Chekhov felt encouraged. But once more he was dismayed at the dress rehearsal, seeing the enervated cast (some of whom still didn't know their lines), ludicrous costumes, and inexperienced direction. His despair was compounded by the anticipation of Lika's attendance, as well as Potapenko and his second wife. In vain he pleaded with Suvorin that the premiere be called off, saying that the audience would be filled with "mean, petty and hypocritical" members of the St. Petersburg *literati*, who wished him ill, and that the opening would go by unnoticed anyway, as the theatre season didn't really get underway until November.[3]

By all accounts, the opening night of *The Seagull* on October 17, 1896 (after only nine days of rehearsal) was one of the notorious scandals of the contemporary Russian theatre. The audience, filled with rowdy admirers of the comedienne Levkeeva, were expecting an entertaining vaudevillian farce. There was also a contingency of those hostile St. Petersburg writers who wished Chekhov ill. Unfortunately, the faction of Petersburg *literati* who would have found the dramatic innovations of *The Seagull* of interest kept away from benefit audiences, so, except for a limited number of friends and family, this could hardly be called a sympathetic audience.

By the middle of Act I, Chekhov's worst fears were already confirmed. In the audience, there was an air of boredom, incomprehension and contempt. An initial burst of laughter came after Komissarzhevskaya, draped in a sheet, began Nina's "men, lions, eagles" monologue during Treplev's play-within-a-play. The laughter was followed by conversation and loud remarks, and the scattering of applause at the act's end was drowned out by hissing, whistling and derisive comments. Chekhov fled the auditorium and stayed in Levkeeva's dressing room for the remaining three acts, while the actors tried desperately to deal with the mounting guffaws, heckling and raucous expressions of derision. Levkeeva sat with him in total silence. Meanwhile, all of Chekhov's friends and family in the audience were shocked, and subsequent notations in their letters, memoirs and diaries—as well as those of the performers—all agree on the universal mood of hostility among the audience and feeling of humiliation among the cast.

After the disastrous performance, friends and family in attendance—Masha, Lika, Suvorin and Leikin—searched for Chekhov in vain. He had fled the theatre, and disappeared into a cold, unfriendly night. Later, they discovered, he had dined at Romanov's restaurant alone (while Lika and Misha waited anxiously in his hotel room). He then returned to Suvorin's at 1 a.m., went to bed and pulled a blanket over his head, refusing to talk to anyone—not even Masha, who arrived at 2 a.m. in frantic search for her missing brother. The following morning, Chekhov took the train to Moscow, and then on to Melikhovo, so upset that he left his suitcase on board.

Chekhov was not the only one who ran from the theatre last night. Lydia Avilova, who was seeing the play as a critic, was waiting in the audience all evening long for the "response" Chekhov had promised her in his play. At the start of Act III, when Nina hands Trigorin the locket as a love-gift, she was thrilled to hear the very same words she had inscribed on her gifted locket to Chekhov: "If ever you need my life, then come and take it."[4] She couldn't wait to return home to verify the page and line of the inscription. But she discovered that the page and line citation in the play were different from the ones she had given him on her original locket. She searched through the volumes of Chekhov's published works in vain. It then occurred to her to search through her own book of stories. There, on the cited page (121) imprinted on Nina's locket to Trigorin and lines (eleven and twelve), she found: "Young ladies should not go unattended to masquerade balls."[5] It was Chekhov's teasing rebuff to her approach in February at Suvorin's soirée in St. Petersburg, and his way of discouraging her romantic pursuit by minimizing their relationship.

Another cruel footnote followed the watch fob saga: Chekhov gave the locket Lydia Avilova had given him to Vera Komissarzhevskaya as a memento of the production. He also told Lika Mizinova he would give her a medallion whose citation referred to a catalogue of Russian plays, page 73, line 1. When Lika looked up the reference, she found the title of a farce called "Ignasha the Fool," a clear reference to Ignati Potapenko.[6] Chekhov seemed to enjoy the game of life imitating art imitating life.

An outpouring of emotional correspondence followed the premiere fiasco. "Stop the printing of the play!" Chekhov wrote to Suvorin the morning after the opening, vowing never to write another play or allow one to be produced.[7] To his brother Mikhail, he wrote: "The play has fallen flat and come down with a crash. There was an oppressive, tense feeling of embarrassment and bewilderment in the theatre. The actors performed abominably—no, stupidly. The moral of the story is: Never write a play."[8]

After a few days, however, Chekhov insisted that he had recovered from the opening night fiasco: "Upon arriving home, I took a dose of castor oil, doused myself in cold water—and now I'm ready to write a new play," he wrote Suvorin.[9] But he smarted from the critics, who trounced the play with undisguised relish. Comments included "absurd," "confused," "tedious," "false," "incomprehensible"—and finally, from Tolstoy, "a bad play." Only Suvorin, who was reviewing for Petersburg papers, praised the play.

Given the universal response to the opening night, imagine Chekhov's shock and disbelief when word came to him, while sequestered in Melikhovo, that the second and third night performances were met with ecstatic response! In attendance were elements of the *literati* who respected Chekhov, and the spirits of the cast, feeling their support, soared. After the performance, Komissarzhevskaya dashed off an exultant letter to Chekhov, reporting the play was now an unqualified success and expressing her regret that he had not been there to hear the audience call repeatedly for the author. Potapenko telegrammed Chekhov, reporting calls for encores after every act.

This dramatic reversal of fortune only confused him. "Why don't you try to write a play?" he wrote to the young playwright Yelena Shavrova. "It gives you exactly the same feeling as when you first creep into an unwarmed bed on a cold night. Try it. Write one..."[10] Some of the letters of praise soothed him temporarily, but the wounds still festered. "It wasn't my play that failed—it was I, myself," he wrote Suvorin, bitterly.[11] "I still can't forget it, any more than I could have forgotten if they had struck me."

Indeed, nothing could console him—neither the steady flow of letters expressing admiration for the play, nor the news that another production of *The Seagull* in Kiev was greeted with positive reviews and audience response, nor the appeals from the editors of *Russian Thought* to publish the text of the play (he refused at first, and then finally gave permission). So stung was Chekhov by the fiasco that he thought of escaping altogether, breaking with the *literati*, even joining the army. Still, he stayed in Melikhovo, nursing his wounds and a new bout of flu, and correcting proofs of his story "My Life," a serialized short novel about a young nobleman who rejects his upbringing and social class. Lika came to visit, and he gave her a baby puppy.

Life imitating art imitating life. As the seagull had been shot down in his play, as Treplev's play had been shot down, so had Chekhov. And yet, despite his vow never to write another play (a vow he was to make each time after the next plays to come), he had accomplished what he set out to do—to experiment with new dramatic forms for the purpose of breathing life into the stagnant contemporary Russian theatre. Moreover, in the process, he had made a important personal discovery. At first, his intent was the same as that of his character Treplev, the avant-garde young playwright, who, in the first act of *The Seagull*, says, impassioned: "We need new forms. We must have new forms, and we don't we might as well have nothing at all."[12] Whereas in the last act, three years later, that same young playwright realized: "Yes, more and more I've come to see…it's not about forms—old forms, new forms—it's about writing, not bound by any forms at all, just writing, freely, from the soul."[13]

Then in November came another cruel and ironic twist of fate—an event prophesized in *The Seagull*. Lika's baby Christina died a few days after her second birthday. Lika came to Melikhovo for comfort, but she waited in vain for Chekhov, who was busy in Moscow. He was now involved with Shavrova, his youngest disciple, who wanted to stage *The Seagull* there. Life imitated art once again.

Chekhov's plays were filled with other prophesies of events to come in his life, as well as events drawn from his life. In November, a fire flared at Melikhovo and destroyed some of the house's interior (an event he would use later in *The Three Sisters*). At New Year's, the largest crowd ever gathered in the quickly restored dwelling. Once again, Chekhov was surrounded with admiring women: Shavrova, the Suvorin's governess Emilie (newly enamored of him), and Lika with her new lover. The family dressed as mummers, a festive touch he would also use in *The Three Sisters.*

Meanwhile, Chekhov hid in his study whenever he could to work on his new story, "Peasants." It had been a long, emotionally draining year, and he needed some quiet.

“The doctors have ordered me to change my way of life.”

(Chekhov, letter to Suvorin, April 1, 1897)

1897

“Between ‘there is a God’ and ‘there isn’t a God’ lies a vast expanse which a wise man finds difficult to cross. A Russian knows only one of these extremes, and the middle ground holds no interest for him. Therefore, he knows either nothing or very little...”
(Diary of A. Chekhov, entry January 10-February 3, 1897)

“Where did you get the idea that I’d forgotten you, esteemed colleague?

I am immersed in work, up to my chin. I write and cross out, write and cross out. To add to that, there are various ‘civic’ duties, such as a census-taking, trips, patients, and multitudes of guests... My head is spinning! Under these circumstances, letter writing is almost a feat.

I wish you a Happy New Year, filled with happiness and hope, as well as an income of 200,000 a week... Above all, I wish you what you forgot to wish me in your letter: the will to live. [...]

Your ‘cher maître’, A. Chekhov”

(Chekhov, letter to Yelena Shavrova-Youst, January 1, 1897, Melikhovo)

“I send you New Year’s greetings, and wish you health, happiness, and lots and lots of money...

I haven’t forgotten that I promised to dedicate ‘The Seagull’ to your wife, but have deliberately have refrained doing so. One of the most unpleasant memories of my life is associated with that play, it repulses me, and therefore a dedication would appear to be tactless.

Yours, A. Chekhov”

(Chekhov, letter to Suvorin, January 4, 1897, Melikhovo)

"Today is my birthday!!

[...] As for the bubonic plague, whether it will reach us or not, nothing definite can be said yet. Even without the plague, however, we have barely 400 out of 1,000 children reach the age of five, while in the villages and in the factories and back streets of the cities you won't find a single adult woman in good health. The frightening thing about the plague is that it will appear two or three months after the taking of the census... So the peasants will interpret that by saying that the doctors have been poisoning off the excess population so there will be more land for the gentry.

Write and send news. I wish you the best."

Yours, A. Chekhov"

(Chekhov, letter to Suvorin, January 17, 1897, Melikhovo)

"I spent twenty days in Moscow and squandered all my royalty advances. Now I'm home, leaving a life of sobriety and chastity. My mind is currently preoccupied with construction (not mine, but the district's)... At the actors' conference no doubt you'll be presented with plans for the enormous people's theatre that we're building. By "we," I mean members of the Moscow intelligentsia (we're collaborating with the capitalists, who are not adverse to the arrangement). A theatre, auditorium, library, reading room, various buffets and so on will be assembled under one roof. The plans are ready, the agreement is being drafted, and now all that's left to do is to raise a half million [...]

There's no news from here—or rather there is, but it's either uninteresting or sad. There's talk of the bubonic plague and the war... Levitan (the landscape artist) will die soon, most likely. He has distention of the aorta.

As for me, things aren't going well. I wrote a long story about the peasants' way of life, but they say that it won't pass the censor and will have to be cut in length by half...

Be happy.

Yours, A. Chekhov"

(Chekhov, letter to Suvorin, March 1, 1897, Melikhovo)

(On March 21, Chekhov suffered a major lung hemorrhage in Moscow and was hospitalized.)

"The doctors have diagnosed extensive pulmonary tuberculosis and have ordered me to change my way of life. The former I understand; the latter, however, is incomprehensible, simply because it's almost impossible. They order me to live in the country, but country life involves constant preoccupation with peasants, animals, and the elements, and to avoid all these cares and woes is just about as hard as avoiding burns in hell. Nevertheless, I'll do my best, and have already put out the word (through Masha) that I'm giving up my practice of medicine in the country. This will be both a relief and a great deprivation. I'm giving up all my official district duties and am buying a dressing gown; I'll sunbathe all day, and eat and eat. I'm under orders to eat six times a day, as they're indignant to learn I eat so little. I'm forbidden to talk much, to swim, etc. etc.

Aside for my lungs, all my other organs are found to be healthy; I've hidden from the doctors the fact that I'm occasionally impotent. Up until now, I've restricted my drinking to an amount that would do me no harm; but as it turns out, I've been drinking less than I had a right to. What a pity!...

There's a constant stream of visitors, they bring flowers, candy, treats. In a word, bliss...

I even can write sitting up now, but as soon as I'm done writing, I have to go back to reclining on my sickbed.

Yours, A. Chekhov"

(Chekhov, letter to Suvorin, April 1, 1897, Moscow)

"Here's the story. Since 1884, every spring I've been finding blood in my sputum. Now it's been determined that mine is an advancing tubercular process, i.e. I've been given the right, if I so wish, to call myself an invalid. My temperature is normal, no night sweats, no weakness, but my dreams are haunted by priests, the future is quite uncertain, and even though the process has not advanced that far yet, it's become necessary, without delay, to write my will, to keep you from getting your hands on my possessions... On Wednesday of Holy Week they'll discharge me, I'll return to Melikhovo, and we'll see what happens next. Meanwhile, they know nothing of my illness at home,

so don't let anything slip out in your letters through that wicked streak of yours...

My regards to your wife and children, from the bottom of my heart, of course.

Yours, A. Chekhov"

(Chekhov, letter to his brother Aleksandr, April 2, 1897, Moscow)

"There's no bad without a bit of good. In the hospital I had a visit from Tolstoy, with whom I had the most interesting conversation—most interesting for me, as I did more listening than talking. We were talking about immortality. He interprets immortality in the Kantian sense; meaning that all of us (both people and animals) will live on in a "principle" (such as reason, or love), the essence and purpose of which remains a mystery. As far as I'm concerned, if this principle or force is an amorphous mass to which my "self"—my individuality, my consciousness—will somehow be fused, then this is an idea of immortality that I don't need. I simply don't understand it, and Lev Nikolaevich (Tolsoy) was amazed that I didn't..."

Yours, A. Chekhov"

(Chekhov, letter to Menshikov, April 16, 1897, Melikhovo)

"Aleksandr Ivanovich, dear friend:

No news. Literature is at a lull. In the editors' offices, they drink tea and cheap wine, without pleasure, just to pass the time. Tolstoy is writing a book about art. He visited me in the hospital and declared that he has abandoned his novel 'Resurrection' because he didn't like it, and was writing only on art, about which he has already read sixty books. His theories aren't particularly new; they've been reiterated in various versions by wise old men from time 'in memoriam'. Old men tend to envision the end of the world and say that morality has sunk to its lowest nadir, that art has degenerated, played itself out, that people have weakened, etc. etc. In his book, he wants to convince us that, in our time, art is in its last stages, that it's entered a blind alley from which there is no exit.

I clasp your hand.

Yours, A. Chekhov"

(Chekhov, letter to the writer Ertel, April 17, 1897, Melikhovo)

"[...] You bemoan the fact that my heroes are gloomy. Alas, it is not my fault! That's just the way I write, and anyway, it doesn't seem gloomy to me; when I work, I am always in a good mood. I've noticed that gloomy people, those of a melancholy disposition, always write cheerfully, whereas the writings of those who love life are depressing. In any event, I am full of the joy of life. At least the first thirty years of my life were pleasurable.

My health is good enough in the morning, and in the evening it's fine. I'm not doing a thing, I don't write, and have no desire to. I've become terribly lazy.

Be well and happy. I clasp your hand.

Yours, A. Chekhov"

(Chekhov, letter to Lydia Avilova, October 6, 1897, Nice)

"Dear Anna Ivanovna,

Many thanks for your letter. You ask about my health. I'm fine, I only have one problem—I spit blood. There's not much of it, but an attack lasts a long time. My last hemorrhage started three weeks ago. As a result I have to endure some deprivations. I don't leave the house after 3 pm, I don't drink anything, don't eat hot foods, don't walk fast (and only on the street)—in short, I am not living but vegetating. And that irritates me. I am always in a bad temper and it always seems to me that at dinner the Russians make stupid and vulgar remarks and I have to control myself not to speak to them impertinently.

For God's sake don't tell anyone about the blood spitting, that's between us...if they find out at home that I'm hemorrhaging, they'll start wailing...

[...] The weather is heavenly here. Warm, mild... I am not moved by nature here, it is alien to me, but I love the warmth and the culture passionately. Here, culture leaps out of every shop window, every wicker basket; every dog reeks of civilization.

Yours, from the heart,

A. Chekhov"

(Chekhov, letter to Anna Suvorina, November 10, 1897, Nice)

"Dear Lika:

I applaud your idea of opening a workshop—not only because, upon coming to dine with you and not finding you in, I would flirt with the pretty dressmakers, but also because it's such a good idea. I won't indulge in moralizing, I'll only say that work, no matter how modest it may seem, whether in a workshop or in a small store, will grant you independence, peace of mind and confidence in your future. I too would be pleased to open something, just for the joy of struggling from day to day, like everybody else. All in all, the privileged position of an idler tires me and bores me hellishly... Every day I ask myself: why don't I get letters from you. Write longer ones. Keep well and don't mope. Don't be tart like a cranberry. Stay as sweet as baklava.

Yours, A. Chekhov"

(Chekhov, letter to Lydia Mizinova, December 27, 1897, Nice)

Determined to forget about the fiasco of the St. Petersburg *Seagull*, Chekhov threw himself into a whirlwind of philanthropic activities. "Never have I had as much work to do, as I do now," he wrote Suvorin on January 17, his thirty-seventh birthday.[1]

His local endeavors included an exhausting census-taking initiative, the planning for a cultural center in Moscow, and other efforts that proved to be all-consuming. He worried about the bubonic plague, rumored to arrive in the district surrounding Melikhovo. He encouraged others to think about establishing a network of charitable institutions that would follow the care of poor patients once they are discharged from the hospital. He sent copies of "The Island of Sakhalin" to fellow physicians and other concerned individuals, and spoke out against corporal punishment. He committed to the construction of yet another school. "A delegation of peasants begged me to do so, and I didn't have the heart to turn them down," he wrote Suvorin. "I'll be spending another summer fund-raising, trying to scrape up the money. In general, country life is a great bother."[2] Meanwhile, he also had his controversial story "Peasants" to finish.

But February at Melikhovo brought more fits of coughing. Then in March, he went to Moscow. He checked into the Great Moscow Hotel, and planned to meet Suvorin (who was staying at the Slavyansky Bazaar, where Trigorin and Nina planned to meet in *The Seagull*), as well as the ever-persistent Lydia Avilova. Chekhov and Suvorin met for dinner at the Hermitage Restaurant on March 22. But as soon as they sat down at the table, blood suddenly started to gush from Chekhov's mouth. Chekhov, who always shunned public spectacle, tried to make light of it and attempted to apply ice applications. But when the flow of blood wouldn't stop, Suvorin hastened him into a cab and returned to his hotel room at the Slavyansky Bazaar. He summoned the hotel doctor, Dr. Obolonsky, who couldn't convince Chekhov to go to the hospital. Instead, Chekhov wrote a note to the footman at his hotel, asking him to find the proofs of his story "Peasants" which he had left in his room and bring them to Suvorin's hotel so he might work on them there.

Although the hemorrhage abated in the morning, Chekhov continued to insist on making light of it. He returned to his own hotel room, and spent the next two days seeing visitors (Suvorin and Shcheglov) and writing letters. He alerted Lydia Avilova that he was ill and apologized for not being able to see her. He wrote to several other writers who had asked them to critique their stories.

But he continued to spit blood. Then on Tuesday, Dr. Obolonsky insisted on taking Chekhov to Professor Ostroumov's clinic associated with Moscow University Hospital. Suvorin found him there laughing, joking, and spitting blood into a large receptacle. But at one moment, Chekhov suddenly asked Suvorin: "Has the ice broken on the Moscow River"? (His question referred to a superstition that the breaking of the ice on the river signified that death would be imminent.)

After a lengthy examination, the doctors found both his lungs—especially the left—badly damaged by tuberculosis. The official diagnosis was pulmonary tuberculosis in both lungs, in an advanced stage. The treatment prescribed included icepacks, rest in a dry climate, and a diet of mare's milk (koumiss). His visiting hours were curtailed, and visitors were barred from asking any questions. He was forbidden to do much talking—a fruitless restriction, as his room in the clinic soon was inundated with visitors (including Tolstoy, who went on a philosophical rant about immortality). Masha came to visit, as did Tolstoy and Lydia Avilova. Friends brought champagne, caviar, roast turkey, and grouse. Flowers and letters poured in, as did manuscripts from hopeful authors who couldn't refrain from asking their mentor to read their work. Chekhov insisted on keeping up his correspondence. Visitors reported that despite weight loss, he was cheery and jocular. "I really should get married," Chekhov joked to Suvorin. "My shrewish wife would cut the visitor flow in half."[3]

When Chekhov suffered yet another severe hemorrhage on March 29, however, doctors forbade all activities except letter writing. Yet he managed to keep contact with his female admirers, including Yelena Shavrova, Lydia Avilova, and Olga Kundasova, who ran errands for him. He longed to return to Melikhovo, but the doctors insisted that come September he would be exiled to the south, where he would remain until the following May.

When he was finally released on April 10 and allowed to return to Melikhovo, the doctors admonished him to give up the practice of medicine, as well as strenuous physical activity (including walking and gardening, which he loved). "I lead a boring, sober and virtuous life," he wrote Lintvaryova, "and if it keeps up like this for another month or two, I'll turn into a goose."[4] To Suvorin, he joked: "I telegraphed you that I am marrying a rich widow. Alas, this is only a sweet dream! Not a single fool would have me, as I've badly compromised myself by having been hospitalized."[5]

Still he continued his local philanthropic activities at the local library and schools. Three days after he returned, on Easter Sunday, sixty-two peasants lined up for Easter gifts at Melikhovo, in anticipation of holiday gifts. Visitors continued to pour in. Chekhov journeyed to survey the school he was building. He continued to despair about the local peasant population. "In the village, they are swilling vodka desperately, and there's a terrible amount of squalor and moral depravity," he wrote Suvorin. "More and more, I'm coming to the conclusion that a sober man can live in a village only with a heavy heart."[6]

His story "The Peasants" was published in the spring, and caused an immediate controversy. (The papers likened the public response to the days when a new novel by Dostoevsky or Tolstoy was published.) The story provoked sharp criticism from those Tolstoyans who accused Chekhov of showing the peasants in a negative light. Still, Chekhov was pleased with the story's popularity (especially in light of *The Seagull*'s disastrous opening). He longed to resume work on stories and plays, but his slow recuperation prevented him from mobilizing himself to write. Moreover, the spring brought endless waves of houseguests, and often he had to wait till they retired before he could sit down to attempt to write. Unable to concentrate, he was content to read Maupassant's stories and Maeterlinck's plays.

While Chekhov was convalescing in Melikhovo, an event occurred in Moscow that would change his life as a playwright, as well as the course of the Russian theatre. On June 22, two young theatre practitioners sat down to lunch at the Slavyansky Bazaar Restaurant in Moscow—a dramaturg and head of drama at St. Petersburg Philharmonic School named Vladimir Nemirovich-Danchenko (aged thirty-nine), and a talented actor/director named Konstantin Sergeevich Alekseev (aged thirty-four). The men couldn't have been more different. Alekseev (whose stage name became Stanislavsky) was tall and imposing, and came from one of the wealthiest *haute bourgeoisie* families in Russia, while Nemirovich, the son of a military family, had no source of income other than his writing. But they shared a dream for the future of the Russian theatre. Stanislavsky dreamed of creating a theatre to match the Maly, one that would take the art form to a wider, more popular audience. Nemirovich, independently, had already submitted a plan to the government to create a new "open theatre."

Their conversation at the Slavyansky Bazaar started over lunch at 2:00 in the afternoon, and ended at 8:00 a.m. the next morning at breakfast. The outcome of this eighteen-hour meeting was the birth of the Moscow Art Theatre, a company they would lead together, with Nemirovich supervising the literary matters and Stanislavsky overseeing the production aspects. Together they began to plan the creation of a new company (recruited from Nemirovich's students) and a budget for a new theatre. It would be a partnership that, despite some fundamental differences, would last forty years.

Meanwhile, Chekhov, sequestered away in Melikhovo, fending off visitors, was unaware of these developments. The traumatic hemorrhage of March and its ensuing bleak diagnosis had left him depleted and irritable. Between April and November he wrote nothing except letters. He gave up the practice of medicine, and curtailed his philanthropic activities to the school he was building. He gardened, pruned his rose bushes, and supervised the planting of trees. His ever-hopeful female admirers (Yelena, Aleksandra, Daria, Lika) lavished attention on him, but their efforts didn't seem to lift his spirits.

By summer, he was so fed up with his endless guests at Melikhovo as well as the pursuits of his female admirers that he leapt at an invitation to travel to France. He departed Melikhovo on August 31, leaving Masha and his mother to renovate the guest cottage for him to live in year-round. (His presence was missed not only by his family, but also by all the Melikhovo inhabitants, whose lives he touched in so many ways.) After visiting Paris and Biarritz he settled down in Nice, at the charming Pension Russe on Rue Gounod near the old city. A few blocks from the sea, this lovely little vine-clad villa was a haven for Russians who sought to escape the cruel northern winters. He installed himself in a second-floor room with a balcony overlooking a charming little garden and large, leafy trees. The pension's comfortable features—including wall-to-wall carpeting, a divan "like Cleopatra's," and Russian cooking—delighted him. He took long walks and ate oysters, his favorite delicacy.

Although the coughing of blood continued, he made light of it. "I go prancing around like an unmarried calf," he wrote Yelena Shavrova.[7] Getting married had become a leitmotif in his correspondence since the lung hemorrhage in March. Clearly, it was on his mind, despite his joking. Slowly, he was beginning to face the reality of his illness.

At the same time, he was finding the solitude extremely productive. Grateful for the distance from the constant flow of visitors, the failure of *The Seagull*, and the harshness of the oncoming Russian winter, he began work again. His short stories that autumn included "The Pecheneg," "Home," "On the Cart" (another story about a schoolteacher), and "A Visit To Friends" (a precursor to *The Cherry Orchard*). He completed them and sent them off to his publisher.

The persistent coughing of blood required him to move downstairs at the Pension Russe, but still he was content. He was reconnecting with his writing. He celebrated the Russian New Year's Eve in Monte Carlo at the roulette wheel with one of his admirers, the writer Aleksandra Khotyanintseva, and engaged in animated discussion about his new passionate interest: The Dreyfus case.

Chekhov and the company of the Moscow Art Theatre at a reading of *The Seagull*

"I'M READY TO GIVE YOU ALL MY PLAYS."

(Chekhov, letter to Nemirovich-Danchenko, May 16, 1898)

1898

"Esteemed Fyodor Dmitrievich:

[...] Here they talk of nothing but Zola and Dreyfus. The overwhelming majority of the intelligentsia is on the side of Zola and believes in Dreyfus's innocence. Zola has added an additional eight feet to his stature; his letters of protest have been a breath of fresh air, and every Frenchman has felt that, thank God, there's still justice in this world, and if an innocent man is condemned, there is someone who will come forward on his behalf... [...]

I clasp your hand, await your article, and remain

Sincerely yours, A. Chekhov"

(Chekhov, letter to the editor Batyushkov, January 23, 1898, Nice)

"The weather is sublime here, it's pure enchantment. Warm, even hot; the sky is blue and clear, the sea sparkles, the fruit trees blossom. I go out without an overcoat and wear a straw hat. I've grown as lazy as an Arab, I do nothing, absolutely nothing, and, looking at myself and other Russians, I've become more convinced than ever that a Russian can't work and be himself unless the weather is miserable.

Potapenko is here. He's also staying at the Pension Russe... We went to Monte Carlo and laughed a lot...

You grow more and more attached to the theatre, while I withdraw from it, further and further. And indeed I regret it, as the theatre has given me much good (as well as a fairly good income; this past winter my plays were more successful than ever in the provinces, even 'Uncle Vanya'). Before, there was no greater delight for me than to sit in the theatre, but now I sit there feeling that any moment they're about to shout "Fire!" And I don't like actors. My experience has a playwright has spoiled it all for me.

Be well.

Yours, A. Chekhov"

(Chekhov, letter to Suvorin, March 13, 1898, Nice)

"Dear Vladimir Ivanovich:

I take you at your word. You write: 'I'll come to see you before rehearsals [for 'The Seagull'] and begin to talk about it.' So come, by all means, please! You can't imagine how eager I am to see you– and just for the pleasure of getting together and talking to you, I'm ready to give you all my plays.

So come! [...]

Yours, A. Chekhov"

(Chekhov, letter to Nemirovich Danchenko, May 16, 1898, Melikhovo)

"Most honorable and esteemed brother!

Everyone is thriving, Father is complaining, Mother is in Taganrog, and I sit [at] home and work, Ivan is off traveling somewhere, Masha is running the household, Misha is in the Treasury Department, enjoying family life...

We're building a district school in Melikhovo. We're soliciting contributions. We're selling apples. As for literature, it's a weak market, as they say. I don't feel like writing, so I do it as if I'm in the sixth week of Lent.

I'm living the life of a bachelor—come fall, I'll start wandering again. Such is life. The position of Suvorin's 'New Times' on the Dreyfus-Zola affair is disgusting and vile...

Be sensible, pure in thought, and meek, like your father, who is gathering apples under the trees so that people won't steal them.

Your bachelor brother, Antonius

P. S. Regards to the family."

(Chekhov, letter to his brother Aleksandr, July 30, 1898, Melikhovo)

"Dear Lika:

Speaking of the devil... If only you knew how much joy your letter gave me! You are callous as well as plump—so how could you possibly understand this joy of mine? Yes, I am in Yalta and shall live here until it snows. You can't imagine how much I didn't want to leave Moscow, but I had to since I am still living in sin with the bacillus. The story that I have put on weight is a complete fabrication—and the one that I am getting married is also a fabrication, spread abroad by you. You know I'd never marry without your permission, and yet you still persist in spreading all kinds of rumors, probably in keeping with the old hunter who neither fires his gun nor lets others do so, but instead grumbles and complains and lies on the stove. No, darling Lika, no! Without your permission I shall never marry, and before I would ever do so I'll make your life living hell, if you'll excuse the expression. So come to Yalta.

I await your letters impatiently, as well as the photograph that you say resembles an old witch. Nemirovich and Stanislavsky have created a very interesting theatre company with lovely little actresses. Had I stayed any longer in Moscow, I'd have lost my head. The older I get, the fiercer and more frequent the pulse of life beats in me. Remember that. But don't be afraid...

I repeat: your letters make very very happy, and I'm afraid that you won't believe me and won't answer soon. I swear, Lika, without you I am bored.

Be happy, well, and successful. Yesterday at supper your ears would be burning from the praise over your singing. May God protect you.

Yours, A. Chekhov"

(Chekhov, letter to Mizinova, September 21, 1898, Yalta)

"Dear Masha:

[...]The sad news—completely unexpected—of Father's death has grieved and shaken me deeply. I am sorry for Father, sorry for us all; the knowledge of your having to endure such distress in Moscow while I live peacefully in Yalta—this I cannot dispel, and it weighs heavily on me. How is Mother? Where is she? If she is not going to Melikhovo (it will be oppressive for her there all alone), where do you intend to settle her? In general there are a great many questions we have to resolve... [...]

Once again, I'm absolutely fine. Write me, please, don't keep me in suspense...

Your Antoine."

(Chekhov, letter to Masha, October 14, 1898, Yalta)

"Dear Lika:

I have two pieces of news. The first is that my father died. His intestines were herniated; they caught it too late, drove him to the station over a terrible road, then performed an operation in Moscow and opened his stomach. Judging from the letters, he died an agonizing death. Masha has suffered a great deal. And I myself feel wretched.

The second is that I'm buying (on credit) a piece of land near Yalta, where I can spend the winters and grow the gooseberries you detest. The bit of land that I am purchasing is located in picturesque surroundings, with views of the sea and the mountains. It has its own vineyard and its own well. It's a twenty minute walk from Yalta. I have already drawn up a plan for the house and have not forgotten the guests, for whom I have allotted a little room in the basement; in their absence, hen turkeys will live there...

[...] Your photos are lovely. You're even pretty, which I never expected. I'd send you one of myself, but I don't have one with me. In any case, you can see my portrait in the Tretyakovsky Gallery [in Moscow]...

[...] Write, Lika. Don't be lazy... Where in the world did you get the idea I have a bald spot? What nerve! I know you are avenging yourself because in one of my letters I made a friendly remark, with no intention of offending you, that you are lopsided, and consequently have still not found a husband. Be well and happy. Don't forget your old admirer.

A. Chekhov"

(Chekhov, letter to Mizinova, October 24, 1898, Yalta)

"Dear Michel:

I know what all of you had to go through at Father's funeral, and I felt terrible about it, I only learned of Papa's death on the thirteenth—for some reason they didn't telegram me...

I am buying a piece of land in Yalta, and shall build there so I have a place to spend the winter. This traipsing about, putting up with hotel rooms, porters, improvised dinners, and so on, has become appalling... I'm not going to supervise the building—it will all be done by an architect. The house will be ready by April. From a city dwellers' point of view, the property is large; it will allow for an orchard, a flower garden, and a vegetable garden. Beginning next year, there will be a railroad in Yalta. [...]

As for your insistence on getting married—what can I say? There's no use marrying except for love; marrying a girl simply because she's agreeable is like buying something you don't need at the market, just because it's of good quality ... The essence of married life is love, sexual attraction, one flesh—and everything else is undesirable and boring... [...]

My 'Uncle Vanya' is on now in the provinces, and it's a success everywhere. You never know, do you, when you're going to win or when you're going to lose. I had no expectations whatsoever for that play.

Be well.

Yours, A. Chekhov"

(Chekhov, letter to his brother Mikhail, October 26, 1898, Yalta)

"Dear Masha:

[...] In Yalta the dogs howl and the samovars hiss... Tell Mother that no matter what, winter must follow summer, old age after youth, misfortune after happiness; man may not be healthy and happy all his life, loss awaits him, he can't protect himself from death. One should be ready for everything. One can only do one's duty, and nothing more. [...]

Your Antoine"

(Chekhov, letter to Masha, November 13, 1898, Yalta)

"Esteemed Aleksei Maksimovich:

'Uncle Vanya' was written long, long ago; I have never seen it staged. In recent years it has been performed frequently in provincial theatres, possibly because I had it published a collection of my plays. In general, my attitude toward my plays is cold. I lost touch with the theatre some time ago and no longer feel like writing for it.

[...] I'm rushing to the post. Be well and successful. I clasp your hand, and thank you again for your letter.

Yours, A. Chekhov"

(Chekhov, letter to Gorky, December 3, 1898, Yalta)

"Dear Masha:

Let me start off with a piece of news. Something pleasant and unexpected. No, I don't think that I want to get married, and I haven't proposed to anyone. I've bought [a villa in] Küchük-Köy [a village just outside of Yalta] on an impulse, I couldn't help it. I paid 2,000 rubles for it and have already signed the papers. In a day or two I'll ride over there with a mattress and some sheets and take possession of it. So now I'm the owner of one of the most beautiful and unusual estates in the Crimea...

Yours, A. Chekhov"

(Chekhov, letter to Masha, December 8, 1898, Yalta)

"My heartfelt gratitude to all [on the opening of The 'Seagull']. Am stuck in Yalta like Dreyfus on Devil's Island. Regret I'm not there with you. You[r] telegram has made me both healthy and happy."

(Chekhov, telegram to Nemirovich-Danchenko, December 18, 1898, Yalta)

"Dear colleague:

[...] In Moscow the gossip is that 'The Seagull' is a success. But since I have bad luck in the theatre, fate has interfered. One of the actors [Knipper] took ill after the first performance, and [two performances of] my 'Seagull' were cancelled.

No, in general, when it comes to the theatre, I'm not lucky—so to the extent that, if I would marry an actress, we would probably beget an orangutan or a porcupine.

Send me another book and write more.

Yours, A. Chekhov"

(Chekhov, letter to Yelena Shavrova, December 26, 1898 Yalta)

It was to be a momentous year—artistically, personally, and politically.

In January, still convalescing in Yalta, Chekhov was caught up with the celebrated cause of Alfred Dreyfus. On January 13th, the French newspaper *L'Aurore* printed a letter, "J'accuse", dated January 13, written by the famous French writer Émile Zola. The letter condemned the French government for trying to cover up the truth—namely that Dreyfus, a captain in the French army court-martialed in 1894 for allegedly selling military secrets to a German attaché, was in fact wrongly charged and was, moreover, the victim of anti-Semitism. Dreyfus had pleaded innocent, but was convicted and sentenced to life imprisonment. (As a result of the letter, Zola was prosecuted, convicted, and sentenced to jail on February 23. He fled to England.)

Chekhov felt passionately that Dreyfus and Zola had been dealt with unjustly. "For me, one of Zola's fingernails is worth more than the whole lot of generals and highborn witnesses judging him now in court," he wrote.[1] He was further upset that his publisher and closest friend, Suvorin, had come out against Dreyfus and Zola. Chekhov identified with Zola as a writer who felt the responsibility to speak out according to his conscience. "Even if Dreyfus is guilty, Zola is still right, because the role of the writer is not to accuse or to persecute but rather to stand up even for the guilty once they are condemned and are suffering punishment," he protested to Suvorin. "Writers and artists should engage in politics only enough to protect themselves from it."[2] Chekhov and Suvorin would remain steadfast in their opposing views, and their friendship would never be the same.

At the end of February, Potapenko and other friends arrived in Nice to cheer their friend Chekhov, who was suffering from dental surgery. To distract him they went gambling together in Monte Carlo. Chekhov was a cautious gambler, and bought books and a miniature roulette wheel to practice at the hotel beforehand. An artist (Josef Braz) was commissioned to paint his portrait for the Tretyakov Gallery in Moscow.

With the advent of spring, Chekhov longed to return to Russia. Masha admonished him, however, not to return until the weather was favorable. After a happy three week visit to Paris, Chekhov was finally able to return to Russia. He arrived in Melikhovo in May, gaunt, his beard graying, swathed in a long black overcoat—clearly an invalid. Then a letter arrived that would change the course of his life as a playwright.

On April 25, Nemirovich-Danchenko wrote to Chekhov with the news of the birth of a new theatre. He had selected six leading actors from the Moscow Philharmonic School, a respected drama program where he taught; Stanislavsky had enlisted his four best actors from the Society for Art and Literature, and together they created the company called the Moscow Art Theatre. It would be the first private theatre to rival Russia's government subsidized theatres in acting ensemble and repertory. Free from the restrictions of the Imperial Theatre Committee, their theatre could select and produce the plays it wanted—especially new ones. With Stanislavsky's personal wealth (his family cotton mill) and Levitan's patron Savva Morozov lending support, the first year's funding was in place.

Nemirovich was determined to include *The Seagull* in his company's inaugural season. Others tried to dissuade him, criticizing the play and reminding him of its disgraceful premiere in St. Petersburg. However, he ignored their warnings and asked the author's permission to produce it. In his impassioned letter to Chekhov, Nemirovich expressed his admiration for Chekhov's gifts as a playwright and for *The Seagull* in particular. He praised the play's innovative blend of tragedy and comedy, and guaranteed that his new company would give it a fresh, imaginative production, free from the deadening conventions of the contemporary Russian theatre. He also apologized to Chekhov, saying that the royalties would be modest, but, on the other hand, promised that Chekhov couldn't find a more reverent director and cast for the play's delicate artistry. He vowed to give the play the love and care that it richly deserved.

Chekhov's response to this letter has been lost, but it must have been a negative one. "Writing plays has spoiled the theatre for me," he had written Suvorin, still smarting from the St. Petersburg disaster.[3] Having retreated from the *sturm und drang* of theatre life, he was now content with the solitary existence of a short story writer. But Nemirovich persisted. He wrote again (twice) on May 12 begging Chekhov to reconsider, saying that his refusal would be a great blow to him as a director, explaining that *The Seagull* was the only new play in Russia that excited him and that Chekhov was the only contemporary writer who was of any interest to him. Furthermore, Nemirovich argued, *The Seagull* had been performed successfully in Kharkov and Odessa and elsewhere in the provinces since its ill-fated premiere in St. Petersburg, so why should he withhold permission for it to be produced in Moscow? Refusal to grant them permission would be an offense, he continued, depriving Moscow audiences unfairly of a great play. Above all, he added, his play would be produced in a theatre where—for the first time in the history of the Russian stage—a director would have complete control over all artistic elements.

Nemirovich's persistence and persuasiveness prevailed. Chekhov answered a few days later, agreeing to meet with Nemirovich and saying that his new theatre company could produce *The Seagull*, and, in fact, any of his plays. From that moment on, the future of the Moscow Art Theatre and the playwright Anton Chekhov would be inextricably bound together.

Overjoyed, Nemirovich responded, saying that he himself would be directing the play and that rehearsals would begin in July. Then he and Stanislavsky plunged into plans for their ambitious first season. In June, the fledgling company gathered at their new summer theatre in Puskhino, the casting for the season was announced, and rehearsals began for the first two productions of the season—*Tsar Fyodor* (by Aleksei Tolstoy, Lev's cousin) and Pisemsky's *A Law Unto Themselves.* The two founders agreed on a kind of artistic co-directorship. Stanislavsky would write a detailed *mise-en-scene* for each play (including set and production elements, plus moment-to-moment movement for each actor), which Nemirovich would then rehearse with the actors. As Nemirovich put it, Stanislavsky would concern himself with "form," while he would deal with "content."

That summer, while the newly formed theatre company began their work, Chekhov returned to story-writing, albeit with difficulty. "When I write, or think about writing, I experience an aversion—as if I were eating cabbage soup from which a cockroach had just been extracted," he wrote the ever-hopeful Lydia Avilova. "Actually, it is not writing itself toward which I feel this aversion—it's the literary entourage that comes with it, from whom there is no escape, just as the earth can't escape its surrounding atmosphere."[4] And yet, characteristically, it was an extremely productive summer. He completed a trilogy of sober, ironic short stories—"The Man in the Case," "Gooseberries," and "About Love"—that appeared in *Russian Thought* in July and August. He also wrote "Ionich," about the life of a provincial doctor, that was published in *The Cornfield.* These stories constitute some of the most haunting portrayals of Russian country life and are among his finest works.

While he was engaged in writing, *Uncle Vanya* was appearing the provinces (Odessa, Kiev, Nizhny Novgorod, Saratov, Tiflis). All these productions garnered praise, and soon royalties from these productions and others of *The Seagull* in the provinces brought in a sizable income. At the same time, Chekhov threw himself into his philanthropic activities with renewed commitment (helping to raise funds for the local school and library).

By midsummer, the time came for the fledgling Moscow Art Theatre to begin work on *The Seagull*. Stanislavsky had confessed to Nemirovich that the play bewildered him, so Nemirovich sat down with him and patiently went through the play line by line, explaining it. At the end of July, Nemirovich took over rehearsals of the first two productions, while Stanislavsky retreated to his brother's estate near Kharkov to work on the *mise-en-scène* for *The Seagull*. Two weeks later, Stanislavsky presented a plan that represented the vision of both founders.

After the first company read-through of the play in late August, Nemirovich wrote a spirited letter to Chekhov, describing the excitement the actors felt for the play and the admiration for its author. He praised Chekhov for his deep sensitivity and artistry, reiterating his faith in his talent, and assuring him that they were penetrating to the heart of the play. Nemirovich reported on the casting: Arkadina would be played by a twenty-nine-year old young actress named Olga Knipper. Vsevolod Meyerhold would play Treplev; Maria Roksavnova would play Nina; Stanislavsky would play Dorn; Maria Lilina (Stanislavsky's wife) would play Masha, and so on. From the beginning, Stanislavsky and Nemirovich disagreed on what part the former should play. Stanislavsky found the role of Dorn to be dull, and kept insisting that he preferred to play Trigorin.

During the first two weeks of rehearsal of *The Seagull* in late August/early September, Nemirovich ran the rehearsals according to Stanislavsky's *mise-en-scène*. He admired Stanislavsky's creative instincts and was excited by a number of his daring directorial choices—such as the play-within-the-play scene in Act I where Stanislavsky had the on-stage observers with their backs to the audience. As Nemirovich discovered more of the play's depth and complexity, however, he saw that some of Stanislavsky's directorial plan needed some adjustment to suit the delicacy of Chekhov's tragicomedy. So Nemirovich wrote a series of lengthy letters, asking Stanislavsky's permission to change certain details in his *mise-en-scène* to suit these shifts of mood. Nemirovich also asked permission to add his own touches. He wanted to tone down some of Stanislavsky's fussy detail, including excessive movement and distracting sound cues. Stanislavsky replied, deferring to Nemirovich's judgment, saying that the latter had a stronger sensitivity and understanding of Chekhov's work than he did.

Later in his memoir *My Life In Art,* Stanislavsky acknowledged that, at the time, he hadn't fully understood the beauty and subtlety of the play, and that it took both Nemirovich and him working together—each digging a tunnel from two opposite sides toward one central meeting point, as he described it—to bring the play to life. So in essence, the direction of *The Seagull* became an evolving collaboration between the two founders—a special blend of Stanislavsky's innovative direction and Nemirovich's insight into the soul of the playwright and his play.

Then Nemirovich invited Chekhov to attend a few rehearsals of *The Seagull*. He came on September 9. According to Nemirovich's description, the company was in a state of nervous agitation and excitement. When Chekhov walked into the room, his presence was electrifying. The company was awed by his presence, as much as he was uncomfortable in theirs. The actors lined up nervously, waiting to be introduced. Aleksandr Vishnevsky, one of the company members, eagerly reminded Chekhov that they had been pupils at Taganrog public school together.

Then the company proceeded to rehearse the first and second acts, after which they awaited his comments. At first, he was at a loss as to what to say. According to reports, he plucked nervously at his beard and kept adjusting his *pince-nez*. But as the reading progressed, Chekhov soon settled in, feeling hopeful for the first time that he was being understood. He came back two days later to watch another rehearsal.

Chekhov's visits to the rehearsal made an indelible impression on one company member in particular—Olga Knipper, who was playing Arkadina. The daughter of an engineer of German descent, Knipper (1868-1959) was a high-spirited young actress who was invited by her teacher Nemirovich to join the Moscow Art Theatre Company. She was the only one of his female students to have graduated with highest honors. Ambitious, impulsive, talented, and garrulous, she loved life, and threw herself headlong into her all-consuming passion: the theatre. Later, she would write that she was attracted to Chekhov and his artistic stature even before she met him, and wasn't the least bit daunted by their age difference of nine years, nor discouraged by his invalid state.

In her memoirs, Olga describes what an inspiration Chekhov's first visit to the rehearsal of *The Seagull* was. Like the other actors, she had been overcome with fear when Nemirovich announced his impending visit. But once they met him, the company was captivated by his charm, modesty, and simplicity. When they finally summoned up the courage, the actors barraged him with questions about the play and their roles. But he was reluctant to give direction or line readings, and instead gave succinct answers that were indirect and inscrutable. At first they thought he was making jokes—but later they appreciated the subtlety of his seemingly casual remarks, and how one small hint would be an epiphany.

After attending the first rehearsal, Chekhov spoke with Nemirovich and Stanislasky, and requested that that the latter replace the actor who was playing Trigorin. Stanislavsky was delighted, and Vishnevsky took over the role of Dorn. At the same time, Chekhov was, like Nemirovich, irritated by Stanislavsky's directorial indulgences, particularly his excessive sound effects (frogs croaking, dogs barking, bell ringing, etc.) and extraneous detail. (Stanislavsky's fussiness as a director would continue to irritate Chekhov in subsequent productions of his plays.)

Meanwhile, Chekhov was taken with Olga Knipper, that young actress playing Arkadina. With her mercurial personality, her passion, her energy, her charisma, and her uncommon beauty (featuring a sharp profile and long, thick, black hair piled high upon her head), she was captivating. He came unannounced to watch her in a dress rehearsal of *Tsar Fyodor* at the Hermitage Theatre a few days later. The theatre was being refurbished at the time; it was unheated, lit only by candles in bottles. The actors, bundled in their overcoats, were delighted and flattered by his presence. Later, he wrote to Suvorin, saying, prophetically: "She was magnificent—her voice, her presence, her warmth. She was so superb, I had a lump in my throat. Had I stayed on in Moscow, I'd have fallen in love…"[5]

Clearly, he was excited by this new theatre company, with its energy and imagination.

"If by chance you are in Moscow," he wrote a medical colleague enthusiastically, "go to the Hermitage Theatre where Stanislavsky and Nemirovich-Danchenko are producing plays. The *mise-en-scène* is fantastic; nothing of its kind has been seen yet in Russia."[6]

But the fall was approaching, and again he began coughing blood. Winter came early, and there was already snow at the end of September in Melikhovo. On doctors' orders, he journeyed down to Yalta, rented rooms in a villa, and strolled along the seaside, consumed with boredom. Impulsively, he bought a villa in Küchük-Köy, a village seventeen miles west on the coast road, so that the family might come visit.

Then came the telegram on October 13 like a bolt—his father had died. Chekhov received the news with a mixture of sadness, guilt (he could not attend the funeral), and ambivalence (his stern, pious, domineering father had clearly been a controversial figure in his life). With his mother now alone, and himself banished to the South by doctors, it was clear that Melikhovo had to be put up for sale. In addition to the villa in Küchük-Köy, Chekhov decided to buy a site at Autka, twenty minutes from the center of Yalta, where he intended to build a house for the whole family. It had a view of the river tumbling down to the sea and the harbor below.

As the fall season progressed, Chekhov struggled with facing his illness. His letters alternated between denial—"I'm fine—I eat like a horse, sleep like a log, drink vodka and wine"[7]—and pleas to his closest friends not to reveal the gravity of his situation. In November, he suffered another lung hemorrhage. It lasted five days. He wrote about it to Suvorin, saying the quantity of blood was more frightening to others than to him, and entreating him to keep it a secret from his family.

In exile, cut off from the world, Chekhov's boredom and frustration increased. There was no one to talk about literature. Newspapers came late. Jokingly, he said he felt like Dreyfus on Devil's Island. He poured himself into his correspondence—most notably, with Maksim Gorky, the flamboyant young writer/revolutionary who thought of Chekhov as his mentor, as well as the ever-hopeful Lydias (Mizinova and Avilova). He distracted himself with civic activities, sitting on committees for local schools and famine relief. He wrote a short story, "The Darling," which was published in a Yalta weekly. And he worried about *The Seagull*.

By that time, both *The Seagull* and *Uncle Vanya* had gathered quite a word-of-mouth reputation. Both had been performed everywhere in the provinces except for Moscow. Chekhov received an ecstatic letter from Gorky, saying that he had seen a provincial production of *Uncle Vanya* and had "wept like an old woman."[8] Gorky went on, in that letter, to praise Chekhov as a dramatist, saying how much he admired his gift. (He singled out one line in the last act of *Uncle Vanya*—Astrov's offhanded remark about the heat in Africa—that Gorky said made him "tremble with rapture" over Chekhov's talent.)

While Chekhov struggled with his invalid status, November passed, and rehearsals for *The Seagull* proceeded with intensity. Both Dr. Altschuller and Masha feared that, with the opening night of *The Seagull* close at hand, another failure would be too much for Chekhov to bear, given his weakening condition. Though she would deny it later, Masha reportedly went to the Moscow Art Theatre and begged Nemirovich and Stanislavsky to postpone the production. But it was too late. Still, Masha hovered around the production protectively, befriending Olga Knipper and Vishnevsky.

On the eve of the opening of *The Seagull*, the stakes were running high. After the success of *Tsar Fyodor*, the next four productions (Hauptmann's *The Sunken Bell*, Shakespeare's *The Merchant of Venice*, Pisemsky's *A Law Unto Themselves*, and Goldoni's *La Locandiera*) did not excite the public, and the box office was poor. Bankruptcy loomed by the end of the year, and Stanislavsky and Nemirovich were counting on Chekhov's play to save their new theatre. To compound their anxiety, they heard the news of Chekhov's latest lung hemorrhage, and feared that another failure of *The Seagull* would be too much for him to bear.

The opening night of *The Seagull* at the Moscow Art Theatre on December 17, 1898, is legendary in theatre history—for reasons markedly different from the traumatic premiere in St. Peterburg two years before. Carriages choked the streets of Moscow surrounding the theatre; patrons jammed into the packed house. According to Nemirovich's account, the cast members were so nervous they took valerian drops (a sedative commonly used at the time). After the curtain fell on Act I, there was a prolonged silence, and the actors, frozen in place, were close to hysteria. Then suddenly, as if "a dam had burst or a bomb exploded" (in Nemirovich's words), there was an outburst of tumultuous applause from all, friend and foe alike. The curtain was lifted, revealing an astonished cast. They were too shocked by the response to bow. At the final curtain, there was a thunderous ovation from the audience. The actors hugged each other and wept, and Stanislavsky performed a spontaneous victory dance before the entire audience.[9]

Nemirovich and Stanislavsky were ecstatic. They telegrammed Chekhov immediately to report the triumphant opening, calling it a huge success, and conveying the audience's demand that a congratulatory telegram be sent to Chekhov. The next day, Nemirovich wrote a long letter describing the opening, likening the mood backstage to Easter Sunday. The cast was in love with the play, he said. And although the company feared that the public might not understand the newness of *The Seagull*, they committed to it totally and poured their hearts into it. Nemirovich actually lived in the theatre, as he described it, for two weeks prior to the opening, supervising every detail of the production, shopping for props himself, checking all the stage equipment personally. After Act I, he reported that the actors were given five curtain calls; after Act III, there was a standing ovation, with cries of "author" and "send him a telegram"; and at the final curtain call, there was another ovation. Nemirovich ranked the performances, placing Olga Knipper's Arkadina at the top. He described her as absorbing the role and capturing its complexities (namely Arkadina's elegance, grace and style on the one hand and her short temper and stinginess on the other). He also praised Lilina's Masha and Kaluzhsky's Sorin. He had critical words for Roksanova as Nina. (She eventually left the company.) *The Seagull* was the talk of Moscow, Nemirovich summarized, and the Maly Theatre was smarting with jealousy over the new theatre company's success.

The next day, Chekhov's sister wrote with a similar report. She had praise for Knipper, Vishnevsky, and Meyerhold. She didn't care for Stanislavsky's Trigorin. On the other hand, the staging was so true to life, she said, that one forgot that it was a play. After only one glitch (Olga Knipper was ill after opening night, and two performances were cancelled), the production continued to play before sold-out houses. There were often queues at the box office all night, and Chekhov was deluged with congratulatory letters and telegrams.

Nemirovich's letter, brimming with joy and elation, ended with a question: "Will you give us *Uncle Vanya*?"[10]

"ART, AND THE STAGE IN PARTICULAR, IS A FIELD WHERE ONE CANNOT WALK WITHOUT STUMBLING AT TIMES."

(Chekhov, letter to Olga Knipper, October 4, 1899)

1899

"Dear Lika:

Your angry letter erupted like a volcano, spewing lava and fire all over me; nevertheless, I've held onto it and read it with great pleasure. First, I love getting letters from you; secondly, I've noticed for some time now that when you're angry at me, things are going well for you.

As for me, I'm living in Yalta as before, I'm bored to tears, and long for spring when I can leave. I have some big news about my life—it's a real event. Am I getting married? Guess! And if so, to whom? No, I'm not getting married, I've sold the publishing rights of my works to Marx... Don't worry, I won't sell Melikhovo to anyone else but you. Let's keep everything as it was.

[...] I'm going to Paris to buy clothes—suits, shirts, ties, and so on, and to see you, of course, unless you've already fled Paris on purpose, as you have before. I'm coming to Paris alone—I always have. The rumors spread by one of my paramours is just gossip, that's all...

I press your hand.

Yours, A. Chekhov"

(Chekhov, letter to Lydia Mizinova, January 22, 1899, Yalta)

"Dear Vladimir Ivanovich:

I haven't written anything to you about 'Uncle Vanya' because I frankly don't know what to say. I gave a verbal promise to the Maly Theatre, so now it's a rather awkward situation. It would look as if I were going behind their back. Be so kind as to make inquiries: is the Maly intending to do 'Uncle Vanya' next season? If not, then of course, the play is yours. And if they are doing it, I'll write another play for you. Please don't be offended; there have been discussions

with the Maly about 'Uncle Vanya' for a long while...
Regards to [your wife] and everyone at the theatre.
Yours, A. Chekhov"
(Chekhov, letter to Nemirovich, February 8, 1899, Yalta)

"Greetings, dear Ivan Ivanovich:
There's no news from here. I'm writing very little.
[...] I have no faith in our intelligentsia; it is hypocritical, insincere, hysterical, ill-bred and lazy... I have faith in individuals, I see salvation in individuals scattered here and there all over Russia, be they intellectuals or peasants—they are a force, though they are few. No man is a true prophet in his own country, and the individuals of whom I speak play an inconspicuous role in society. They do not dominate, but their work has an impact. Whatever you may think, science is steadily advancing, self-awareness is growing, moral issues are more provocative, and so on. And all this is happening despite the magistrates, engineers, and tutors, despite the intelligentsia en masse, despite everything.
I press your hand, be well, successful and happy. Write!
Yours, A. Chekhov"
(Chekhov, letter to his friend Orlov, February 22, 1899, Yalta)

"If only you knew how desperately the Russian village needs a sensible, educated teacher! A teacher must be an artist, dedicated to his calling; instead, in Russia, he is an uneducated itinerant, who goes into the village to teach children as though he were in exile. He is starved, downtrodden, terrorized by the fear of losing his livelihood... Whenever I see a teacher, I feel ashamed for him, for his timidity, for his shabby demeanor. And I feel that I myself am to blame for the teacher's wretched state..."
(Chekhov in a conversation with Gorky, spring, 1899)[1]

"[...] A writers' court of honor is senseless, it's an absurdity, since they do not constitute a corporate group such as lawyers or army officers. In an Asiatic country where there is neither freedom of the press nor of conscience, where the government and nine-tenths of society regard the journalist as an enemy, where people live herded together

in such wretched conditions and with little hope of better days, follies such as mud-slinging, courts of honor etc. put writers in the ridiculous and pathetic position of small animals, who, trapped, bite off each other's tails.

[...] I'm well. When are you coming to Moscow?

Yours, A. Chekhov"

(Chekhov, letter to Suvorin, April 24, 1899, Moscow).

"What's happening? Where are you? You seem determined not to give us any news, so we have no choice but to turn to idle speculation. Have you forgotten us, or have you married someone in the Caucasus? And if so, whom? Will you give up the theatre? The writer has been forgotten, how awful, how cruel, how treacherous! Everyone sends their greetings. No news. No flies, either. Nothing. Even the calves aren't biting...

I take your hand in mine, if you'll allow me, that is, and wish you the very best.

Yours, A. Chekhov"

(Chekhov, letter to Olga Knipper, June 16, 1899, Melikhovo)

"Dear Aleksei Maksimovich:

Greetings, once again! In response to your letter, I am in general opposed to dedications [of literary works] to living people. I used to do it, but now I feel it may not be the right thing to do... However, it's up to you; all I can do is to bow and thank you. If you can, strip the dedication of as many words as possible ....and leave it at that...

Another bit of advice: eliminate qualifying nouns and verbs wherever you can. Your writing has so many of them that they tax the reader and tire him out. It's enough when I write, for example: 'The man sat down in the grass'. It's enough because it's clear and doesn't distract the reader. On the other hand, it would be unintelligible and distracting if I were to write: 'The tall, skinny man of average height, with a short red beard, sat down in the green grass, which had already been trampled by passers-by; he sat down noiselessly, timidly, and glanced around him nervously.' One's brain cannot comprehend this, and yet fiction must be grasped at once—on the spot.

One more point: you're a natural lyricist, the pitch of your soul is gentle. Were you a musical composer, you wouldn't write marches. Being offensive, sounding off, mocking, and denouncing in a frenzy—all this doesn't suit your talent...

Be well, health and happy.

Yours. A. Chekhov"

(Chekhov, letter to Gorky, September 3, 1899, Yalta)

"My dear, my extraordinary actress, you remarkable woman, if only you knew the joy your letter gave me. I bow low before you, very, very low, so low, in fact, that my forehead touches the bottom of a well that is fifty feet deep. I've grown used to you and now I am inconsolable, I simply can't bear the thought that I won't see you before the spring, it's driving me mad...

[...] I kiss your hand hard, hard.

Yours always, A. Chekhov"

(Chekhov, letter to Olga Knipper, September 3, 1899, Yalta)

"At your request, I hasten to answer your letter, in which you ask about the last scene between Astrov and Yelena [in 'Uncle Vanya']. You write that Astrov comes on to Yelena like the most impassioned lover, that he 'snatches at his feelings like a drowning man grasps at straws.' But that's utterly and completely wrong! Astrov is attracted to Yelena, he's captivated by her beauty, but in the last act he already knows that nothing will come of it and that Yelena is lost to him forever. He speaks to her in this scene in the same tone as speaks of the heat in Africa, and kisses her simply because there doesn't appear to be anything else to do. If Astrov plays this scene with turbulent emotion, then the whole mood of Act IV– which is quiet and low-key - will be lost... [...]

It's turned cold here in Yalta all of a sudden. Oh, how I long to be in Moscow, dear actress! But of course you have no time for me... I haven't sent you my photograph because you never sent me yours, you snake! Yes, you're a great big snake. (Isn't that a flattering thing to say?)

I take your hand in mine, I bow low, my head touches the ground, o gracious one.

I'll be sending you another present soon.
Yours, A. Chekhov"
(Chekhov, letter to Knipper, September 30, 1899, Yalta)

"Dear actress,

You really did exaggerate in your gloomy letter, that's obvious, since the reviews of opening night in the papers have been very positive. Still, one or two unsuccessful performances are no reason to feel dejected or to lose sleep. Art—especially in the theatre—is a domain you cannot enter without stumbling across the threshold. There may be many more days of failure ahead, whole seasons, even, there will be huge misunderstandings and deep disappointments, but you have to be prepared for that, you must expect it and follow your path, come what may.

And of course you're right, Stanislavsky shouldn't be playing Ivan [in 'The Death of Ivan The Terrible']. Acting is not his calling. When he directs, he's an artist, but when he acts, he's just a rich young merchant who wants to dabble in art.

I've been ill for the past three-four days, and now I'm sitting at home. There's a deluge of visitors. Idle tongues are waging and I'm bored and in a wretched mood. I envy the rat that lives under your theatre's floor.

I see you wrote your last letter at 4:00 a.m. If you insist on imagining that 'Uncle Vanya' is not the success you wanted it to be, then please, go to bed and sleep it off. Success has spoiled you awfully, so that you can no longer tolerate the humdrum of theatre life. [...]

Write me more often. As you can see, I write to you almost every day. An author writing to an actress so often—that will start hurting my pride. I've forgotten that they call me the Inspector of Actresses. Be well, little angel.
Yours, A. Chekhov"
(Chekhov, letter to Knipper, October 4, 1899, Yalta)

"My dear, good actress,

You wrote and asked me if I'd get agitated about the opening, but 'Uncle Vanya' was performed on the 26th and I only learned about it on the 27th when I received your letter. The telegrams started coming on the eve of the 27th, when I was already in bed. They read them to me over the telephone. Each time I awoke and ran to the telephone in the dark, barefoot. It was freezing. Then no sooner did I got back to bed than the telephone rang again, and again. It's the first time when my own fame kept me from sleeping. The following night, when I went to bed, I kept my slippers and a dressing gown by my side, but there were no telegrams.

The telegrams talked only of the curtain calls and the brilliant success, but there was a subtle suggestion that you weren't entirely pleased. The newspapers that I received today have confirmed my hunch. Yes, my actress, all you actors at the Art Theatre have had mixed reviews for a change. You got knocked around a bit in the press. To speak plainly, you're spoiled by all this constant talk of success, of full houses, you've been poisoned by it and in two-three years nothing will be good enough for you. Get over it!

How are things, otherwise? As for me, I am neither one thing nor the other. I work, I plant trees.

I've had visitors, and so it's been impossible to write. They stayed over an hour, wanted tea, so we had to light the samovar. Oy, how boring it is!

Don't forget me, don't let your friendship die, let's go somewhere in the summer. Farewell! We probably won't see each other before April. What if you come to Yalta in the spring, do some performances, and rest? That would be marvelously artistic.

One of these guests will take this letter and mail it.

I take your hand in mine...

Yours, A. Chekhov

P. S. Write to me, actress, in the name of all that's holy, otherwise I'll be dejected. I feel like I'm in prison, and I'm irritable, irritable."

(Chekhov, letter to Knipper, October 30, 1899, Yalta)

"I understand your mood, dear actress, really I do, but if I were you, I wouldn't get so worked up into such a state. Neither the role of Yelena nor the play ['Uncle Vanya'] is worth getting so upset over. It's a play written long ago, it's out of date, and it has all sorts of flaws. If more than half the

actors weren't able to get the right mood, then it's the fault of the play. That's for starters. Secondly, once and for all, you must stop fretting about success or failure. Your job is to work step by step, from day to day, quietly, carefully, prepared to face the inevitable mistakes and failures, in short, to follow your artistic path and leave the competition to others

Thirdly, your director [Nemirovich] telegrammed me that the second performance went wonderfully, everyone was superb, and he was very pleased.

I take your hand in mine.

Yours, A. Chekhov"

(Chekhov, letter to Knipper, November 1, 1899, Yalta)

"Dear Actress,

Vishnievsky wrote and told me you'd only give three kopeks to be able to see me. That's what you told him. Thank you, how generous of you! But in a few months' time you won't even give two kopeks!

How people change!

In the meantime, for the chance to see you, I'd give seventy-five rubles...

Be well!

Yours, A. Chekhov"

(Chekhov, letter to Knipper, November 19, 1899, Yalta)

"Dear Vladimir Ivanovich:

Please forgive me for my silence. My correspondence is at a standstill. First of all, I've been writing my stories; secondly, I'm reading proofs for Marx; thirdly, I'm deluged with ailing itinerants who for some reason are flocking to me for care...

Of course I'm bored to death here. I work during the day, but in the evening I ask myself what I am doing, where am I going—and by the time Act II has begun at your theatre, I'm in bed. I get up while it's still dark, as you can imagine. It's dark, the wind roars, the rain beats against the windowpane...

I'm not writing a play. I have a title—'The Three Sisters'—but until I finish the stories that have been in my head for so long, I can't concentrate on a play. So next season you'll have to go ahead without me—that's for certain.

My Yalta dacha has turned out very nicely. It's a warm and cozy place. The garden is going to be exceptional. I'm planting it all myself. Hundreds of rose bushes, the best varieties...

In your letter, there's a note that keeps ringing like an old bell—and that's when you write about the theatre and how the daily details of the theatre are wearing you down. Oh, no! Don't wear yourself out, don't lose your enthusiasm! The Art Theatre soon will occupy the foremost pages of the book to be written on the contemporary Russian theatre. It's your pride and joy, and it's the only theatre I love, although I've never even set foot in it. If I lived in Moscow, I'd try to join your theatre's staff, even as a watchman, just to be a part of it, to help in any way I can, to prevent you, if possible, from cooling toward this institution that is so dear to my heart.

There's a heavy downpour, it's dark in my room. Be well, be happy and gay. I take your hand in mine. Bow low to everyone for me, but bow lowest of all to Olga Leonardova [Knipper].

Yours, A. Chekhov"

(Chekhov, letter to Nemirovich, November 24, 1899, Yalta).

"Dear Vladimir Ivanovich:

[...] You're right, of course—for the tour [of 'The Seagull'] to St. Peterburg, it's absolutely essential that we work on Stanislavsky's interpretation of Trigorin. Liven it up a bit, or something to that effect. In Petersburg, where the majority of our writers live, Stanislavsky's Trigorin—played as hopelessly impotent—will provoke general disbelief. Recalling Stanislavsky's acting is so depressing and I can't dispel the memory of it. And there's no way I can believe that he's good in 'Uncle Vanya', although everyone writes unanimously that he's not only good but very good.

Be well... I press your hand and embrace you.

Yours, A. Chekhov"

(Chekhov, letter to Nemirovich, December 3, 1899, Yalta)

This was to be a year of deepening of relationships—with a new publisher, with contemporary writers, with the Moscow Art Theatre, and above all, with a young actress in the company who would play a major role in his few remaining years.

In January, Chekhov gave the rights to all his work (except for his plays) to Adolf Marx, the publisher, thereby ending a professional relationship of over thirteen years with Aleksei Suvorin, to whom the bulk of his correspondence about his life as a writer had been written. "I've become a Marxist," he quipped to his friends, in an effort to deflect the discomfort he felt in curtailing this long-term friendship. Chekhov made the change for financial reasons; he recognized the gravity of his illness, and he needed the increased cash flow. Moreover, Suvorin's conservative political views and his position against Dreyfus (tinged with anti-Semitism) had altered their relationship irrevocably. Now came the enormous task of collecting hundreds of short stories from all the journals that had published them over the past two decades. He put his sister Masha, his brother Aleksandr, and even the ever-hopeful Lydia Avilova to work on it.

That winter, Chekhov suffered from his usual seasonal *ennui*. "God doesn't give a bad-tempered cow any horns," he wrote ruefully to Lydia Avilova.[2] Searching for a new outlet, he engaged in an intense correspondence with the young writer Maksim Gorky, who was achieving widespread popularity at the time. It was a correspondence of mutual admiration and support. Gorky admired Chekhov greatly, and his letters of praise for Chekhov as a man of genius were effusive. In the ensuing years Gorky would lavish praise on *Uncle Vanya* and *The Cherry Orchard* in particular for their departure from realism, their new forms, their depiction of social change in Russia, and their keen understanding of human suffering. Chekhov, on the other hand, admired the fiery spirit of the younger writer, as well as his passionate commitment to social causes. He found Gorky to be lively, stimulating, spontaneous, and fiercely idealistic—a refreshing change from the Moscow *literati*. "He looks like a tramp," he described Gorky, "but his soul is quite elegant."[3] Gorky, on the other hand, gave us an unusual glimpse into the darker side of Chekhov, describing with compassion how his illness made him solitary, pensive and disillusioned. Gorky's reminiscences of Chekhov are among the most touching written about him in his final years.

Meanwhile, Chekhov tried to make the most of his life in Yalta, planting his own garden and a small orchard. He boasted to Masha of his cherry trees, as well as the mulberry, almond, and pear. As in Melikhovo, he threw himself into local philanthropic activities, contributing the first of his royalties from Marx towards the construction of a local village school. Strangers flocked to him for all sorts of reasons—financial assistance, literary advice, and above all, medical care. Ironically, he found himself caring for dozens of itinerant victims of consumption, the disease from which he himself suffered. He arranged for them to be lodged in a communal dwelling, and continued to raise money for a local clinic, never for a moment imagining that he would want to move there himself. "My house is being built, but my muse has collapsed altogether, I'm not writing a thing and don't feel like working," he reported[4]

But Chekhov grew restless from the boredom of Yalta life and the monotonous role of an invalid. "I'm tired of playing the role of the man who, instead of living, simply vegetates 'for his health's sake.' I walk along the quay like a priest without a parish," he wrote Suvorin.[5] So he fled in the spring to Moscow, without the permission of Dr. Altschuller, his attending physician. He stayed with his mother and sister until he couldn't bear the flow of visitors any longer, and then found a flat of his own. There he was touched by a visit from Tolstoy, with whom he was developing a friendship. He warded off repeated advances from Lydia Avilova, who was passing through Moscow at the time (with her three children) and persisted in harboring illusions that Chekhov was in love with her. As they parted, he gently affirmed that this was to be their last meeting. (Decades after his death, Avilova would romanticize this last encounter in her sad memoir *Chekhov In My Life.*)

Indeed, Chekhov had another woman on his mind. On Easter Sunday, while in Moscow, he paid a surprise visit to the family of Olga Knipper, the charismatic young actress who had attracted his attention the previous fall during the reading of *The Seagull*. Next, he invited Olga to attend an exhibit of Levitan's paintings. Then on May 1, he attended a private performance of *The Seagull* at the Moscow Art Theatre arranged especially for the author, since he had not been able to attend the opening in December. According to Stanislavsky, he insisted on seeing it, saying he would be unable to write anything else until he had seen a performance of *The Seagull* and could believe it was the success that everyone said it was.

The special performance of *The Seagull* expressly for Chekhov (and only ten other spectators) proved to be a labor of love on the part of the company. Since the season was over by that time, the Nikitsky Theatre had to be rented out for this one performance only, all the production elements had to be reassembled, and the actors needed to rehearse anew. Stanislavsky was extremely anxious over Chekhov's response. While he seemed energized by being in a theatre again, Chekhov was nonetheless evasive about the production itself. Reportedly, he disliked Stanislavky's elaborate sound effects, and complained about the dragging tempo of Act IV. (Chekhov jokingly suggested that the play end with Act III.) He was especially displeased with the performance of Maria Roksanova as Nina, and, according to Stanislavsky's memoir, asked that she be replaced. When Stanislavsky asked him how he liked his performance as Trigorin, Chekhov replied: "You're a wonderful actor, only that's not my character. I didn't write that… [Trigorin] wears checkered trousers and shoes with worn soles."[6] Though Stanislavsky tried to press him for an explanation, Chekhov refused to elaborate. Stanislavsky was hurt—after all, he was proud of Trigorin's elegant costume, consisting of white trousers, a white vest, and white hat. But a year later, when he was playing the part again, he realized what Chekhov had meant. He would treasure those insightful gems of advice that Chekhov gave him for the rest of their working relationship. (Later, Stanislavsky would refer to Chekhov's remarks to actors as "little diamonds."[7])

Soon after, Chekhov was photographed with the cast in a picture that would become a historic one. In it, Chekhov sits amongst them, pince-nez in place, pretending to read a copy of *The Seagull*, while the actors surround him in a respectful, admiring pose. In the center of the group, in an arresting profile, sits the charismatic young actress, Olga Knipper, who played Arkadina.

After the performance, Chekhov invited Olga to visit him at Melikhovo, where they spent three sunny spring days together. Chekhov proudly showed her his "domain"—the pond, the gardens, the flowers, the little cottage where he wrote *The Seagull*. Olga immediately bonded with his mother and sister. (Olga had met Masha earlier that winter, when Vishnevsky brought her to her dressing room following a performance of *The Seagull* and liked her right away.) It was an altogether felicitous beginning. Thereafter, on June 16, Chekhov wrote her his first letter and she responded. Their exchange of letters would last six years (until the end of his life) and would eventually constitute one of the great romantic correspondences in theatre history.

Soon after Olga's visit to Melikhovo, Chekhov put the house and property up for sale. She immediately invited herself to Yalta to visit him while his new house was being constructed. They spent the summer together, and their relationship deepened. She worried how he neglected his health; he noted her abrupt mood changes. They returned to Moscow in August, where Olga resumed rehearsals with the company, and Chekhov remained briefly, until the onset of autumn forced him to return with his mother and sister to Yalta, to take up residence in his new home.

Chekhov was pleased and relieved to be settled at last in his new study in Yalta. It was a cozy room, with a fine view of the garden. He was surrounded with Levitan paintings and photos of writers he admired, including Tolstoy and Turgenev. (A "no smoking" sign was placed above his desk, one that Chekhov would not enforce if a careless guest inadvertently lit a cigarette.) At last he could return to his writing. That autumn he wrote two stories that constituted major additions to his collection of prose—"In The Ravine" and "The Lady with the Dog"—and as well as made notes for future ones. (The latter was a lyrical love story between two married individuals who struggle to preserve their love in the face of insurmountable obstacles. The elements of love, longing, fate, and an uncertain future foreshadow themes of his next play, yet to be written.) He rejected the suggestion of a friend to write an autobiography. "Autobiography? I have an illness: autobiographobia. To read details about myself, or worse, to write about myself for publication, is a true ordeal for me."[8] Instead, his thoughts were with Olga, who was deep in rehearsal on another one of his plays.

The story of *Uncle Vanya*'s rewriting—and how it came to be produced by the Moscow Theatre—is both a colorful and a mysterious one. First, the mystery: scholars do not seem to agree on when *Uncle Vanya* was actually written. We know that it is a masterful rewrite of his earlier comedy *The Wood Demon*, which failed so miserably in 1889. But "when" Chekhov actually made this dramaturgical transformation is another matter, as he was very secretive about it. He first refers to it in a letter to Suvorin dated December 2, 1896: "My plays are being printed with amazing slowness, slower than my stories…Up until now, I have proof-read only *Ivanov* and the vaudevilles. Two long plays are not yet published: *The Seagull*, known to you, and *Uncle Vanya*, unknown to anyone on earth…"[9]

The reference suggests that he may have done the rewrite of *Uncle Vanya* in the late summer/early fall of 1896, as *The Seagull* was opening in St. Petersburg. We know that he gave a copy of it to his publisher in October, along with *The Seagull*, *Ivanov*, and two vaudevilles, *The Bear* and *The Proposal*. Despite the scandal of that opening night on October 17 and his vows ("I shall never write another play again"), Chekhov must have felt that he was finding his way as a playwright, that he had discovered the "new forms" that his character Treplev longed to create, and that, like Treplev, he was writing "freely, from the soul." Other scholars put the rewrite much earlier (after the failure of *The Wood Demon* and before Chekhov left for Sakhalin), prompted by his reference in a letter to Gorky dated December 3, 1898, that *Uncle Vanya* was written "a long long time ago."[10]

But the tightness of the dramaturgy would suggest the former theory—that the revisions on *The Wood Demon* resulting in *Uncle Vanya* were indeed written in the late summer/early fall of 1896 (i. e. after the writing of *The Seagull*). The skill, confidence and economy with which he transformed the old play into the new one reflects a mature dramaturgical talent. Indeed, the metamorphosis is remarkable.

First, he reduced the cast from thirteen to eight, adding only one new role (Marina, the old nurse), and eliminating characters who seemed to serve as doubles or foils of the principal ones. Instead of offering a main protagonist as he had in his earlier plays of the 1880s (*Platonov, Ivanov, Uncle George)*, in *Uncle Vanya* (as in *The Seagull*) he provided an ensemble of characters. Second, he transformed three characters from *The Wood Demon* into richer, more complex portrayals in *Uncle Vanya*. Uncle George, who kills himself melodramatically at the end of Act III, becomes Uncle Vanya, who lives to face the misery of his hopeless life. The saintly Dr. Khrushchov becomes the eccentric, enigmatic, reclusive Dr. Astrov. Sonya, a simple country girl in the earlier play, becomes the stoical, heartbreaking figure in the later one.

Third, he reduced length of the older play by almost one-third, creating *Uncle Vanya*, the shortest of his plays, a chamber piece and a jewel of simplicity and economy. He redrafted most of Act I, preserved most of the magical Act II, rewrote the first part of Act III (adding the "map scene" between Astrov and Yelena), and completely rewrote Act IV. Not only did he cut, but also he significantly refined the text. Instead of scenes on three different estates in *The Wood Demon*, he unified the action of *Uncle Vanya* into one location, subtitling the play "scenes from country life" and intensifying the atmosphere. Whereas, in the earlier play, nature was given a fairy-tale-like treatment, in the later play it becomes a place of duality—of beauty and majesty on the one hand and impenetrability and danger on the other.

Above all, there was a significant change in the play's tone. *The Wood Demon* was Chekhov's "romantic comedy"—his attempt to please the audience and critics, to be all things to all people, having felt that he failed with tragedy in *Ivanov*. By altering the most crucial action of the play—having Vanya live instead of committing suicide, like Uncle George—Chekhov changed the tone of the play dramatically. With this deftly chosen plot adjustment, Chekhov transformed his earlier, awkward play into a masterpiece of tragicomedy.

Set on the Voynitsky family estate, *Uncle Vanya* follows the lives of Ivan Voynitsky, his family and friends, over a three month period one summer. Vanya, as he is called by all, is a forty-seven year old landowner struggling with a mid-life crisis. An educated, cultured man, Vanya has spent his adult life managing the family estate with his niece Sonya, supporting his aging mother, and dutifully copying the manuscripts of his brother-in-law, Professor Serebraykov, whose first wife was Vanya's late sister and Sonya's mother. Vanya is unmarried, unfulfilled, and deeply unhappy. Over this particular summer, the Professor arrives for a visit with his lovely new wife, Yelena. Vanya, who despises his brother-in-law, falls irrationally in love with her. During their sojourn on the estate, a series of love entanglements develop involving Vanya, Yelena, Sonya, and Astrov, a country doctor and Vanya's closest friend, whom Sonya loves deeply. As the summer progresses, Vanya spins more and more out of control, neglecting the estate, fawning over Yelena, drinking excessively, arguing with everyone, and making a fool of himself.

When the Professor suddenly announces his intentions to sell the estate out from under him, however, a horrified Vanya is finally provoked into action. Enraged, he first attempts to shoot the Professor—twice—and misses. He then attempts to poison himself, and fails at that, too. In the end, the Professor and his wife leave, and Vanya and Sonya are left, as before, to live out the rest of their days alone and unfulfilled. "Everything will be as it was," says Vanya, pronouncing his own sentence to an unfulfilled life. He will continue to run the family estate with his niece and copy his brother-in-law's worthless scholarship, knowing that despite all his hopes and dreams he will never amount to anything, let alone "a Schopenhauer, a Dostoevsky."

As in *The Seagull*, there is no Aristotelian plot to speak of, no hero striving with courage and conviction toward a noble goal. Instead, there are people who come and go, who ruin others' lives, whose own lives in turn are ruined, who move on, who stay behind. This would be the pattern, or rather non-pattern, of every one of Chekhov's mature plays. As such, Chekhov is dramatizing his deep perception of human behavior, one he gained after many years of observation. Characters don't shoot themselves onstage, like Ivanov. Instead, they endure, as Nina says, or work, Sonya says. Vanya alive, facing the truth of his wasted life day after day, is more truthful and more tragic, in Chekhov's view, than Vanya dead. As Chekhov once remarked to the young writer, Goroditsky:

"In life, one does not shoot oneself in the head, hang oneself, or declare one's passion at every fencepost, and one does not pour out profound thoughts in a constant flow. No, mostly one eats, drinks, flirts, makes stupid remarks: that is what should be seen on stage. One must write plays in which people come and go, have dinner, talk about the rain and the sunshine, play cards—not because this is the author's whim but because this is what happens in real life… Nothing must be fitted into a pattern."[11]

As in *The Seagull*, there is no one major theme in *Uncle Vanya*. Rather, the play is about a number of elements—love, country life, nature, and the inexorable passage of time –all of which run through his later, mature plays. The "scenes from country life" that were romanticized in *The Wood Demon* are now scenes of a far different nature. While Chekhov himself glorified country life when he was a young medical student summering in the south, once he became a landowner himself at Melikhovo, he experienced its harsh realities. Through his character Astrov, he shows us his view of the difficulties of the life of a country doctor—"impassable mud on the roads, frosts, blizzards, enormous distances, a brutal, savage population, poverty, disease," as Yelena describes it. Just as Treplev and Trigorin were two sides of Chekhov the writer, so Vanya and Astrov are two sides of Chekhov the landowner and country doctor. This corresponding duality in nature and human nature emanates from Chekhov's own experience.

As for *Uncle Vanya,* Chekhov seemed to have been content to transform a failed comedy into a new form for its own sake. "I don't want to write on pain of punishment or for money," he wrote Suvorin. "I'm quite satisfied with things as they are, and want to write a play just for the sake of writing it."[12] Moreover, he seemed confident enough in the quality of *Uncle Vanya* to forbid the publication of *The Wood Demon* in a new collection. "I hate this play and I'm trying to forget about it," he wrote his publisher about *The Wood Demon*. "Whether the play itself is to blame, or rather the circumstances under which it was written and staged—I don't know, but it would be a true blow if someone were to bring it out from hiding into the light of day and force it to live again."[13]

Chekhov was pleased that the provincial productions of *Uncle Vanya* during 1898—in Odessa, Kiev, Nizhny Novgorod, Saratov, Tiflis—were garnering unanimously positive reviews. At the same time, with shadows of *The Wood Demon*'s failure still haunting him, he was reluctant to commit to a St. Petersburg or Moscow production.

Then, in 1898, the Maly, the most prestigious theatre in Moscow at the time, approached him with an offer to produce *Uncle Vanya* in its 1899 season. Regretful that they hadn't produced *The Seagull*, the Maly administrators were determined not to lose out on *Uncle Vanya*. The Maly theatre was an "official theatre"—traditional, government-owned, and the very opposite of the innovative Moscow Art Theatre. Chekhov was flattered by the invitation—after all, the Maly had been Moscow's leading theatre for almost a century, and it would mean official recognition, whereas the Moscow Art Theatre was only a few months old. There were also financial considerations—the Maly would pay him more. So Chekhov entered into conversations with the theatre in early 1899, and fended off Nemirovich's anxious inquiries to produce *Uncle Vanya* with an apologetic response that he had already given a verbal promise to the Maly.

The rest, however, is history. The ensuing interaction between the Maly and Chekhov is almost comical. As the Maly was a government-run theatre, any new work needed to be approved by a government-appointed committee of so-called literary authorities. Upon reading *Uncle Vanya* in February, three of the scholars on the committee found it dramatically imperfect and socially irrelevant. They deemed it unfit to be performed in an Imperial Theatre, and demanded that Chekhov make certain specific revisions according to their direction. For example, they were offended by the notion that Uncle Vanya, an educated, cultured man, would fire a shot at Serebraykov, a university professor. Chekhov reluctantly agreed to make certain specific revisions.

Meanwhile, Nemirovich and the actors at the Moscow Art Theatre were terribly upset by Chekhov's intentions to give the play to the Maly. Once he heard the objections of the literary committee (of which he himself was a member), Nemirovich countered with an offer that the Moscow Art Theatre would accept the play as written and that there would be no need for Chekhov to make any revisions. According to Nemirovich, Stanislavsky liked *Uncle Vanya* even better than *The Seagull*. Ultimately, Chekhov, who found the committee's response more amusing than offensive, declined the Maly's offer and gave the play to a thrilled Nemirovich and the Moscow Art Theatre.

Rehearsals for *Uncle Vanya* began in September. Before returning to Yalta, Chekhov attended several rehearsals, and was unusually vocal, expressing his annoyance at the slightest deviation from his authorial intentions. Because of his specific attention to the actresses in the cast, he was accordingly nicknamed "The Actress Inspector." When the cast asked specific questions, he would offer brief, elliptical responses in a serious tone, followed by diverting laughter. "It's all there in the stage directions," was his favorite response to the actors' questions. To illustrate his point, he answered a question about the character of Uncle Vanya by indicating the stage directions: "Enter Vanya, adjusting his dapper tie." At first, the cast found this comment cryptic and puzzling. But after Chekhov explained that the elegant silk tie signified Vanya's status as an educated, cultured man, they realized that the costume element expressed Vanya's desperation to live a life he was not living. The cast came to appreciate Chekhov's illuminating gems of wisdom—these "diamonds," as Stanislavsky called them—and the way in which he offered them.

In response to Olga's entreaties for a fuller interpretation, he gave her specific direction on how she should play Yelena and on the tone of each act. According to Chekhov, Act IV should be quiet and subtle. As he explained to Olga, Astrov "speaks to her in this scene in the same tone as speaks of the heat in Africa, and kisses her simply because there doesn't appear to be anything else to do."[14] Meanwhile, his view of Stanislavsky's acting wasn't any more positive than it had been during *The Seagull*. Privately, he described Stanislavsky's acting as that of a rich young merchant/dilettante.

Nemirovich, too, was concerned about Stanislavsky, who was spreading himself thin in his multiple roles as co-artistic director, stage director and actor. The Moscow Art Theatre had nine productions in their 1899 season; Nemirovich and Stanislavsky were overseeing the entire season together and working around the clock, with Stanislavsky directing two of them in addition to *Uncle Vanya*. Stanislavsky was frequently absent from rehearsal of *Uncle Vanya*, even though he was both directing it and performing in it. (On the first day of rehearsal, reportedly, he hadn't even decided which role he wanted to play—Astrov or Vanya. He eventually chose Astrov.)

Concerned, Nemirovich wrote Stanislavsky a tactful letter, noting with compassion that he was over-extended. He politely tried to organize Staislavsky's time, but to no avail, and the tension between the two men deepened. On the morning of the opening of *Uncle Vanya*, Nemirovich wrote a second, more urgent letter. After several apologetic paragraphs he finally got to the point, and enumerated his concerns: 1) that Stanislavsky curb his artistic indulgences and not, for example, wear a handkerchief over his head in Act I to keep the mosquitoes away, a detail that was not indicated in Chekhov's text; 2) that he memorize his lines; 3) that he pick up the pace, instead of dragging out certain scenes with the purpose of calling attention to certain moments; 4) that he not brutalize props, set furniture, and so on, thereby setting a bad example for other actors.[15]

After four dress rehearsals, the Moscow Art Theatre's production of *Uncle Vanya* opened on October 26, with Vishnevsky as Vanya, Stanislavsky as Astrov, Olga as Yelena, Lilina (Stanislavsky's wife) as Sonya, Vasily Kaluzhsky as Serebryakov, and Aleksandr Artyom as Waffles. The next morning, Nemirovich telegrammed Chekhov with a euphoric report of the opening's success. The following letter he wrote to Chekhov that day, however, was less than euphoric, reflecting the beginning of artistic differences within the company that would deepen over the years. Nemirovich reported that although the audience's response was enthusiastic (eleven curtain calls after Act III), the reviews were mixed, citing a slowness in pacing and an ambivalent response to the character of the Professor (a concern which the Maly had predicted). Nemirovich praised Stanislavky's Astrov, although he remained critical of Stanislavsky's direction, including slow pacing, overemphasizing of certain lines, and the excessive use of sound effects. Still, Nemirovich assured Chekhov that the play would run successfully, and that these reservations were only trivial—assurances that Chekhov received with dubiousness. As for Olga Knipper, Nemirovich also reported that her performance had been erratic thus far, owing to nerves, causing her to overact at times.[16]

Indeed, Knipper was very distraught over her performance. After opening night, she also wrote a long letter to Chekhov, saying that her acting was appalling, explaining that differences with Stanislavsky over her role had thrown her into a panic. Stanislavsky was trying to impose another interpretation, she said, and she felt lost and confused. While *The Seagull* had taken a physical toll on her, she wrote, *Uncle Vanya* was taking a psychological one. She hid at home, depressed, ashamed of her performance, afraid to face anyone. She begged Chekhov's forgiveness for her treatment of Yelena, imploring him not to judge her to harshly. In any event, she assured him that, despite her acting, the play was a great success.

But Chekhov doubted both Nemirovich and Knipper's assurances. He enlisted his devoted sister Masha to attend performance. She corroborated Olga's report of her nervousness on opening night, but reported that the second performance was much better than the first, and that people were talking of nothing else but *Uncle Vanya*.

In her struggle with the role of Yelena, however, Knipper had penetrated to the heart of the matter. In acting Chekhov's plays, she wrote later in her memoirs, it was not enough to play one's individual role well. On the contrary, she explained, playing Chekhov was all about the ensemble, their collective love of the author, their sensitivity for his plays and their deep humanity. Her understanding of the ensemble and the need to feel the "mood" of each act went to the heart of the newness of his plays, their settings, their themes, and the challenges they posed to the young company.[17]

As for Chekhov's contemporaries, there were sharply divergent responses to *Uncle Vanya*. Gorky was euphoric—he wrote to Chekhov that he'd seen the production twice and planned to go again. Tolstoy, on the other hand, disliked *Uncle Vanya*, openly complaining to the actors and others that the play was totally devoid of dramatic conflict and moral content. When word of Tolstoy's response reached Chekhov, he shrugged it off with a smile. Chekhov never let Tolstoy's continuing disapproval of his plays diminish his admiration for the older writer, nor mar their friendship. Meanwhile, Tolstoy continued to express his open displeasure for Chekhov's dramatic work (with the exception of *The Bear*). At the same time, Tolstoy maintained an admiration for Chekhov's short story writing, as well as a strong paternal affection for the younger writer.

The exchange of letters between Chekhov and Olga Knipper after *Uncle Vanya*—her mercurial mood swings, her entreaties for support, his reassurances—served to intensify their relationship. Meanwhile, the emotional turmoil surrounding the production deepened Chekhov's ambivalence toward the theatre even more. On the one hand, he was frustrated by the slightest misinterpretation of his work on the part of Stanislavsky, and uncomfortable by any news of friction between the players. On the other hand, he was drawn deeper and deeper into the vortex of theatre life, even from afar.

November and December found Chekhov facing the realities of daily life in Yalta. "Snow on the mountains. A cruel wind is blowing. Anyone who lives in the Crimea now is a fool," he wrote Masha.[18] A letter to his brother Mikhail that month describes the quotidian routine of visitors, phone calls, worries about finances, and dealing with sick consumptives who kept coming to him for treatment from all over. His dreams of going abroad or to Moscow seemed more remote than ever, and the prospect of a winter in Yalta, away from the excitement of the Moscow Art Theatre, was bleak. "How terrible it is to go to bed at nine," he continued in his letter to Masha, "furious, knowing you have nowhere else to go, no one to talk to, and nothing to work toward since no one will either see or hear the fruits of your fruitless labor. The piano and I—we're two inanimate objects spending our lives together in silence, wondering why we're put here when there is no one to play us."

Then came Olga's letter at the end of December, reporting that the company was taking *The Seagull* and *Uncle Vanya* to St. Petersburg. If only they would come to Yalta, he hoped—then he would have something to look forward to in the Centennial.

Act Four: *Yalta*

"I FEEL AS IF I'VE BEEN LIVING IN YALTA FOR A MILLION YEARS."

(Chekhov, letter to Korobov, January 29, 1900)

1900

"Dear Mikhail Osipovich:

... I fear Tolstoy's death. If he were to die, it would leave a great void in my life... Firstly, I'm not a religious man, but of all beliefs his are closest to my heart and suit me most. Secondly, as long as Tolstoy is among the ranks of the 'literati,' then it's easy and agreeable to be a writer. Even the realization that you haven't done much or ever will is bearable, since Tolstoy makes up for us all. He practices what he preaches—that is to say, what he writes. Thirdly, Tolstoy stands tall, he represents an enormous authority, and while he's living, bad taste in literature, vulgarity, and vanity is eclipsed. His moral authority alone keeps our literary standards high. Without him, we would be like a flock without a shepherd, unable to find our way.

[...] I'm happy to be a member of the Writer's Academy... although I'd be just as happy to lose my title over some misunderstanding. And one is bound to occur, since the learned academicians are very much afraid that we'll be shocking them. After all, they elected Tolstoy, and to them he's some kind of nihilist... On this misapprehension, I congratulated him with all my heart.

Greetings to your family.

Yours, A. Chekhov"

(Chekhov, letter to the journalist Menshikov, January 28, 1900, Yalta)

"Dear Aleksei Maksimovich:

Thank you for your letter, for your comments about Tolstoy and 'Uncle Vanya', which I haven't yet seen performed—in general, thank you for not forgetting me. Here in blessed Yalta, without letters one could simply keel over. Idleness, a stupid winter with temperature about zero, a complete absence of interesting women, pig snouts walking along the boardwalk—all this could wear a man out in no time. I'm exhausted, and it seems that this winter is lasting ten years.

...You're a young man, strong and hardy. If I were in your place, I'd escape to India or who the hell knows where. I'd also get two or more university degrees. Plans, plans—you're laughing, I'm sure, but it pains me that I'm already forty, short of breath, and afflicted with all kinds of nonsense that prevents me from living freely. All things considered, be a good fellow, and don't be annoyed with me that I'm sermonizing like a priest.

Nothing's new. Be well, I press your hand hard."
(Chekhov, letter to Gorky, February 3, 1900, Yalta)

"Dear actress:

...Why are you in such low spirits? Why? You're alive, you're working you have hopes, you drink...what more do you want? For me, it's quite another matter. I'm uprooted from my native soil, I don't live a life, I can't drink, although I love to, I love noise and there isn't any, I'm like a transplanted tree wondering whether to take root or wither away. If I sometimes complain to you of boredom in my letters, I have reason to, whereas you?

[...] I won't write to you any more until you send me your portrait. I kiss your little hand.

Your Antonio Academicus

P. S. Thanks for your good wishes on the occasion of my marriage. When I told my fiancée of your attention to come to Yalta, just to tease her a little, she said that when that 'evil woman' arrives she would keep a tight rein on me. I replied that being kept in such close quarters wasn't very hygienic in hot weather. She got angry, and said that the theatre was a bad influence and that my intention not to write any more plays was a good one. Then she asked me to kiss her. I replied that at the moment, with the title of Member of the Academy, it wasn't appropriate to kiss so often. She burst into tears and I left."
(Chekhov, letter to Olga Knipper, February 10, 1900. Yalta)

"Dear actress:

The photographs [you sent] are very good indeed, especially the one in which you look so sad, with your elbows resting on the back of the chair. Your expression is one of modest melancholy, behind which lurks a little imp. The other one is excellent too, but you look like a little Jewess, almost like a musician who is attending the conservatory but who is also studying the mysteries of dentistry...

Of the seventy rosebushes I've planted in the garden last autumn, only three haven't taken root. The lilies, irises, tulips, and hyacinths—all are coming up. The willow is blossoming, the grass around the bench is luxuriant. The almond tree is flowering. I've placed little benches everywhere, not wrought-iron ones but wooden ones which I'm painting green. I've put three bridges across the stream. I'm planting palms. There's so much that is new that you won't recognize the house, the garden or the street... I've heard no music or singing since autumn, and I haven't seen one good-looking woman either. Wouldn't you be melancholy, too?

I wasn't going to write you, but since you sent the photos, and since I don't think I'm in your good graces, I decided to write, as you can see...

Oh, and I was only joking when I wrote that you looked like a little Jewess in your photo. Don't be cross, my jewel. I kiss your hand and remain your devoted

A. Chekhov"

(Chekhov, letter to Olga Knipper, February 14, 1900, Yalta)

(The Moscow Art Theatre came to Yalta in April; thereafter, Chekhov went to Moscow and traveled in the Caucasus with Gorky. Olga rejoined him in Yalta in July).

"Darling, glorious, marvelous actress,

I'm alive, well, and thinking of you, dreaming of you, pining away that you're not here. I'm back in Yalta, my prison. A cruel wind is blowing, the boats aren't sailing, the sea is swelling, people are drowning, there's not a drop of rain, everything is withered and faded—in a word, it's been terrible here since you left. Without you, I shall hang myself. Be healthy and happy, my good little German. And don't be sad, sleep well and write soon. I kiss you hard, hard, 400 times.

Your Antonio"

(Chekhov, letter to Olga Knipper, August 13, 1900, Yalta)

"Dearest, I don't know when I'm coming to Moscow because, if you can believe it, I'm writing a play. It's not even a play, it's some sort of muddle. There are many characters—and it's possible that it won't work and I'll stop writing...

Be well, my little German, don't be angry with me, and don't betray me. I kiss you, hard.

Your Antoine"

(Chekhov, letter to Olga Knipper, August 14, 1900, Yalta)

"Hello, my darling good little actress:

I'm writing a play but our guests are driving me crazy. Yesterday they were here from nine in the morning till the evening, and today they're back for lunch. My head is spinning, my mood is mercurial, I get frustrated and have to start all over again.

The headmistress of the local girls' school has just arrived, together with two of her young relations. They installed themselves in my study, and have just started drinking tea. [...]

...So I've left the study and am hidden away in a corner of my bedroom, writing. If our visitors don't interrupt me and I don't get angry, then I'll finish the play between the first and fifth of September... Then I'll come to Moscow...

Be well, don't be sad.

Your Antonio"

(Chekhov, letter to Olga Knipper, August 17, 1900, Yalta)

"My dearest:

I'm working away in Yalta, being tortured terribly at every turn. The play is in my head, it's already taking form and flowing smoothly, and all it asks is to get written down, but no sooner do I pick up a piece of paper, some ugly mug or other peers through the door. I don't know what will be, but the beginning of the play is going smoothly.

Shall we see each other? Yes, we shall. When? In early September, most likely. I'm bored and irritable. Money just seems to disappear, and I'm going broke. There's a cruel wind today, storms, the trees are withering.

One of the cranes has flown away.

Yes, my sweet little actress, I could run across a field with such rapture, past woods, streams, sheep. Funny, but I haven't seen real grass in two years. How boring, my darling!...

Your Antonio"

(Chekhov, letter to Olga Knipper, August 18, 1900, Yalta).

"My dearest:

What's happening?!! You write that you've only received one of my letters so far, but I write to you every day, or almost every day! What could this mean? My letters never get lost.

[...] The play is off to a good start, it seems, but now I've grown cold, it seems so vulgar to me and I don't know what to do. A play should be written without stopping, without a break, and this morning is the first time I've been alone without any interruption. Never mind, what does it matter...

[...] I'm dreadfully bored without you.

Your Antoine"

(Chekhov, letter to Olga Knipper, August 20, 1900, Yalta).

"Hello, my dearest:

...Stanislavsky came to visit yesterday. He stayed until nine, and then we went (or more accurately, I took him) to visit the headmistress of the local girls school. There was a pleasant Hungarian woman who speaks very funny Russian. She played the harp and amused us. We stayed until twelve.

[...] I'm writing the play, but I'm afraid it will turn out to be a bore. I'll keep writing it, and if I still don't like it, I'll set it aside until next year or until that time when I feel like writing. A season without a play by me isn't the end of the world. In any case, we'll talk about it when I'm in Moscow.

[...] Write soon, don't be stingy. I'll reward you for it—I'll make love to you wildly, like an Arab. Don't forget to write and think often of your

Antoine"
(Chekhov, letter to Olga Knipper, August 23, 1900, Yalta).

"My dearest, my angel:

I haven't been writing to you, but don't be angry with me, don't give in to human weakness. I've been working on the play all along, doing more thinking than writing, which is to say that I'm writing and not rushing it. So it's possible that I'll be coming to Moscow without having finished it. There are so many characters that it's getting crowded, and I fear that it will come out murky and bland, so I think it's best to put it off till the following season.

We have guests: the headmistress of the local high school again with two young ladies. I'm writing with interruptions.

[...] There's no rain in Yalta. The trees are withering, the stream dried up long ago; the wind howls every day. It's cold.

Write to me more often, your letters warm my heart and lift my spirits, which are parched and black every day, like the Crimean earth. Don't be angry with me, my darling.

The guests are leaving. I'll see them out.

Your Antoine"
(Chekhov, letter to Olga Knipper, September 5, 1900, Yalta).

"Dear fellow countryman Aleksandr Leonidovich:

Huge thanks for your letter and for your kindness. We'll see each other soon. All I think about is Moscow since you've left. I'm bored to distraction, to despair. I'm writing the play, I've written a lot already, but since I'm not in Moscow, I can't judge it. Perhaps it won't be a play after all, but some kind of boring Crimean nonsense. It's called 'The Three Sisters' (as you already know), and I've written the role of the director of the high school for you. He's also the husband of one of the sisters. You'll be wearing a school uniform with a decoration around your neck.

If the play isn't produced this season, I'll rework it for next season.

... I envy you that you frequent a place where I haven't been in six years— the baths. I'm covered from head to toe with fish scales, I'm shaggy, I walk about without a stitch on and howl like a wild one. The young ladies are afraid of me.

... Be well and happy, my compatriot, work hard, enjoy it, and don't forget

Yours, A. Chekhov"

(Chekhov, letter to the actor Vishnevsky, September 5, 1900, Yalta).

"As for my play, it will be finished sooner or later, in September or October, or even in November, but whether I decide to let it be performed in this season, who knows, my sweet baboon. I may decide against it, since, first of all, the play may not be ready yet and should lie on my desk for a while, and secondly, I simply must be present at rehearsals, I must! Four crucial female roles, four intelligent young women—I can't leave them in Stanislavsky's hands, no matter how great my respect is for his gift and understanding. I must keep an eye on rehearsals myself.

[...] I kiss you passionately, till I swoon, till I go mad. Don't forget your

Antoine."

(Chekhov, letter to Olga Knipper, September 15, 1900, Yalta).

"My darling Olya:

[...] Ah, what a part there is for you in 'The Three Sisters'! What a part! Give me ten rubles, and you can have it, or else I'll give it to another actress. I'm not giving them 'The Three Sisters' for this season; the play needs to sit for a while, or as the merchants' wives say when they put a pie out on the table, 'let it breathe'...

Nothing else new.

Your very own Antoine"

(Chekhov, letter to Olga Knipper, September 28, 1900, Yalta)

"My darling:

What an idiot I am! I arrived here in Vienna and found

that all the shops are closed—it's German Christmas! So here I sit empty-handed in my room, without a clue, not knowing what to do, and feeling very foolish. Yes, there are some restaurants open, but they're filled with dandies next to whom I look like a beggar. What was I supposed to do!

Tomorrow I leave for Nice, and meanwhile I'm sitting here looking lustfully at the two beds in my hotel room, ready to sleep and dream! What a pity that I'm here alone, without you, my little scamp, my darling. How are things going in Moscow? How do you feel? How are rehearsals? Have they gotten very far? Write everyday, and tell me everything, darling, down to the smallest detail! Or else God only knows what kind of mood I'll be in.

[...] Write, little one....

Your Antoine"

(Chekhov, letter to Olga Knipper, December 12, 1900, Vienna)

"My dearest:

Strange as it seems, I feel as if I've landed on the moon. It's warm, the sun shines everywhere, it's too hot to wear a coat, and everyone is walking around dressed for summer. The window in my room is wide open, and so, it seems, is my soul. I'm doing rewrites on the play and am amazed that I'm writing such a farce, let alone why. Oh my darling, why aren't you here? You'd rest, look around, listen to the street singers and the musicians who pass through the courtyard from time to time, and above all bask in the sunshine.

I'm going down to the sea now to sit and read the newspapers, and then, after I return, I'll start the rewrites. Tomorrow I'll send Nemirovich the rewrites to Act II and the day after I'll send Act IV—or both together. I've made some changes in Act III—and added just a little bit, but not much.

Send me your photograph, my darling, do.

There are [a] lot of flies here.

I'm meeting a lot of Russians...

I hug you fiercely, I kiss you a thousand times. I'm eager for a letter from you, a long one. Meanwhile, I bow low before you.

Your Antoine"

(Chekhov, letter to Olga Knipper, December 15, 1900, Nice)

It was to be a momentous year for the ailing writer—the Centennial, his fortieth birthday, and the writing of a new play, the very first specifically for the Moscow Art Theatre and its company. Though plagued intermittently by a wracking cough, hemorrhages, influenza, fever and related ailments, Chekhov hardly had time to ail, so swept up he was in the whirlwind of events.

The year began with his election into the Academy of Sciences—a distinction that Chekhov brushed off with his usual self-deprecating humor, finding amusement in signing his letters "Antonius Academicus." He made light of his fortieth birthday as well ("my elevation to the ranks of the immortal"), and it passed without much note.

February and March provided the year's only lull. Already the Art Theatre was pressuring Chekhov to write a new play (Nemirovich even enlisted his sister Masha to keep after him). In a letter to Nemirovich, he admitted that a new idea was "pecking its way out of the shell"[1] but that he hadn't started on it yet. He was out of sorts. "I am bored," he wrote Gorky, "not in the same sense as *weltschmerz*, nor in the sense of existential weariness, but simply bored from lack of people, from lack of music, which I love, and from lack of women of whom there are none in Yalta. I'm bored without caviar and sauerkraut."[2]

Alone in his Yalta, his "prison," his "hot Siberia" as he called it, he filled the emptiness with tending his orchard, playing with his dogs and his new pet crane. "If I hadn't become a writer, I'd have been a gardener," he wrote.[3] He continued to deal with dozens of indigent consumptive patients referred to him by doctors from all over Russia. Their poverty and their status as society's rejects distressed him terribly.

Above all, he immersed himself in a blossoming correspondence with Olga. Hitherto, the bulk of his prodigious correspondence had been to family members (Aleksandr, Masha, Mikhail), publishers (Suvorin, Leikin), fellow writers (Gorky), young aspiring writers (Leontyev-Shcheglov, Shavrova, Avilova) and so on. But as their relationship deepened during this centennial year, the object of his correspondence would shift to Olga. Alternating with paragraphs of teasing, joking and tender affection, these intimate letters contain an almost day-to-day account of his life in Yalta—expressing his loneliness, his boredom, his longing to be in Moscow, his persisting ailments, and a haunting sense of the passage of time. Had she forgotten him? Why must she feel so low? And why is she so angry with him? He wrote, half-teasing, half serious. And she responded: Why couldn't he come to Moscow? Why is he so callous? Why didn't he understand? He complained of aging, she complained of their separation, of not understanding him. Back and forth the letters flew, as their affection intensified and deepened.

Then the idea occurred to him: why not invite the entire theatre company to come to Yalta? He submitted an invitation to Stanislavsky, who loved the idea, hoping that a company tour to Yalta with *The Seagull* and *Uncle Vanya* would inspired Chekhov to get to work on the new play. The tour was set for April, and turned into one of the major artistic events of the Centennial Year. Chekhov awaited their arrival in excitement and anxious anticipation, fearful that they might cancel and not come. "For me, no winter has ever lasted as long as this one," he wrote Suvorin.[4] The company arrived in Sevastopol (a town near Yalta) with great fanfare to start their Crimean tour, bringing the sets for *The Seagull* and *Uncle Vanya* with them. (Chekhov had experienced a violent hemorrhage only a few days before their arrival, but managed to pull himself together.)

Hidden away in the back of the director's box in the local theatre, Chekhov watched as the company gave a passionate performance of *Uncle Vanya* for the author, who was seeing it for the first time. He also saw their performance of *The Seagull*. Chekhov's house in Autka (on the outskirts of Yalta) became the center of daily gatherings, lunches, teas, suppers, laughter, and gaiety. It was a festival-like atmosphere, with many artists and writers in attendance, including Gorky, Ivan Bunin, Chaliapin, and Sergei Rachmaninov. Chekhov never got to bed before 3 a.m. During that euphoric two week visit, Chekhov and Olga became lovers. Try as they might, they couldn't hide their intimacy from Chekhov's mother and sister, provoking discomfort and disapproval from the latter two.

At the end of April, the Moscow Art Theatre company moved on. They departed from Yalta, leaving the swing and bench from the set of *Uncle Vanya* in Chekhov's garden as a souvenir of that happy visit. Chekhov couldn't bear the void, and restlessness overcame him. He fled Yalta to Moscow, and traveled to the Caucasus with Gorky. When the tour ended in July, he and Olga were joyously reunited in Yalta.

Then Olga left for Moscow and the start of a new season at the Moscow Art Theatre. Stanislavsky was convinced that the success of the theatre rested on another play by Chekhov, otherwise it would lose its prestige. At the same time, Stanislavsky was worried that he might not be well enough to write. But that week, Stanislavsky wrote a letter in the strictest secrecy to Nemirovich, saying that he had cajoled a piece of news out of the ever-elusive Chekhov—that in fact he was beginning work on a new play. It featured four young female roles and included a corps of military men. It would be the very first play he would write expressly for the Moscow Art Theatre and would feature the first role he would create especially for Olga. Stanislavsky and Olga together pressured Chekhov to finish the play for this season. "I gave him my word to finish it by no later than September," Chekhov wrote Olga. "You see what a good boy I am?"[5]

Chekhov's letters to Olga over the two month period during which he was writing *The Three Sisters* (from mid-August to mid-October) are among the most colorful and revelatory of his entire correspondence. In these spontaneous, intimate letters, written almost daily, he would pour his heart out over the enormous struggle to write his most complex play to date. The constant stream of visitors to his house in Autka (Yalta) proved to be a great source of distraction and annoyance. He dealt with the frustration with these vexing visitors (including a headmistress of the local school and her friends) by amusing himself and putting details of his daily Yalta life in the play.

For inspiration, Chekhov drew from a variety of events in his past, notably two memories. The first was his stay in the provincial garrison town of Voskresensk in his medical school days, where one of the officers of the resident military unit had proposed to his sister Masha (a proposal for which Chekhov had tacitly withheld his support).

The second source of inspiration was from his summer in the Ukrainian countryside near the village of Luka on the Psyol River in 1888. Chekhov had rented a dacha there in on the estate of the Lintvaryovs, a family of the impoverished gentry class who lived a genteel, old fashioned, high-minded life. There were three sisters in the family: the eldest, Zinaida, was a doctor, who was blind and suffered from epilepsy. The middle sister, Yelena, was also a doctor. Natalia, the youngest and most spirited, was a teacher. The family was cultured, genteel and highly individualistic, and Chekhov passed an idyllic summer with them. The sense of warmth, well-being, appreciation of culture, beauty and tradition that they evoked would be a source of inspiration for the three Prozorov sisters he was conjuring up in his dramatic imagination.

In actuality, Chekhov and his brothers had been involved with a number of trios of sisters over the years. There were also the three Golden sisters—Anna, Anastasia, and Natalia—whom Chekhov knew in 1881 while writing comedic sketches for *The Spectator*. They were Orthodox Jews, and became intimately involved with the Chekhov brothers during those early years. Anna Golden was a secretary in the magazine's office, and became Nikolai's common law wife. Natalia, the youngest, fell in love with Chekhov. Next came the three Markova sisters that occupied his summer of 1884, the year he graduated medical school. The Chekhov brothers became romantically entangled with this trio, as well.

In the colorful coterie of characters, Chekhov included his long-favored, under-appreciated provincial schoolteacher, who had appeared in a number of his short stories ("The Man In The Case," "The Teacher of Literature") as well as in *The Seagull*. There were also other Chekhovian types: the cultivated army officer ("The Kiss") and, of course, the doctor, who was represented in all his previous plays as well as in his short stories ("Ward No. 6" among numerous others). These he included in the ensemble of *The Three Sisters*, the most populated of his full-length plays.

As for the provincial setting of the play, Chekhov mentioned in a letter to Gorky that he imagined "a town like Perm."[6] This large but remote town was situated just west of the Ural Mountains, the range that divides the vast land into European Russia and Asiatic Russia. Presumably Chekhov picked Perm because, while it was still in the western part of Russia that looked to Europe as its cultural model (in contrast to Asiatic Siberia), it was nonetheless a far cry from the civilized, cosmopolitan cities of Moscow and St. Petersburg.

Set in this imagined town a year after the death of their father, a prestigious Colonel in the artillery, the play tells the story of the three Prozorov sisters (Olga, Masha, Irina) and their brother Andrey. Well-educated, cultured, talented, they had enjoyed an idyllic upbringing and a fine education in Moscow. Then they moved to this provincial town with their father's regimen, where they had been living for the past twelve years, never giving up their dream to return to their city of origin.

During the three year period that the play spans, the lives of the Prozorov sisters become fatefully involved with members of their father's artillery unit. Those officers include Tusenbach, an upright young lieutenant (and a baron of German descent) who falls in love with Irina, the youngest sister; Solyony, a delusional captain who becomes Tusenbach's rival for Irina's heart; Vershinin, a handsome (married) major who captures the heart of the unhappily married Masha, the middle sister; and Chebutykin, an aging army doctor who was once in love with the three sisters' mother. Meanwhile, Andrey, the sisters' talented brother, falls in love with Natasha, a local girl beneath his family's social status. Ultimately, the artillery unit moves on, leaving the three sisters stranded in the town with no hope of ever escaping, and leaving Andrey trapped in a miserable marriage.

The isolation and growing desperation of the Prozorovs corresponded with Chekhov's own intense feeling of exile in Yalta, so far from Moscow and its vibrant cultural life. Indeed, the sisters' desperate cries "To Moscow, to Moscow"! were an expression of his own.

Although more "happens" than in its predecessors *The Seagull* and *Uncle Vanya*, the play essentially follows the same pattern as the previous two: a group of people (in this case, the military) come, a group of people go, life goes on as before, with an uncertain future. As in the previous plays, there is no moral or message. There is only work, the answer to the hopelessness of life. "Endure," says Nina in *The Seagull*. "Work," says Sonya in *Uncle Vanya*. "Live," says Olga in *The Three Sisters*.

The complaints that Chekhov expressed in his letters to Olga over the interruptions and distractions masked a more significant source of frustration—namely, his continuing insecurities as a dramatist. In calling *The Three Sisters* a "muddle" or a "hodge podge" as he did in his letters to her, Chekhov was revealing both excitement and concern over the ambitious scope of this play. In addition to its having the largest cast and the most intricate, intertwining story lines of his later plays, it was his most complex in yet another way. He was experimenting with a delicate and subtle technique similar to that of the pointillist painters, an offshoot of the French Impressionist movement of that same epoch. In Act II of *The Three Sisters*, for example, set in the Prozorov drawing room on a snowy February evening, Chekhov divides his characters in groups on stage, some philosophizing downstage, others playing cards center stage, others strumming the guitar and singing softly upstage, while shadowy forms of mummers appear through the windows. He "layers" them, very much as the French pointillist painter Georges Seurat layered his figures in the famous painting "La Grande Jatte" (1884) the decade before. Downstage, Tusenbach (the pragmatic), Vershinin (the romantic) and Masha (the idealist) engage in philosophizing. What will life be like in 200-300 years? they ask. 1,000 years, even? "And the meaning of all this is…?," asks Masha. The answer offered by Tusenbach, is: "Look, it's snowing outside. What is the meaning of that?"

In the scene, as in Seurat's painting, it is as if time is standing still. And yet so much is going on. Who are the important figures? Where should the audience focus? Is what they are saying important, or what they are doing? Or not doing? Chekhov seems to be redefining the very essence of dramatic action, where every detail (like those in a pointillist painting) can mean something, or nothing, as it fades into the "bigger picture," like the endless, fruitless philosophizing of Chekhov's characters on that snowy evening (and the tiny daubs of paint delineating Seurat's figures on the banks of the Seine).

It was clear from the letters he wrote Olga—over these eight weeks as he struggled with *The Three Sisters*—that his identity as a playwright was becoming inextricably associated with the Moscow Art Theatre. For the first time, he was bringing characters to life based on individual company members (Olga as Masha, Vishnevsky as Kulygin, and so on). He corresponded with the actors, Stanislavsky, and Nemirovich as he wrote the play. The theatre and its company—especially the leading lady—were in his dramatists' eye; and despite his fear he might not be able to deliver, they were alive in his imagination and were helping to bring his vision to life.

Even with all the unwelcome distractions (including several bouts of flu and a fire that burned down the Yalta Theatre), Chekhov pressed on, writing to Olga that he wouldn't come to Moscow until he'd finished the play. He tried to distract her with amusing endearments ("my little granny," "crocodile of my soul," "golubchik," "my little Jewess") and offered her bows, kisses and "fierce hugs" above his signature. "One of the sisters has gone a little lame," offering it as a reason for his not coming yet. "And anyway, I'm afraid you'll become disenchanted with me. I'm losing my hair at an alarming rate, so much so that I'll be bald within a week. I'll look like an old monk."[7] She replied, offering her Uncle Sasha's remedy for baldness, and at the same time expressing frustration over their separation, accusing him of not wanting to come to Moscow and falling in love with someone else—an accusation that he also returned, although teasingly. "If we're not together," he responded," it's neither my fault nor yours, but that of the demon, who's put the bacilli in me and a love of the theatre in you... Don't be angry with me, golubchik, and don't mope, be a good girl."[8] He amused her by putting her remedy for baldness in the play.

Finally, on October 16, he wrote to Olga that the play was finished. A week later, he journeyed up to Moscow. He stayed at the Hotel Dresden, where he and Olga spent the night together—an arrangement they devised to avoid Chekhov's sister and mother any embarrassment, although the latter were increasingly distressed by their intimacy. He attended the company's first read-through of *The Three Sisters* on October 29. According to various reports, the company's high spirits at the onset of the reading descended into a heavy and awkward silence. Chekhov smiled, coughed, and attempted to dispel the tension with small talk and humorous remarks. But he smarted from the actors' comments that the play was more an outline than a play, that it wasn't ready yet, that the characters weren't fully drawn. He took special offense when some actors asked whether *The Three Sisters* was a tragedy or a comedy. When they questioned him in detail, he gave brief answers, such as "Andrey appears in this scene in his slippers" or "Here the character simply whistles," etc. He retreated to his hotel, stung by the company's response, and set about the daunting task of rewriting the first two acts. His cough increased, he was plagued by headaches, and, meanwhile, Moscow was getting colder and colder.

Reluctant to face another dreary winter in Yalta, Chekhov impulsively decided to leave Russia altogether. In December he set out for Nice, where he would have peace of mind to continue the rewrites on *The Three Sisters*. He settled into the Pension Russe, the charming little hotel a few blocks from the sea where he had previously stayed. There he could sit out on the balcony overlooking the courtyard and take meals downstairs with the other guests. The weather was lovely and summer-like, the air was warm, and the roses were in bloom. He enjoyed wearing a new light-weight coat, practicing his French and strolling down to the seaside to read his newspaper in the morning.

Still, his mind was on Moscow and the progress of *The Three Sisters*. In December, while Nemirovich and Stanislavsky began rehearsing Acts I and II in Moscow, Chekhov made changes to Act III and rewrote Act IV almost entirely—all within a week. Included in these significant changes was the addition of Dr. Chebutykin's crucial line in Act II: "Balzac was married in Berdichev"—providing a closing, absurdist note to the deep philosophical discussion between Vershinin, Tusenbach and Masha.

Later in his memoir (*My Life In Art*), Stanislavsky expressed his great admiration for this rewrite, citing as an example the original version of Act IV, where Andrey delivered a significant speech describing the behavior of women before and after marriage. In the revised Act IV that he sent Stanislavsky in December, Chekhov cut the entire speech and substituted it with the laconic, ironic phrase: "A wife is a wife." In one masterful stroke, Chekhov was able to condense this entire speech into five words, summing up Andrey's bewilderment and despair over his marriage to Natasha. Stanislavsky singled out this change as an example of Chekhov's dramatic genius.

Meanwhile, Chekhov wrote Olga: "The play is now finished and has been sent off. I've added a lot more for you in Act IV. You see, there's nothing I wouldn't do for you."[9]

Olga wrote during the early weeks of rehearsals with reports. Stanislavsky had once again written a detailed *mise-en-scène*, and was directing. Olga was displeased with the actor Serafim Sudbinin, whom nobody felt was right for Vershinin and was approaching the role in a coarse, off-hand manner. But she loved the part of Masha, and was pleased with the deep-toned voice she was developing for the role, as well as the walk. She described how much the company was enjoying rehearsing the "porch" dance in Act II. Both Stanislavsky and Nemirovich also wrote Chekhov with their reports of the rehearsals' progress. Chekhov scrutinized their every word, and answered their questions immediately in detail, even giving line readings and stage directions. "In Act III," he wrote Nemirovich urgently, "the last words that Solyony says are essential: (looking at Tusenbach): 'Tsip tsip tsip…' Elongate this line, please."[10]

His deepening relationship with Stanislavsky, Nemirovich and the cast, however stressful, was resulting in his most intense collaboration to date, binding him closer than ever to a theatre that was clearly his artistic home.

Chekhov and Olga Knipper

"Do you know how many more years I'll be read? Seven... But I have even fewer years to live than that..."

(Chekhov, spoken to Bunin, 1901)[1]

1901

"Give me a wife who, like the moon, does not appear in my sky every night."
(Chekhov, letter to Suvorin, March 23, 1895, Melikhovo)

"Esteemed Konstantin Sergeevich:

I wish you everything: a new year, good fortune, a new theatre, which you'll soon be building, and a new crop of great plays, too. As for that old play 'The Three Sisters', it must not be read at the Countess's soirée under any circumstances, I beg you, or else you'll distress me greatly.

I sent off the rewrites to Act IV some time ago before Christmas, addressed to Nemirovich. I've made a lot of changes. You write that in Act III, when Natasha is making the rounds of the house at night, she puts out lamps and searches for thieves under the furniture. But it seems to me that it would be better if she walked straight across the stage in a straight line, not looking at anything or anyone, à la Lady Macbeth with a candle—it's simpler and scarier.

[...] I press your hand hard.

Yours, A. Chekhov"
(Chekhov, letter to Stanislavsky, January 2, 1901, Nice)

"Are you feeling down, my darling, or gay? Don't despair, my sweet— live, work, and write to your Wise Old Antonio more often. It's been a while since I've received a letter from you, apart from the one dated December 12th, which I only received today, in which you describe how you cried when I left. What a wonderful letter it was! You didn't

write it yourself, did you, you probably got someone else to do it. An amazing letter.

Nemirovich hasn't come to see me yet. I sent him a telegram the day before yesterday, asking that he come to see me 'seul'.... We need to meet and talk about the letter I received from Stanislavsky...

Describe at least one rehearsal of 'The Three Sisters', please. Does anything need to be added, or cut? Are you acting [the role of Masha] well, my darling? Listen to me: don't put on a sad face, not even in one act. Angry, yes—but sad? No. People who are used to carry sadness inside just whistle and are lost in thought. So when others are talking on stage, you often become pensive. Do you understand? Of course you do, you're brilliant... I kiss both your hands, every one of your ten fingers, your forehead, and wish you peace and happiness...

Your Toto"

(Chekhkov, letter to Olga Knipper, January 2, 1901, Nice)

"Esteemed Ioasaf Aleksandrovich:

...Here are answers to your questions:

1) *Irina doesn't know that Tusenbach is going to a duel, but she guesses that something extraordinary has happened the evening before that could have major and possibly unfortunate consequences. And when a woman suspects something, she always says: 'I knew it, I knew it.'*
2) *Chebutykin only sings the following lyrics: 'Won't you please take this sweet fig...' These are lyrics from an operetta which was put on at the Hermitage. I can't recall the title... Chebutykin shouldn't sing more than that, otherwise it will prolong his exit.*
3) *Solyony really and truly thinks he looks like Lermontov, but of course he doesn't—it's funny even to think of it... He should make himself up to look like Lermontov. The likeness will be significant, but only in Solyony's mind, of course.*

[...] No one is writing to me about the play. When he was here, Nemirovich said nothing and I got the impression that the play bored him and that it won't be a success. So thank you for you letter which has cheered me up considerably.

I wish you health and the very best.

Yours, A. Chekhov"

(Chekhov, letter to Tikhomirov, a cast member of '*The Three Sisters*' January 14, 1901, Nice)

"My darling Actress-ella, plunderer of my soul:

... How is 'The Three Sisters'? Judging from your letters, you're putting up with utter nonsense. Noise in Act III? Why?! There is only noise in the distance offstage, indistinct, muffled, while on the stage everyone is exhausted... If Act III is spoiled, then the play is ruined and I'll be hissed off the stage in my twilight years. Stanislavsky praises you in his letters, and so does Vishnevsky. And even though I'm not there to see you, I praise you too. As for "tram-tam-tam," Vershinin sings to you as if he's posing a question, while you answer him, and it's so novel that you respond with a smile... Masha sings 'tram-tam' and then laughs, but not loudly, just a little. We don't need a character like the one in 'Uncle Vanya', but rather a younger, more vital one. Remember, you're quick to laugh, and quick to anger... I'm counting on you, my darling, you're such a good actress...

Meanwhile, I already wrote that Tusenbach's body mustn't be carried across the stage during your scene, but Stanislavsky insists that nothing can be done without that body. I wrote to him about it, but I don't know whether he received my letter. If the play fails, I'll go to Monte Carlo and gamble and drink myself into a stupor.

Be well.

Your Wise Old Antony"

(Chekhov, letter to Olga Knipper, January 20, 1901, Nice)

"My precious:

Masha's confession in Act III isn't just a confession but simply a frank conversation. Play it with tension but not desperation, don't shout, smile from time to time, and, in essence, try to feel the exhaustion of the night. As for people feeling that you're smarter than your sisters, it's you yourself who must think so, at least. As for the song, do it your way. You're my brilliant one.

[...] I am still writing, of course, but without any desire to do so. Either 'The Three Sisters' has worn me out or else I'm sick of writing and getting old. I don't know. Perhaps I'll take five years off from writing, travel, and then come back and settle down...

Be well, my darling better half. I remain your loving

Academic Toto"

(Chekhov, letter to Olga Knipper, January 21, 1901, Nice)

My dearest, most wonderful woman:

I didn't go to Algiers after all. The sea was too rough and my companions refused to go. So I'm giving up and returning to Yalta. Anyway, they say it's supposed to be warm there, and meanwhile Mother is alone.

I'll send my photograph to you.

[...] You wrote to me that in Act III of 'The Three Sisters' you lead Irina by the hand...Whatever for? Is it in the mood of the moment? You shouldn't get up from the sofa. Shouldn't Irina come to you? Really! Colonel Petrov [a military advisor to 'The Three Sisters'[2]] has sent me a long letter, complaining about Fedotik, Rode and Solyony; he also complains about Vershinin, and his lack of morality in carrying on with another woman! I do believe, however, that he's done what I asked him vis à vis their military uniforms. Meanwhile, he has praise for the three sisters and for Natasha, as well as Tusenbach.

I kiss you.

Signed, Priest Antony"

(Chekhov, letter to Olga Knipper, January 24, 1901, Nice)

"My dearest, most marvelous darling:

I embrace you and send you hot kisses. I've been traveling for fifteen days, receiving no letters, thinking you've fallen out of love with me—and suddenly they all appeared—from Moscow, from Petersburg, and from abroad. I left Italy for Yalta early because there was snow and it was cold and because life was suddenly dreary without your letters and no news. I found out about 'The Three Sisters' here in Yalta—in Italy, I only got hints. I had the impression it had flopped because everyone who read the newspapers kept quiet and meanwhile Masha was gushing praise in her letters. Never mind.

You ask when shall we see one another?... I don't know, we'll figure it out, my marvelous clever one, my famous little Jewess.

I kiss my darling once again.

Your monk, Antony"

(Chekhov, letter to Olga Knipper, February 20, 1901, Yalta)

"Hello, my little darling! I'll certainly come to Moscow, but I don't know if I'll go to Sweden with you this year—I'm not sure. I'm tired of roaming around, my health is like an old man's—and anyway, I'd look more like your grandfather than your husband. I while away the days in the garden, the weather is marvelous and warm, everything's in bloom, the birds sing, we have no company, no life, but plenty of raspberries. I've put literature aside entirely, and when we get married, I'll make you give up the theatre and we'll live together like farmers. Wouldn't you like that? Keep acting for five more years, and then it will be clear.

[...] Write me, my dear darling, your letters give me such joy. You're deceiving me, because, as you put it, you're a human being and a woman. So fine, deceive me then, only stay the good, glorious person that you are. I'm an old man, too old to deceive you, I know that very well, but if in fact I should, then you'll forgive me, since you understand that while there may be grey in my beard, there's a devil in other parts, right?

[...] I embrace you, traitress, a hundred times, I kiss you passionately, Write, write, my joy, or when we're married, I'll beat you.

Your Wise Old Man Antoine"

(Chekhov, letter to Olga Knipper, March 16, 1901, Yalta)

"My darling, glorious Knippschitz:

[...] I'll be in Moscow in early May, and if possible, we'll get married and go down the Volga or else take a trip down the Volga first and then get married, whichever you prefer... Wherever you want to go, we'll go. I'll spend most of the winter in Moscow in the same apartment with you. As long as I stay well... My cough saps all my energy, I think only vaguely about the future and have no desire to write. You do the thinking about the future, be the mistress of my house, and I'll do whatever you say—otherwise we won't live, we'll swallow life at the rate of a spoonful an hour, and that's all.

So you don't have any new roles to play? That's nice... It's raining today, there's an awful wind blowing, still it's warm outside, which is very pleasant. My dog is hurt, I have to bandage his paw, and there's a smell of iodine everywhere...

What will I find playing in your theatre now? What's in rehearsal? 'The Wild Duck'? I'd really like to write a four-act vaudeville for the Moscow Arts Theatre, or a comedy. I'll do it, as long as nothing prevents me, although I won't be able to deliver it until the end of 1903.

I'll telegram you, tell no one and come to the station alone. Do you hear? So, goodbye my sweet, my dearest little girl. Don't be sad and stop imagining God only knows what; on my word of honor, there is nothing I'm hiding from you, not even for a moment. Be good, don't be angry.

I kiss you fervently, doggie.

Your Antoine"

(Chekhov, letter to Olga Knipper, April 22, 1901, Yalta)

"Little doggie Olya!

I'm coming in early May... Find a cheap hotel room... If you agree, we'll go down the Volga together...

[...] If you give me your word that no one in Moscow will know about our marriage until it actually takes place, then I'll marry you the day I arrive. For some reason I have a terror of weddings, the congratulations, the champagne, standing around with a glass in your hand and a vague grin on your face. Let's not drive home from the church, but go straight to Evenigorod. Or let's get married there. Think

about it, do, my sweet! You're so clever, they say.

[...] I embrace you, Ol'ka.

Your Antoine"

(Chekhov, letter to Olga Knipper, April 26, 1901, Yalta)

"My precious sweetheart,

I leave Yalta on May 5, or at the latest, on May 10th, according to the weather. Then we'll go along the Volga, in a word, we'll do just as you wish. I'm in your power.

Meanwhile, if you ever marry Vishnevsky, it won't be out of love, but rather out of self-interest on his part. But you may decide that he's not so bad after all—so then marry him. Clearly, he's counting on the fact that you'll soon be a widow, but tell him that I'm vindictive and am preparing a will in which I forbid you from ever marrying again.

Be that as it may, my precious, glorious Olya, we'll be together soon and talk it all over. It's evening now, I feel better than I did before. I'll probably arrive in Moscow in the morning, since there's an express train running, starting from May 4. I'll send a telegram...

Farewell, doggie!

Your Antoine"

(Chekhov, letter to Olga Knipper, May 2, 1901, Yalta)

(Chekhov and Olga were married on May 25.)

"Greetings, dear Masha:

I'm always getting ready to write to you, and then don't, there's so much going on, all busy work, of course. About my having gotten married, you already know. I don't think this will change my way of life in the least, nor the circumstances under which I've lived up until now. Mother is probably saying God knows what, but just tell her that there will be no changes at all – everything will remain as it has been. I shall keep on living as I have and Mother will too; and my relationship with you will remain unchanged—warm and pleasant—just as it has always been..."

Your Antoine"

(Chekhov, letter to his sister Masha, June 2, 1901, Aksyonovo)

"Dear Masha,

Your letter, in which you advise me not to get married, was forwarded to me here from Moscow, and I received it yesterday. I don't know if I've made a mistake or not, but I got married mainly because, firstly, I'm over forty; secondly, Olga comes from an upstanding family; and thirdly, if we ever need to separate, I'll do so without the slightest hesitation, just as if I'd never married at all. She's an independent, self-supporting person. Moreover, this marriage doesn't change my way of life at all, nor of those who have lived and continue to live around me. Everything, absolutely everything, will remain as it has been, and I'll go on living on my own in Yalta just as before.

Your desire to join us in the Ufa province pleases me very much. In fact, if you do decide to come, it would be wonderful. Come in July; we'll stay here and take the cure [mare's milk, "koumiss"], then we'll go down the Volga to Novorossisk, and from there back to Yalta...

I'm sending you a check for five hundred rubles. If you feel it's too much and don't want to keep it at home, then deposit some of it in the bank in your own name...

My humble respects to Mama... Write more often, please.

Yours, Anton"

(Chekhov, letter to Masha, June 4, 1901, Aksyonovo)

"Dear Masha,

I bequeath to you my dacha in Yalta for the duration of your lifetime, as well as the income from my dramatic writings. To my wife Olga Leonardovna I leave my dacha in Gurzuf [near Yalta] and 5,000 rubles. You may sell my real estate [the house in Yalta], if you so wish. Give my brother Aleksandr 3,000; to Ivan, 5,000; and to Mikhail, 3,000... After your death and Mother's death all that remains, except the royalties from my plays, is to be placed at the disposal of the Taganrog municipality for public educational programs. The income from the plays is to go to my brother Ivan and after his death, similarly to the Taganrog municipality. I have pledged 100 rubles to the peasants of the village of

Melikhovo to help pay for the highway... Help the poor. Take care of Mother. Live in peace.

Anton Chekhov"

(Chekhov, letter to his sister Masha, August 3, 1901, Yalta)

"My marvelous wife, my dearest friend,

Yesterday I returned to Yalta, again. Sevastopol was fine—there was a strong wind in the morning, I expected rough seas but there weren't any, and everything is fine. Now I'm at home, sitting at my desk, writing to you. How are you? What have you found in Moscow? How was your reunion with your fellow company members? Write me everything, my glorious girl, I'm thinking of you constantly.

The armchair in your room is gloomy and morose, I'm having it moved into mine. Your room on the first floor is quiet and lonely...

Arseny [the servant] still hasn't shown up...

My clothes haven't been brushed today—your absence is already keenly felt. My shoes haven't been cleaned, either. But don't get upset—I'll get it done. Masha will take care of it...

I love you, my darling, so very much. Send Mother, Uncle Sasha, Uncle Karl, Vishnevsky, Nemirovich, and everyone my regards. I kiss you and embrace you, my precious, priceless one. I bless you. Write, write, write everyday, or else you'll be beaten. I'm a strict husband, and a severe one, too, you know.

Your Antoine

P. S. It rained yesterday in Yalta. Everything is fresh in the garden."

(Chekhov, letter to Olga Knipper, August 23, 1901, Yalta)

"My dearest darling:

[...] Last night I had an attack of something akin to cholera—vomiting, etc., Extremely unpleasant. From what, I haven't a clue... I'm all right now...

You write to me about your kitten Martin, but—brrrrr!—I'm afraid of cats. I do like dogs, though... Anyway, my darling, keep a crocodile if you like, whatever, I'm ready for anything, I'll sleep with the kitten, if needs be.

Farewell, my darling, be well. I kiss you, my doggie...
Your Anton"
(Chekhov, letter to Olga Knipper, August 30, 1901, Yalta)

"Greetings, darling little Olga!

I didn't write yesterday because, first of all, I had so many guests and, second of all, because I had no time. Once the guests all left, I started working on a story ['The Bishop']...

Thank you, my joy, Mother was delighted with your letter. She read it and then she gave it to me to read to her aloud. Then she sang your praises. You write about being jealous, and you may be justified, but at the same time it doesn't become you. You write that Masha will never accept you and so on. That's nonsense! You exaggerate, as usual, your thoughts are silly, and I'm afraid that no matter what you'll end up quarrelling with her. Here's my advice: be patient and don't say anything for a year, and everything will become clear to you. Whatever anyone may say to you, just be reticent. For newly-weds, this non-resistance in the early months will result in happiness. Listen to me, my darling, and be smart about this!...

Write, write, darling, write! I'll never love another woman, ever.

Be well and happy!

Your husband, Anton"
(Chekhov, letter to Olga Knipper, September 3, 1901, Yalta)

"Greetings, my darling doggie:

In your letter you asked about the weather. It's quiet, and warm, but foggy... The garden is in good shape, the chrysanthemums are blooming, the roses too... I've been reading proofs all day yesterday and today – I hate it, and I've just finished once and for all, so they won't have any more to send me.

I haven't felt quite myself yesterday and today... But I'm glad you're well and happy, my darling, it makes my heart lighter. I desperately want you to have a little half-German, to make you happy and fill your life. You must, my darling! What do you say?...

Olya, my wife, congratulate me: I've had a haircut! Yesterday I polished my shoes for the first time since I arrived. But my clothes still haven't been cleaned. Still, I change my shirt every day and wash my hair...

I'm sending you a poster of 'Uncle Vanya' from Prague... I'm living like a monk, and think only of you. And though it's embarrassing to be declaring love at the age of forty, I can't stop telling you, my doggie, that I love you deeply and tenderly. I kiss you, embrace you and hold you close.

Be well, happy, gay!

Your Antoine"

(Chekhov, letter to Olga Knipper, November 2, 1901, Yalta)

"Hello, little actress!

I'm feeling better, there's no blood, but I'm still weak. It's been a long time since I've been eating properly. I think that in two or three days I'll be feeling much better. I'm taking pills, powders...

You write, that you were a little tipsy on the evening of December 8. Oh my sweet, if only you know how much I envy you! I envy your spirit, your youth, your health, your mood, I envy the fact that you can drink without spitting blood. Once upon a time I used to drink heartily, too...

[...] God bless you, don't forget me, don't leave me. I kiss you a thousand times.

Your Anton"

(Chekhov, letter to Olga Knipper, December 13, 1901, Yalta)

"My darling:

You're being silly. Never, as long as I'm your husband, have I reproached you for working in the theatre, on the contrary, I'm overjoyed that it is your work, that you have something to do, that you have a purpose in life, and that you don't talk foolishness, like your husband. I'm not writing to you about my illness, because I'm feeling fine now. My temperature is normal, I eat five eggs a day, drink milk, and then there's dinner which, when Masha is here, is delicious. Keep working, my sweet, don't get wound up, and above all, don't feel low...

Masha is annoyed that you haven't written to her...

So, my little flea, farewell for now, be well! Don't you dare be sad... Laugh. I embrace you, and, unfortunately, not much else.

No letter from you yesterday. How lazy you've become! Ah, doggie, doggie!

So, my darling, my good and glorious wife, I kiss you fervently and embrace you yet once again. I think of you often, so often—think of me, too.

Your Antoine"

(Chekhov, letter to Olga Knipper, December 29, 1901, Yalta)

The rewrites of *The Three Sisters* may have been completed and sent to Moscow, but Chekhov continued to worry. Restless and bored in Nice, he sent anxious letters to Olga, begging for news from the Moscow Art Theatre. The erratic mail delivery from Moscow (from Olga, Stanislavsky and others at the theatre) increased his anxiety and frustration. Letters would be delayed from Russia to Nice for weeks, and Chekhov accused Olga of not writing, not caring, and above all, not sending any news about the progress of the play. "Describe one rehearsal at least," he wrote to her, pleading to report if any lines needed adding or cutting. He accused Nemirovich and the company of thinking the play was dull. Moreover, he predicted that it would be a disaster and that he'd never again write for the Moscow Art Theatre.

When he finally received Olga's letters, however, he became even more distressed. She sent details from the rehearsal room, describing the extraneous touches that Stanislavsky was so fond of adding to Chekhov's plays, ones that irritated him deeply, such as the sound of a mouse scratching in Act II during Masha and Vershinin's first love scene, and so on.

Moreover, Stanislavsky's letters to Chekhov contained questions of interpretation that drove him to distraction. In particular, Chekhov found one of Stanislavsky's directorial ideas—having Tusenbach's dead body carried across the stage at the end of Act IV while the three sisters stand center stage—to be particularly preposterous. Letters flew back and forth between them, and between Chekhov and Olga, on the topic. His alarm was further compounded by a letter from Colonel Petrov, a military consultant to the production, complaining about the verisimilitude of the costumes and other details. Chekhov had insisted that the Colonel attend rehearsals and scrutinize all aspects of military dress and behavior, to ensure that the officers were played realistically and not as caricatures.

As January passed and opening night drew nearer, correspondence intensified between Chekhov and various members of the cast who were writing Chekhov in Nice with anxious questions regarding their roles. He counseled Olga never to play Masha with a note of sadness. "Angry, yes—but sad? No," he wrote.[3] Olga responded, begging Chekhov to settle disputes between her and both Stanislavsky and Nemirovich over her interpretation of the role. In Act III, for example, Nemirovich wanted Olga to play Masha's confession of love for Vershinin with joy, while Olga felt it should be played with tension. Chekhov replied, instructing her to play it quietly, almost as a frank conversation. He even tried to correct some of Stanislavsky's direction long-distance. "You shouldn't get up from the sofa [in Act III]," he wrote her. "Shouldn't Irina come to you? Really!"[4] To other actors, he wrote specific notes down to minute costume details.

Meanwhile, Nemirovich had returned to Moscow from France in January, to find Stanislavsky near exhaustion. It was the first time Stanislavsky was directing a Chekhov play alone without Nemirovich's presence and collaboration, and he was in a state of high anxiety. Moreover, the entire company was suffering from influenza. Feeling that the production needed an objective eye, Nemirovich took over and made some adjustments. He toned down the frantic tone of Act III, delegating more noise offstage while creating a feeling of emptiness onstage. He simplified Stanislavsky's directing, and discarded unnecessary, fussy detail. He recast the role of Vershinin, now to be played by Stanislavsky—and recast the role of Solyony too, now to be played by Gromov. He sent Chekhov a detailed report on the rest of the cast and how their roles were developing. In general, he was pleased with Savitskaya as Olga, Olga Knipper as Masha, Maria Andreeva as Irina, Vishnevsky as Kulygin, and Meyerhold as Chebutykin. Staniskavsky's wife Lilina's interpretation of Natasha especially excited him. He requested a few cuts in the final speeches of the three sisters, and at the same time reassured Chekhov that the play was not overwritten, as he had originally thought.

Chekhov's fortieth birthday (January 17) passed unnoticed. Aware of his anxiety, Masha, Chekhov's ever-loyal sister, attended the first dress rehearsal of *The Three Sisters* and wrote in haste to report how moved she was and how copiously she wept. She especially loved the scene in Act III between the three sisters. (Masha was also pleased to report that she successfully persuaded Olga to get rid of the unflattering red wig that she insisted on wearing in the role.) Masha predicted a great success. Chekhov would not receive that letter for weeks.

As opening night drew near, Chekhov became so restless that he left Nice and journeyed to Italy, visiting Pisa, Florence and Rome with Kovalevsky, a friend. Perhaps because he was convinced that Stanislavsky had once again misunderstood his play, he feared that *The Three Sisters* would be a failure and wanted to avoid news of the audience and critical response. Finally on February 4, four days after the opening in Moscow (January 31), Chekhov received a telegram in Rome from Nemirovich, reporting that the play was a success and that the actresses did well in particular, although the second act felt a bit long. Olga was singled out for praise. Admirers mobbed her at the stage door, or flocked to her flat seeking autographs.

Although he was pleased by Olga's success, Chekhov would soon see through the kindness of Nemirovich and other friends. The truth was that the critical and audience response was mixed, finding the pacing of the play to be slow and the complex characters difficult to comprehend. Chekhov was prepared for this criticism. Nonetheless, he wrote to Nemirovich, saying that he accepted that it was "a failure," and making his characteristic threat that he would never again write for the theatre. The weather suddenly turned cold in Italy, and, abandoning his plans to go on to Naples and Corfu, he sailed for Yalta by way of Odessa in early February.

Later, in his memoirs, Nemirovich would look back on *The Three Sisters* as the best production of the Moscow Art Theatre of any of Chekhov plays, because of the superb ensemble work, and because of Stanislavsky's direction (his best, Nemirovich wrote, despite some of the excesses that had to be toned down). Stanislavsky himself also later wrote that, with *The Three Sisters*, he had made a breakthrough in his understanding of Chekhov's characters and their determination to live despite their deep personal sorrow. As for the dramaturgy of the play itself, Nemirovich praised Chekhov for his fine craftsmanship and for his keen understanding of the specific actors for whom he had written the roles. Nemirovich and Gorky recognized *The Three Sisters* as the most profound of Chekhov's plays to date, but it took the critics and the public several years to agree.

With the announcement that the production of *The Three Sisters* would go to St. Peterburg in February, Chekhov's anxiety increased. He had bitter memories of the St. Petersburg opening of *The Seagull* in 1896—indeed, he never recovered from the scandal of that "failure" on the first night. The intellectual and artistic snobbery of St. Petersburg *literati* filled him with dread, and he warned Olga of it. His irritability increased, along with a growing fear of another disaster. His fears were founded. As it happens, the critics were harsh. One of them published a particularly cruel skit parodying the play, called "Nine Sisters and Not a Single Groom," in which Vershinin's and Masha's love song ("tram tam tam") and Solyony's taunt ("tsip tsip tsip") were included. This particularly upset Chekhov, as it was published in his friend Suvorin's *New Times*. On the other hand, the St. Petersburg audiences loved *The Three Sisters*, and Olga wrote glowing letters of the warm reception there. Gorky saw a performance there, and wrote Chekhov that the play was wonderful, better than *Uncle Vanya*.

Still, Chekhov smarted from the negative St. Petersburg reviews. He begged Olga not to read the newspapers: "Listen to your old wise one," he wrote[5] His bitterness toward St. Petersburg hardened even more. Once again, he threatened Olga that he was giving up writing for the theatre completely, complaining that in Russia (unlike Germany, Sweden and Spain) playwrights are not respected. "My next play will be very very funny, at least that's my intention," he promised.[6] (This is the first mention of his intention to write a "comedy," which later became *The Cherry Orchard*.)

Sequestered at home with his increasing cough, he spent February and March working in the garden, fending off visitors, and writing to Olga, begging her to come to Yalta, tempting her with the promise of perfumes that he brought back from abroad. His correspondence was filled with teasing, love and longing, signed "Your Priest," "Your Monk," "Retired Physician and Part-time Playwright," "Titular Councillor and Cavalier," "Your Toto" [her nickname for him]). He further amused her by inventing endlessly imaginative salutatory terms of endearment, including: "Knippschitz," "red-haired doggie," "glorious girl," "little granny," "poopsik," among others.

It was during the run of the play in St. Petersburg that the question of marriage surfaced in their correspondence. For several years, Chekhov had mentioned marriage jokingly in his letters to others. He continued with this practice after he met Olga. "So you heard I was getting married?" he had written to Suvorin a few months before the opening of *The Three Sisters*. "It's not true. I'm off to Africa, to hunt crocodiles."[7] But Olga's friends were expecting it. In response to the pressure he was feeling, Chekhov demurred, deflecting the issue with joking comments in his letters to her, such as "You need a husband, or rather, a spouse with mutton chops and a hat covered with medals and decorations. Meanwhile, what am I? Nothing much,"[8] or "I'd look more like your grandfather than your husband,"[9] or "You'll give up the stage and we'll live together like farmers."[10] His affectionate diversions ("there may be gray hairs in my beard but a devil in my extremities"[11]) only frustrated her further. She responded with requests that he stop joking. They discussed marriage during her brief visit to Yalta in March, but reached no conclusion. Then Olga threatened not to return to Yalta again in the summer, citing his sister and mother's disapproving glances as being too much to bear.

Finally, in April, Chekhov agreed: "You do the thinking about the future, be the mistress of my house, and I'll do whatever you say, or else we won't live, we'll swallow life at the rate of a spoonful an hour, that's all."[12] He qualified, however, that it would be done with as discreetly as possible, as he hated the fuss surrounding weddings. Still he continued to joke about it. Up until a few weeks before their marriage, he was teasing her about her running off with Vishnevsky.

The events surrounding the marriage of Anton and Olga,

which finally took place on May 25, resembled one of Chekhov's own farcical vaudevilles. The couple asked Vishnevsky (the actor who had played *Uncle Vanya*) to arrange for a little wedding party in Moscow. The guests gathered, but Anton and Olga failed to appeal. While the guests waited at a restaurant in vain, the couple were married quietly in a church on the outskirts of Moscow. Significantly, the groom had not notified his mother or his sister of the event. (Later, he sent a telegram to his mother and wrote to Masha, informing them.) The newlyweds journeyed down the Volga River to a sanatorium at Aksyonovo, where his doctors had ordered him to take a "cure" of koumiss. At the end of June, he returned to Yalta for the summer with his new wife to face his mother and sister.

That summer *en famille* in Yalta was stressful, to say the least. Masha, who had devoted her life to Anton (as secretary, housekeeper, and caregiver) and who was also a close friend of Olga, found herself feeling betrayed, jealous, and depressed. She had written to Anton earlier in the spring, advising him not to marry because of his health, and was devastated to learn that the couple, to whom she had been supremely loyal, had eloped behind her back. Anton's perfunctory telegram to his mother and letters to Masha following his marriage—assuring her that everything would remain as before, even inviting Masha to join them on their honeymoon—upset her even more. While his mother adjusted to the marriage, Masha did not, and her relationship with Olga would never be the same. Even Chekhov's letter to Masha on August 3, outlining his last will and testament and clearly favoring his sister (and other family members) over his wife, did not appease her.

In September, Olga returned to Moscow, and preparations at the Moscow Art Theatre for *The Three Sisters* in the upcoming season began. Reluctant to face the separation once again, Chekhov journeyed to Moscow and attended rehearsals. Frustrated anew by Stanislavsky's fussy direction and excessive realism, Chekhov insisted that he eliminate the sound of doves cooing made by backstage actors as the curtain went up on Act I.

Then Chekhov returned to Yalta, and resumed their correspondence, now as husband and wife. They exchanged each letters every other day, at least—letters filled with love and longing, as well as the daily detail of domestic life (1901 yielded the most voluminous exchange of letters in their six years together). He teased her—was his "little German" falling out of love with him? Was she getting used to living without him? She barraged him with questions. Was he taking care of himself? Was he eating properly? Did he miss her? His letters revealed intense loneliness; gardening was his sole consolation. His habitual joking covered up the progressing symptoms and the realization that he would be an invalid permanently.

As the fall progressed, his letters grew sadder. He wasn't writing and consequently was feeling worthless. "Today I caught two mice. So no one can say that I'm not doing anything," he half-joked.[13] He feared she was tiring of him, that they were growing apart. He wrote about having a child. "I desperately want you to have a little half-German, to make you happy and fill your life. You must, my darling! What do you say?"[14]

Meanwhile, her letters grew livelier, describing a whirlwind of activities that included rehearsals, performances and all-night carousing with the company. He begged her to speak with Nemirovich and Stanislavsky and insisted that she be given the holidays off to join him in Yalta. Stanislavsky refused. Frustrated, guilty, she threatened to give up the theatre. Chekhov calmed her down, saying that would be inconceivable and tried to cheer her with promises to go abroad in the summer. At the same time, he too threatened to give up writing for the theatre. As the letters passed between Moscow and Yalta, it became clear that on the first New Year's Eve of their marriage, Chekhov would spend it in Yalta, alone. "I'll go to bed at nine so as not to see the New Year in," he wrote her. "As you're not here, I don't want anything."[15]

Meanwhile, in the last weeks of 1901, Chekhov received a letter from Nemirovich, saying that he'd heard from Olga that her husband might be starting work on a new play for the Art Theatre, and entreating him to do so. As it happened, several ideas for a new play had been turning around in his head. He had written to Olga earlier in the year about a strong urge to write a full-length vaudeville for the Moscow Art Theatre. "I've been dreaming about writing a funny play in which the devil goes around as a dragonfly," he joked in a letter to Olga later in December.[16]

Clearly, his impulse was to write a comedy. Eventually, under extraordinary circumstances, an idea would take shape in the coming year.

"We get along just fine, as all married people do, God willing..."

(Chekhov', letter to Kniper, December 2, 1902)

1902

"I'm an old man already...."
(Chekhov, letter to Knipper, December 17, 1902, Yalta)

"What a silly fool you are, my darling!

Why are you in such a state, over what? You write that you're worthless, that your letters bore me, that you feel your life is closing in and so on and so on. How silly! I didn't write to you about my next play—not because I have no faith in you, as you write, but rather that I have no faith in the play! It's barely forming in my mind, like the earliest rays of dawn, and even I don't know what it is or what will come of it. Anyway, it changes every day. If we were together, then I'd tell you about it, but I can't write about it, because I'd only write nonsense at this point and then I'd grow cold to it. In your letter you threaten never to ask about my writing, never to interfere in it—why are you doing this, my darling? You're too good, your rage will turn to mercy when once again you realize how much I love you, how close you are to my heart, how I can't live without you, my little silly. Stop moping! Laugh! I'm allowed to mope, because I live in a desert, I have nothing whatsoever to do, I see no one, I'm ill every week... whereas you? Your life is so very full.

[...] By the way, Gorky is writing a new play about life in a homeless shelter ['The Lower Depths'], although I've advised him to wait a year of two and not to rush it. A writer must write, but he mustn't hurry. Isn't that so, my better half?

On January 17, my birthday, I was in a terrible mood—one, because I didn't feel well, and two, because the phone never stopped ringing with congratulations...

You write, saying: don't be sad, we will see each other

soon. Meaning when? Holy Week? Or sooner? Don't upset me, my joy. In December you wrote that you would be coming in January and you got me all excited in anticipation, then you wrote that you would be coming in Holy Week and I told myself to stay calm, to get a hold of myself, and now you're stirring up another storm on the Black Sea. Why?

[...] So, my good and golden wife... remember your husband, in the evening at least as you go to bed. And above all, don't be sad. Your husband isn't a drunk, or a profligate, or a thug. I behave like a perfect German husband: I even wear long underwear.

I hug you 101 times. I kiss my wife endlessly."

Your Antoine.

P. S. You write: 'Wherever I turn, there are walls everywhere.' So where did you turn?!"

(Chekhov, letter to Olga Knipper, January 20, 1902, Yalta)

"Again on a spree, my debauchée?!

Fine, wonderful, in fact, and I love you for it, only don't wear yourself out.

[...] You'll come for two days? That's all? It's like giving a starving man a teaspoonful of milk after forty days' fast. It will merely upset me, give us another separation to suffer—and isn't it better, my darling, for you to delay your coming to until the end of Lent? Just think about it. To come for two days—that's cruel! Two days—that's Nemirovich's gift, is it? Then no thanks!

If I can hold out till February, I'll endure it till the end of Lent. Two days will simply tire you out and unnerve me first with expectation and then again with parting. No, no, no!

[....] I love you, little doggie, I can't help it... I embrace my frivolous one.

Your Ant.

P. S. If you don't give up your intention of coming at the end of Shrovetide, then I'll agree to a five-day visit—no less! Five days, six nights."

(Chekhov, letter to Olga Knipper, January 29, 1902, Yalta)

(Olga paid Chekhov a visit in Yalta from February 22-28.)

"My wife, my darling Olya:

How was your journey? Have you arrived safely? I'm so worried. Your sore spots and the cruel weather have spoiled my entire day, and I won't rest easy until I get a letter from you. Well? For God's sake, write, my darling...

Come back soon. I can't live without my wife...

Your hermit Antony"

(Chekhov, letter to Olga, February 28, 1902, Yalta)

"My darling, my silly little doll, my wily, wicked wife:

Yesterday I didn't receive a letter from you. Meanwhile, I have written to you every single day (except for yesterday)...

I am not writing a play and have no desire to do so, as there are plenty of playwrights around at the moment and working on plays is boring and tedious enough. [...]

Write, little darling, don't be lazy, be a proper wife. I hug and kiss you hard...

Your submissive husband,

Antoine"

(Chekhov, letter to Olga Knipper, March 16, 1902, Yalta)

(Olga had a miscarriage twelve days later on March 29 in St. Petersburg, unbeknownst to Chekhov at the time.)

"My dearest sweetheart:

I'm just going to visit Tolstoy. The weather has been marvelous. Are you getting tired of St. Petersburg? Are you bored? Is it cold there?

[...]Was Gorky's play successful? Well done! [...]

I'm in fine shape. Tomorrow, I'm having my last set of fillings done at the dentist...

And so, my wife, farewell! Soon we shall be together, and none of these dogs can tear us apart till September or October.

I embrace you and kiss you a thousand times.

By the way, was [Ibsen's] 'The Wild Duck' a flop?

Your faithful husband Antoine

P. S. There wasn't a letter from you today."

(Chekhov, letter to Olga Knipper, March 31, 1902, Yalta)

(Olga wrote to Chekhov on March 31 by post, informing him of the miscarriage. He did not receive the letter until April 5, and was consequently unaware of this event for six days.).

Wire with health details.
(Chekhov, telegram to Olga Knipper, April 5, Yalta)

...I'm so worried, telegram every day, I beg of you.
Anton
(Chekhov, telegram to Olga Knipper, April 6, 1902, Yalta)

Nemirovich has arrived. Bring a midwife with you as far as Sevastopol,
Then come alone; telegram me. I wait impatiently.
(Chekhov, telegram to Olga Knipper, April 10, 1902, Yalta)

Dear Konstantin Sergeevich:

Dr. Strauch came to Lyubimobvka [Stanislavsky's estate] today and found that all is well. He only gave Olga one restriction—traveling over bumpy roads and excess movement in general. But he gave her his permission to take part in rehearsals without any reservation, to my great delight. She can start work as early as August 10. She's been forbidden to travel to Yalta, however. I'll go there alone in August, and then return in mid-September and stay in Moscow till December.

I like Lyubimovka very much... The weather is good, the river is fine, we eat and sleep like bishops. I send you thousands of thanks, from the bottom of my heart. I can't remember spending a summer like this. I fish every day, five times a day, the catch isn't bad (yesterday we had fish chowder), and I can't describe how lovely it is just to sit on the riverbank. In a word, everything is delightful. There's only one thing: I'm lazy, I don't do a thing. I haven't started the play yet, I'm only thinking about it. I'll probably start work on it before the end of August.

Olga sends you her greetings... I clasp your hand.
Yours, A. Chekhov"
(Chekhov, letter to Stanislavsky, July 18, 1902, Lyubimovka)

"Dear Aleksei Maksimovich:

I've read your play ['The Lower Depths']. It's original and very good, no doubt about it. The second act is particularly good, and when I read it—especially the ending—I almost jumped for joy. The mood is bleak, heavy, and the audience may walk out of the theatre, so you can say goodbye to your reputation as an optimist. My wife will play [the role of] Vasilisa...

[...] I'm living in Stanislavsky's dacha at Lyubimovka, and I fish all day from morning till night. It's a wonderful river, deep and full of fish. I've grown so lazy it's disgusting.

Olga's health seems to be improving. She sends her heartfelt greetings.

Yours, A. Chekhov"

(Chekhov, letter to Gorky, July 29, 1902, Lyubimovka)

"Home at last, my darling.

The trip was fine, quiet, although quite dusty. I knew a lot of people on the ferry, and the sea was calm. They were overjoyed to see me at home, asked after you, and scolded me for not bringing you. But when I gave Masha your letter and she read it, she was very quiet, and Mother was very sad... Today they gave me your letter; I read it and was quite dismayed. Why were you so cruel to Masha? I gave you my word of honor that if Mother and Masha invited me home to Yalta, it wasn't alone but with you. Your letter was extremely unfair, but it's written and nothing can be done about it, God help us. I repeat: I swear to you that Mother and Masha invited us both—never me alone—and that they have nothing but warm feelings for you.

I'll come to Moscow soon, I can't live here... And I won't be able to write a play here.

[...] I kiss you and embrace you. Be well...

Your Anton"

(Chekhov, letter to Olga Knipper, August 17, 1902, Yalta)

"My dear, my own:

Once again I've received a strange letter from you, heaping all sorts of nonsense on my poor head. Who told you that I didn't want to return to Moscow, that I was leav-

ing for good and would not return in the fall? You know very well that I wrote to you clearly, in the Russian language, that I'd be returning in September for certain and would live with you till December. Didn't I?... I simply don't know what to do with my wife and how to write to her. You write that you tremble when you read my letters, that it's time for us to part, that you don't understand the whole situation... It seems to me, my dearest, that neither of us is to blame for this muddle, but rather someone else you've been talking to. The seed of mistrust – of my words, my movements—has been planted in you somehow—you're suspicious of everything, and I can do nothing about it, I can't. I won't even try to change your mind, it's useless. You write that I am capable of living with you and saying nothing, that I need you only as a pleasant female companion, while you are in effect living alone, a stranger to me... My sweet, dearest darling, you are my wife, you know you are, for heaven's sake get it into your head once and for all! You the nearest and dearest person to me on earth, I love you without limit and always will...

I'm feeling better, though I'm coughing terribly. There's no rain, and it's hot... You write that I should show Masha your letter; thank you for trusting me. By the way, Masha is guilty of absolutely nothing, you'll come around to seeing it sooner or later.

...When you arrive in Moscow, send me a telegram... Don't forget my fishing rod; wrap it up in paper. Be happy, don't be sad, or at least try to look happy... If you can drink wine, let me know, and I'll bring some. Write, if you need money, or if you can last until I arrive....

We're catching mice.

Write and tell me what you're doing, what roles you're playing, and which ones you're learning. You're not as lazy as your husband, are you? My darling, be my wife, be my friend, write me cheerful letters and stop being melancholy, don't torture me, please. Be a good and wonderful wife, the kind you really are. I love you more than ever, and as your husband I am blameless—understand that once and for all, my joy, my little scribbler.

Farewell, be well and happy. Write me every day, for certain. I kiss you, poopsik, and embrace you.

Your Anton"

(Chekhov, letter to Olga Knipper, September 1, 1902, Yalta)

"Olya, my sweet little muzzle, greetings!

Judging from your recent letters, you've sunk into a deep melancholy, so much so that you've become a little nun, and meanwhile I'm longing to see you! I'll come soon, soon, and I repeat—I'll live with you till you throw me out...

[...] You write that if we were to live together inseparably, that I'd grow tired of you, and would take you for granted, like a table or a chair... I don't know about that, my darling—I only know that the longer we live together, the broader and deeper my love for you will become. Remember this, little actress: if it weren't for my illness, you wouldn't find a more constant and devoted homebody than I. [...]

Meanwhile, Dr. Altschuller is coming tomorrow to examine my chest for the first time this fall. I've kept putting him off, but now it's become too awkward. He keeps frightening me, threatening to write to you. (Everyone here in Yalta for some reason thinks that you're very strict and domineering.)

What else, then? I kiss my little bug... I stroke your back and embrace you. Farewell!

Your Anton"

(Chekhov, letter to Olga Knipper, September 20, 1902, Yalta)

(Chekhov was in Moscow with Olga from October 14 to November 27).

"Greetings, my little actress!

[...] I'm writing a story... I'd rather be writing a vaudeville, but I can't seem to get around to it; anyway it's too cold to write—it's so cold, in fact, that I'm resorting to pacing around the rooms in order to warm up. It's far warmer in Moscow. There's not a ray of sun. One consolation: the days are getting longer, and soon spring will come.

My nails have grown long, but there's no one here to cut them.... I broke a tooth. A button fell off my vest.

During the holidays, I'll write you once a day—even twice—so you won't feel sad.

[...] I hug my respectable, intelligent, unusual, superb wife, I pick her up, twirl her around, turn her upside down and hug and kiss her fiercely.

Your A.

P. S. My mother thanks you for the hat. She likes it very much."

(Chekhov, letter to Olga Knipper, December 12, 1902, Yalta)

"My sweetheart, my poor old doggie:

You'll have children, or course you will, the doctors say so. All you need to do is to regain your strength. You're in good health, so don't worry, all you need is to have your husband with you for a whole year. So come what may, I'll find a way to live by your side; you'll have your little boy who will break your dishes and pull your dog's tail, and you'll watch and be comforted.

Yesterday I washed my hair and caught a chill, most likely, because I can't seem to get down to work today. My head hurts. I went into town for the first time; it was deadly, all you see are people who look like rats, there isn't one decently dressed woman.

As soon as I get down to writing 'The Cherry Orchard' I'll write you, doggie. In the meantime, I'm working on a story, but it's not very interesting, not to me, at least. In fact, it's boring.

In Yalta the grass is green. It's lovely to look at, when there's no snow. [...]

There's a cruel gale blowing. [...]

The pig you gave me has a torn ear.

So, light of my life, God bless you, be good, don't be sad, don't be melancholy, and remember your husband every once in a while....I hug and kiss you a thousand times.

Your Anton"

(Chekhov, letter to Olga Knipper, December 14, 1902, Yalta)

"My dear little friend:

I received a telegram from Stanislavsky saying:

'Gorky's play and the theatre have had a huge success. Oga Leonardovna gave a stellar performance to a very discerning public.' Celebrate, my sweetheart! Your husband is very proud and would drink to your health, if only Masha would bring some schnapps.

... Today the weather is gloomy; it's warm and there's still no breath of spring. I've been sitting on the balcony in the sun thinking of you, and Fomka [the dog], and crocodiles, and the lining of my jacket which is torn. And I thought how much you need a little son to occupy you and fill your life. A son or daughter—you shall have one, my own, believe me, you only need to wait and regain your health. I'm not lying, and I'm not hiding one word of what the doctors say, I give you my word.

Misha sent some herring. What else can I say? We have many mice again. Every day I catch them in a mousetrap. Apparently, the mice have gotten used to this arrangement—they seem to accept it good-naturedly, and are no longer afraid. There's nothing to write about, life goes along dully and colorlessly.

I cough. I sleep well, but dream all night, as lazy-bones are wont to do.

Write me, little one, write in detail, so that I feel that I'm not in Yalta, but rather in the north, and that this joyless, colorless life hasn't swallowed me up. I dream of coming to Moscow no later than the first of March, that is in two months, but who knows if that's what's going to be. God bless you, my good wife, my red-haired doggie. Imagine that I'm scooping you up in my arms and carrying you around the room for an hour or two, kissing and embracing you...

... Think of your husband.

Your A."

(Chekhov, letter to Olga, December 20, 1902, Yalta)

In the turbulent year of 1902, unexpected, traumatic events in Chekhov's personal life would consume all his energy and attention, eclipsing his artistic activities.

Signs of trouble surfaced as early as January. There were Olga's letters, describing her fast and furious lifestyle, with back-to-back rehearsals, performances, and dinners. She would stay out all night with the cast at parties, drinking champagne and eating caviar. She would return home at nine in the morning with a few cast members, drink coffee, sleep till noon, then go off to rehearsals and hair dresser appointments. Chekhov responded to this news indulgently and good-naturedly, chiding his "dissolute wife," as he called her in his salutations, begging her to come home early and go to bed. But behind his teasing was the edgy question: "You are being a good little wife, aren't you?," which became a leitmotif in his letters. She would respond with self-reproach—that she wasn't a good wife, that she didn't deserve him, that her devotion to the theatre was selfish, that it was taking her away from him, and so on. She protested that Stanislavsky was working her too hard, and that she couldn't come to Yalta over New Year's to be with him. At the same time she complained that she felt excluded from Chekhov's life as an artist, and that he shut her out of his inner thoughts.

Letters from others corroborated Olga's mercurial behavior. Masha wrote, expressing disapproval of her brother's leniency toward Olga's life style, and reporting on Chekhov's name day (January 17) that Olga was out carousing past dawn with a crowd of men from the theatre. Even Stanislavsky's wife Lilina mentioned jokingly in a letter to Chekhov that Olga was flirting with her husband. Chekhov responded to Lilina with humor, as if to deflect the implications of her message: "Thanks to you, I shall now take measures to start divorce proceedings. I'm sending the initial papers off today with your letter enclosed, and come spring I imagine that I'll be a free man. But before May, I plan to take my wife in hand."[1] As for Stanislavsky, he himself noted that the décolleté of Olga's rehearsal clothes caught the attention of the theatre owner. Meanwhile Olga continued to write, lamenting their separation, indicating that she had physical needs. Couldn't he come to Moscow? She said she felt lonely, though she was constantly surrounded by people.

Then, in February, Olga wrote a letter to Chekhov, filled with shame. After several evasions, she revealed that she had debts, serious ones, in the amount of 7,000 rubles. She begged Chekhov to use the 8,000 royalty he had just received from the Moscow Art Theatre to pay off her debt. Chekhov complied.

Meanwhile, acknowledging that the stress of their separation was taking a toll on Olga, Nemirovich finally succumbed and allowed her to visit Chekhov in Yalta at the end of February for two days. At first Chekhov protested, saying that a long journey for such a short stay would hardly be worth it, that they could hold out till Easter, and that if she came, they would only have time for farewells. She finally convinced Nemirovich to give her a longer break, and so she journeyed south to Yalta. They spent five days together (February 22-28) in seclusion. Then on March 1, on the train journey back to Moscow, Olga wrote to Chekhov with reports of pains in her abdomen, nausea, and weakness, and said that a fellow traveler suggested she might be "expecting."[2]

No more was mentioned of her condition in their exchange of letters in March, save for one oblique reference, obscured in a typically jocular comment. "So soon you'll be a famous actress?" Chekhov wrote Olga. "The next Sarah Bernhardt. Will you drop me? Or will you hire me to count your box office receipts? P.S. I have no objection to your becoming a famous actress and earning 25-40,000 rubles a year, only first try to have a little Pamphil" (the name they had invented for the child they'd been hoping to have one day).[3]

Meanwhile, Olga was in St. Petersburg, performing every single night. Chekhov was distracted by the political storm surrounding Gorky's election to the Academy of Sciences, which had been annulled by the government because of his political views. Friends were pressuring Chekhov to resign from the Academy in protest. Olga's letters to him in March were filled with reports of her successes on the stage, accompanied by exasperation with the theatre and longing for him. He, in turn, wrote of loneliness, restlessness, and dreams of their upcoming summer together.

Then, after March 29, her letters stopped. Meanwhile, Chekhov wrote regularly during that last week of March, about trips to the dentist, a visit to Tolstoy, and other quotidian detail. "Hello, my little debauchée," he wrote jokingly. "No letter from you today" was the leitmotif, as he worried about her silence.

Then on April 5 he finally received Olga's letter from St. Petersburg dated March 31, revealing that apparently she had been pregnant, but didn't know it, even though she kept feeling ill. On March 29, she realized she was having a miscarriage. Two doctors were summoned, she was taken to a clinic, given chloroform, and operated on at midnight by Dr. Ott and an assistant. The company had been visiting her, so there was no need to worry. How sorry she was that was to be no little "Pamphil," she said.

Upon receiving her letter, Chekhov telegrammed her in great alarm and agitation, demanding details. He wanted desperately to come up to St. Petersburg, but everyone agreed it would be best (because of the harsh northern weather) that Olga convalesce in Yalta, and journey down as soon as she was able. Stanislavsky telegrammed him, promising there was no danger, and meanwhile Nemirovich and his wife journeyed down to Yalta on April 6 to reassure Chekhov.

Meanwhile Olga had written a second letter dated April 4, saying that she was having terrible pains in her left side due to an inflamed ovary. She reassured him that she wasn't in danger, and begged him to tell Masha and his mother. She was inundated with flowers and visitors—all this reported on the day before Chekhov received her first letter, informing her what had happened.

The fact that Olga delayed sending a letter for two days after the procedure raises several provocative questions. Why had Olga written, rather than telegrammed, with this urgent news? What was her reluctance in letting Chekhov know about the miscarriage? Why did the Petersburg surgeons perform an emergency operation in the middle of the night for an early miscarriage? According to biographer Donald Rayfield, her symptoms (intermittent bleeding, ovarian pain, swollen abdomen, peritonitis) indicated an ectopic pregnancy, which typically occurs eight to twelve weeks after conception. If this were the case, the biographer indicates, conception would have occurred before Chekhov and Olga's reunion in Yalta at the end of February.[4]

Meanwhile, Olga wrote several more letters to Chekhov from the Petersburg clinic, filled with guilt and remorse. The company rallied around her. Moskvin, one of the actors, tried to cheer her with a joke: "Our leading lady is in disgrace: to have a child with such a great man and lose it smacks of carelessness."[5] He meant well, but the joke fell flat and made her feel worse. Olga left the clinic on April 6 and journeyed south to Yalta on the train, accompanied by a midwife, at Chekhov's insistence. She arrived with a high fever and in terrible pain. She had to be carried off the steamer on a stretcher to Chekhov's house, where she remained until the end of May.

So began the most difficult chapter of their marriage. The convalescence was strained, and yet they put on brave faces. Olga was depressed and defensive, imagining that Masha and Chekhov's mother blamed her for losing the baby (even though Masha lovingly helped take care of her). With his typical discretion and tact, Chekhov did not speak of their loss. Whatever his thoughts may have been on the entire episode, he kept them to himself. Any questions he may have had would remain unanswered.

Then on May 24, they journeyed together to Moscow, where Olga fell acutely ill again. The diagnosis was peritonitis, and a second operation was threatened. Chekhov cared for her, never leaving her side, but his health was failing, too, so the actor Vishnevsky (who played Uncle Vanya) volunteered to look after them both, together with Nemirovich, who visited every day. (In anticipation of a long convalescence, Stanislavsky had already hired Vera Kommissarzhevskaya, the original "Nina" in the ill-fated St. Petersburg production of *The Seagull* in 1896, to take Knipper's place in the upcoming season.)

Meanwhile, Chekhov's vigil over the ailing Olga took its toll, and his own health declined. In keeping with his pattern of behavior, anxiety over his health made Chekhov restless, and he longed to escape the unrelieved tension of the past traumatic months. Using the excuse that he needed to think about the next play for the Moscow Art Theatre, he left Olga in his mother and Vishnevsky's care, and set off on June 5 with Savva Morozov (the theatre's benefactor) to the Urals for a holiday, retracing the honeymoon route of the previous year. This episode was puzzling. Why had he left Olga's side? Was he suspicious of the pregnancy? Mistrustful of a potential liaison Olga may have had with another? Heartbroken over the miscarriage? Or simply exhausted from the emotional upheaval of that year?

During that trip, it was clear that Chekhov's illness was progressing to an advanced stage. Still, he relished the time there, especially in the company of Tikhonov, a young writer whom Morozov asked to serve as Chekhov's companion while Morozov returned to Moscow on business. They walked in the forest together, fished, and talked of politics and writing. Tikhonov was greatly affected by these conversations, and deeply moved by the dignity with which Chekhov endured his illness. Tikhonov described Chekhov as an invalid, with a sunken chest and graying hair. He shuffled along like an old man, stopping often to catch his breath. Tikhonov was awakened one night to hear Chekhov's terrible coughing in the next room. He found him convulsed and breathless, blood spurting out of his mouth. Chekhov apologized for keeping him awake. He returned to Moscow, to Olga's side, on July 2.[6]

Then came the invitation from Stanislavsky that Olga and Chekhov should spend the summer convalescing at his country house in Lyubimovka, a lovely spot near Moscow surrounded by woods and meadows. There they spent two happy months. Olga regained her strength walking and rowing on the river, while Chekhov fished and took notes for the next play. The coterie of personalities on the estate gave him rich source material—an English governess who spoke halting Russian, a clumsy servant named Yegor who attempted in vain to speak with erudition, and a pert serving girl named Dunyasha. Olga and Chekhov indulged themselves in the bounties of the region—freshly caught fish, fresh milk, and wild mushrooms. "We're eating and sleeping like archbishops," he reported to Stanislavsky.[7]

Still Chekhov was restless. He experienced two more hemorrhages, which he hid from Olga, who had in the meantime been given permission by her doctor to return to rehearsals.

In mid-August, he returned to Yalta—a decision which sparked an open conflict between Olga and Masha, and put the marriage to its second test. Olga wrote an angry, hurtful letter to Masha in Yalta, accusing her and her mother of inviting her husband to return to Yalta alone without her in a deliberate attempt to cause a rift in their marriage. Chekhov read the letter and was horrified by Olga's anger and cruel accusations, as well as those she meted out to him, saying he had abandoned her while she was ill and that he had returned to Yalta alone because he wanted them to part. "But I've been with you since Easter," he pleaded, "never leaving your side for a moment, and wouldn't have ultimately done so had I not begun spitting up blood."[8] As for her treatment of his mother and sister, he wrote Olga, calling her letter to Masha rude and unfair. These would be the sharpest words he would ever use in their marriage. "You must always be pure and fair-minded, after all, you're such a good and compassionate person. Forgive me, my sweet, for saying so, I'll never do it again," he wrote, attempting to soften the blow of his words.[9]

Once again, Chekhov found himself in the middle, attempting to placate both his wife and his sister. He wrote warm, loving, letters to Olga in Moscow, filled with endearments and reassurances that he loved her, that they would certainly have children—reassurances that he sensed she needed. "Don't leave me yet," he entreated her, "not until you've given me a little boy or a little girl. Then you can do whatever you want."[10] Still, marital relations were strained. Behind the warmth and reassurances of his letters, there was the sense that Chekhov was relieved by the respite from the emotional turbulence of the year. While he lamented his solitude in Yalta, he seemed to find peace from it. As Olga often noted, he remained, in a sense, detached from those closest to him (while seeming to be intimate), and his innermost feelings were inscrutable.

Meanwhile, the Moscow Art Theatre was experiencing its own turbulence. By now, the company had established itself as the premiere Russian theatre, and Savva Morozov, the company's patron, was putting up money for the purchase and renovation of a new building. At the same time, a rift was developing between the theatre's co-founders, Stanislavsky and Nemirovich—one that would have long-term implications. Firstly, Morozov was taking more and more control over the daily operations of the theatre—a development that Stanislavsky supported and Nemirovich opposed. Secondly, the Art Theatre's much anticipated production of *Julius Caesar*, with Stanislavsky as Brutus, was not a success. The co-founders clashed over artistic issues, and exchanged angry letters. Thirdly, the concept of the theatre as an "artistic collective," upon which the co-founders had agreed, was going awry. Some but not all members were invited to become shareholders, and this exclusionary policy found the principals on opposite sides of the issue—Stanislavsky in support, and Chekhov and Nemirovich emphatically against.

Back in Yalta, Chekhov turned to other matters, namely the "Gorky case," and his ultimate decision to resign from the Academy of Science in protest over Gorky's exclusion. As for writing his new play, despite the constant pressure from Olga, Stanislavsky and Nemirovich, Chekhov chose instead to refine his vaudeville *On the Harmful Effect of Tobacco*. His favorite work, this would be the fifth time he would revise it, ever in search of finding the right tragicomedic balance in its tone.

By the fall, Olga had fully recovered, and Chekhov was anxious: "What does Dr. Strauch say about your trying again to have children? Now or later?," he wrote. "Ah, my darling, my darling, time is passing! By the time our child is a year and a half, I'll most likely be bald, gray, and toothless, and you'll look like your Aunt Charlotte."[11] He wrote in September that Dr. Altschuller found his health improved and that he could come visit Olga in Moscow. "My jackets and trousers are worn," he wrote her. "I'm beginning to looks like a poor relative… You'll be embarrassed to be seen on the streets of Moscow with me, so I'll just walk along, pretending we don't know each other—not until we buy some new trousers."[12] Thinking that a visit would stimulate work on the new play, he traveled north on October 14, and plunged into Moscow life, frequenting restaurants and theatres, visiting with Gorky, the singer Chaliapin, and Diaghilev, founder of the Ballets Russes. He saw performances of *Uncle Vanya* and *The Three Sisters* at the Moscow Art Theatre.

But after six weeks, the coughing bouts became too much for him, and he had to return to Yalta at the end of November. He had stayed in Moscow long enough to leave with the hopes of her becoming pregnant again. But Olga wrote him on December 9 with disappointing news in that regard. He responded, reassuring her that she would have a "half-German" one day, but he was tired—of commuting from north to south, of keeping his and Olga's spirits high, of fluctuating climates and fluctuating health, and of his inexorable downward spiral.

"It's cold here, and the silence is oppressive," he wrote Olga.[13] Dispirited, he tried to resume work on *The Cherry Orchard*. But the traumas of the past year had taken a toll, and he was unable to get into a writing rhythm. He offered all kinds of excuses: a gale was blowing, the pipes were broken, the house was too cold to work. "Tomorrow I'll sit down and write," he promised. "I'll write from morning to dinner time and after dinner till bed. I'll send you the play in February."[14] Still, he procrastinated. "All I feel like doing is to lie in bed and eat sweets," he wrote Olga.[15] He couldn't seem to concentrate; instead, he wrote to Olga, reassuring her of his love, reiterating his loneliness, and attempting to cheer her with his endlessly inventive new endearments ("my chubby one," "my philosopheress, "*Frauchen*," "baby baboon," "my little muzzle," "my perch," "my Astrakhan," "my little bug," "my crocodile," etc.). In answer to her questions, he reported: "I take cod liver oil regularly, in fact it's my only activity."[16] His restlessness returned. Already he was dreaming of returning to Moscow, and asked her to order a new fur coat. "Without a light fur coat I'll feel like a tramp…" he joked.[17]

But it was December, and he had to remain in Yalta. By Christmas he was suffering from pleurisy, and Masha came down to Yalta to care for him. And so he faced another New Year as an invalid, without his wife.

"...MY DARLING: HOW HARD IT WAS FOR ME TO WRITE THAT PLAY..."

(Chekhov', letter to Olga Knipper, October 14, 1903)

1903

"Happy new year, my little actress, my wife!

I wish you everything your heart desires, everything you deserve, and above all I wish you a little half-German who will rummage through your closets and smudge ink all over my desk, to your delight.

[...] Write to me, my own, comfort me with your letters. My health is superb. I got a tooth filled. In short, everything is fine, more or less. Except I'm without a wife.

[...] They're calling me to tea now. Be well and happy, little actress, God be with you. I kiss, embrace and bless you.

Your Anton"

(Chekhov, letter to Olga Knipper, January 1, 1903, Yalta)

"My own:

You write that your conscience torments you because you live in Moscow, and not with me in Yalta. But just think: if you lived with [me] in Yalta all winter, your life would be spoiled and I would feel guilty, and that would hardly be an improvement. I knew very well that I was marrying an actress— meaning that you'd be spending the winter in Moscow. I don't feel hurt or neglected—not for a millionth of a second—on the contrary, it seems to me that everything is fine, or at least as it should be, so have no regrets, my darling. We'll be together again in March and won't feel the loneliness we're feeling now. Be calm, my own, don't worry, just wait and hope. Hope, and nothing more. [...]

Your spouse. A."

(Chekhov, letter to Olga Knipper, January 20, 1903, Yalta)

"Little actress:

I haven't heard from you in two days. You've deserted me, is that it? Or don't you love me any more? If that's the case, then write, and I'll send you your nightgowns that are hanging in my closet, and you can send me my galoshes. But if you still love me, let's leave things as they are.

Shapovalov [the Yalta architect] arrived yesterday, bringing my peppermints and the Order of the Seagull from Stanislavsky. I'm eating the peppermints and I've hung the seagull on my watch chain....

It's forty-seven degrees in my study, no more. Arseny doesn't know how to heat stove, and it's cold out—first wind, then snow, with a high wind that won't let up. I can manage to write six or seven lines a day—I couldn't do more if my life depended on it.

[...] Why don't you write to me, my sweetheart? Are you angry? If so, why? Without your letters I'm anxious and depressed. If you're angry, never mind, write anyway. And if you can't manage a kind letter, then write an abusive one.

[..] And so I kiss you on your neck and both hands, and tenderly embrace my joy. Be well, laugh, live in hope.

Your passionate husband"

(Chekhov, letter to Olga Knipper, February 5, 1903, Yalta)

"My superb little sweetheart:

You've sent me your address at last... Then this morning I received a tear-stained letter from you...with no address! I was ready to divorce you on the spot, but then your telegram arrived at noon!

[...] I'll come to Moscow the week after Easter, before your return from St. Petersburg, and meet you not at the station but at home, after I've been to the baths and done some work on the play. It's not going well, by the way. One of the main characters isn't fully developed yet, so I'm a little blocked. But by Easter, I think, the character will be clearer and I'll be past the difficulties.

[...] I'll write again tomorrow. Don't talk nonsense—you're not in the least to blame that we don't live together in the winter. On the contrary, we're a solid married couple, and do not interfere in each other's work. You do love the

theatre, don't you? If you didn't, it would be another matter... We'll be together soon, and I'll hug and kiss you forty-five times. Be well, little one.

Your A."

(Chekhov, letter to Olga Knipper, March 18, 1903, Yalta)

(Chekhov arrived in Moscow on April 24 to be with Olga. He returned with her to Yalta in July, and she left for Moscow in mid-September).

"How cruel of you, my sweetheart!

All yesterday, all last night, all day today, I've been waiting for your telegram... I thought the boat had sunk, or that you didn't have a ticket, and so on and so on. That's not right, my better half... Don't make promises you can't keep.

I feel better today, although I still don't feel right. Weakness, a bad taste in my mouth, no appetite. Today I washed all by myself... The water wasn't too cold. I feel your absence keenly. And if I weren't so angry with you about the telegram, then I'd tell you how much I love my little horsey. Write in detail about the theatre. I feel so far from it all, that I've begun to lose heart. I feel dried up as a writer, and every phrase I write seems worthless... I forget to take my pills, even when they're right under my nose.

[...] I kiss you, my little wife, my golubchik. If my letters seem ill-tempered and pessimistic, don't worry, it's all nonsense.

Your A."

(Chekhov, letter to Olga Knipper, September 20, 1903, Yalta)

My darling, horsey:

I've already telegrammed you that the play is finished—all four acts are written. I'm already making a copy. The characters have come out alive, it's true, but as for the play itself, I really don't know. I'll send it to you; you'll read it and you'll see for yourself.

[...] The sea is rough, but the weather is fine...

Regards to Schnapp, and thank him for not frightening you.,..

[…] So, little horsey, I stroke you, and feed you the very best oats and I kiss your forehead and your little neck. God be with you. Write me and don't be too angry if I don't write every day. I'm copying the play….

Regards to all.

Your A."

(Chekhov, letter to Olga Knipper, September 27, 1903, Yalta)

"My horsey:

Don't write depressing letters, and don't forbid me to come to Moscow. Come what may, I shall come to Moscow, and if you won't let me stay with you, then I'll find a hotel somewhere. My health is much better, I've gained some weight, I cough less, and by November I'll be in excellent shape. I'm in fine spirits. I'm copying the play, it will be finished soon, my golubchik, I give you my word. When I'm ready to mail it, I'll telegram you. I promise you that every extra day is worth it, as the play is getting better and better and the characters are clearer. Only I'm afraid that there are parts that the censors will want to cut, and that will be terrible.

My own, my dove, my sweetheart, horsey, don't worry, everything isn't as bad as you think, things are fine. I swear to you a thousand times that the play is finished. If I haven't sent it yet, it's only because I'm copying it slowly and making changes as I go along.

It's raining today, and it's cool. They've brought us two live quails.

Darling, I'll come to Moscow for certain, even if you kill me. I'd have come anyway, even if I weren't married. That way, if I'm run over by a cab, you won't be guilty.

Perform well, diligently, study, my darling, and observe—you're still a young actress. Above all, don't be depressed, for God's sake! […]

I embrace my joy. God be with you, be calm and happy.

Your A."

(Chekhov, letter to Olga Knipper, October 9, 1903, Yalta)

"And so, little horsey, our patience has finally been rewarded! The play is finished, truly finished, and tomorrow, or on the morning of the 14th at the latest, I'll send it to

Moscow. I've also enclosed some commentary. If there are any rewrites needed, they won't be extensive, I don't think. The only problem with the play is that I wasn't able to write it in one spurt but rather over a long, long period of time, so it might feel a little belabored. Oh well, we'll see.

My health is improving, I don't cough too much now. Since Masha has gone, the meals are much worse; today for example we had mutton which I'm not allowed, so I didn't get anything hot to eat... I can manage eggs...

My darling, how hard it was to write that play!

Tell Vishnesky to find me a job as a tax collector. I've written a role for him, but I'm afraid that, after Antony [in 'Julius Caesar'], the part written by Anton will seem very inelegant and awkward to him... Your role is well delineated in Acts I and III but not much more than an outline in the others. But never mind, I won't lose heart. Meanwhile, Stanislavsky has gotten cold feet—and it's a shame. He started out so boldly, playing Trigorin as he liked, but now he's discouraged because Efros [the critic] doesn't praise him.

So my little peasant, don't complain about me, God be with you. I love you and shall always love you. I might even beat you. I embrace and kiss you.

Your A."

(Chekhov, letter to Olga Knipper, October 12, 1903, Yalta)

"What are you complaining about, granny!... I sent for Dr. Altschuller today, I'm sick of my condition... Without you is like being without hands. I feel as if I'm on a desert island.

The play has been sent—you should receive it at the same time you receive this letter... Please give it to Nemirovich, and tell him to telegram me, so I know what he thinks. Ask him to keep its contents a secret, so that Efros [the critic] doesn't find out about it... [...]

Be well, little horsey. Read the play carefully. There is also a horse in my play. I bless you and hug you many times. God be with you.

Your A.

P. S. When you've finished reading the play, read these comments:

1) You'll have to play the role of Lyubov Andreevna, as there is no one else in the company who can play it. She doesn't dress elaborately, but with great taste. She's intelligent, kind, distracted, and gentle to everyone. There's always a smile on her face.

2) The role of Anya must, above all, be played by a young actress.

3) Varya: perhaps Maria Petrovna can play her.

4) Gaev: that's the role for Vishnevsky. Ask him if he knows how to play billiards, and have him write down the terminology of the game. I myself don't play—or rather, I did once, but have forgotten everything. With Vishnevsky's help, I can correct what's necessary.

5) Lopakhin: Stanislavsky

6) Trofimov, the student: Kachalov

7) Simeonov-Pishchik: Gribunin

8) Charlotta: a question mark. I want to give her more lines in Act IV– but last night I had an upset stomach while I was copying it, and I couldn't add anything new. In Act IV, Charlotta plays a trick on Trofimov with his galoshes. Raevskaya can't play the role. They'll have to find an actress with a sense of humor.

9) Yepikhodov: perhaps Luzhsky

10) Firs: Artyom

11) Yasha: Moskvin

If the play will be produced then, say that I'll send rewrites where necessary and requested. I have the time, but, honestly, I'm tired of the play. But if something isn't clear, then write me.

The setting is an old manor house, gentrified and elegant. People once lived there in style, and that should be reflected in the furnishings. Stylish and comfortable.

Varya is rather blunt and foolish, but very good-hearted."

(Chekhov, letter to Olga Knipper, October 14, 1903, Yalta)

"Greetings, my dearest horsey, sweetheart!

I didn't write to you yesterday, because I was waiting anxiously for a telegram all day. Late last night your telegram arrived, and this morning I received a 180-word telegram from Vladimir Ivanovich [Nemirovich]. I was so worried, so afraid. The elements that concern me most are the slowness of the second act and the unfinished quality of the role of Trofimov, the student. After all, Trofimov is always being expelled from the university and sent into exile. How can you dramatize this? [...]

Will my play be performed? If so, when? [...]

The Odessa papers have given a summary of the plot of my play. It doesn't resemble it one bit. [...]

And write me who will play Charlotta. Will it really be Raevskaya? If so, she won't be Charlotta, she'll be unfunny and pretentious...

I have [guests]. They just arrived.

Your A."

(Chekhov, letter to Olga Knipper, October 19, 1903, Yalta)

"My darling little horsey:

[...] Today I received a telegram from Stanislavsky, in which he calls my play a work of genius, thereby overpraising the play and robbing it of the moderate success it would receive under the most favorable conditions. Nemirovich hasn't sent me the casting list yet, but I fear the worst. He's already telegrammed me that Anya resembles Irina, meaning that he wants to cast Maria Fedorovna in the role. But Anya resembles Irina as much as I resemble Burdzhalov. Anya is, above all, a child, happy till the end, unaware of life; she never cries, not once, except for in Act II when she has tears in her eyes... Who will play Charlotta?

[...] When will they put on my play? You'd understand my impatience if you lived, as I do, in this hot Siberia. But I've become accustomed to it, and have learned to work here.

So my horsey, my Hungarian, I embrace and kiss you hard. Don't forget, I'm your husband and have the right to give you a thrashing.

Your A."

(Chekhov, letter to Olga Knipper, October 21, 1903, Yalta)

"Horsey:

You write that Efros [the critic] can't spoil my play with his lies. But all the newspapers are reprinting his article, and today I even saw it in the 'Moscow Courier.' What a beast he is!

You write that Vishnevsky can't play Gaev. Well then, who can? Stanislavsky? Then who will play Lopakhin? They can't give Lopakhin to Luzhsky, not under any circumstances. He'll either play him colorlessly or else like a clown. Luzhsky is supposed to play Yepikhodov. No, please don't take it away from Vishnevsky.

There's absolutely nothing new here. I get up in the morning, get through the day somehow, and in the evening I go to bed and fall asleep quickly, that's about it. Hardly anyone comes to see me.

Nemirovich writes that there are a lot of tears in my play, and also a certain amount of roughness. Write me, sweetheart, and tell me what you think isn't right and what they're saying, and I'll correct it. It's not too late – I could even rewrite an entire act.

So the actors like the role of Pishchik? I'm so glad. I think Gribunin will play him splendidly.

I bow very low before you, darling, I kiss and hug you... I can't wait to get to Moscow—I'm dying for some corned beef and cutlets. And I want to pet my horsey, too.

Your A."

(Chekhov, letter to Olga Knipper, October 23, 1903, Yalta)

"Dear Vladimir Ivanovich:

When I gave 'The Three Sisters' to your theatre, and an announcement about it appeared in the 'News of the Day,' both of us—you and I—were upset.

I spoke with Efros [the critic], and he promised that it would never happen again. And now, all of a sudden, I'm reading that Ranevskaya lives abroad in Asia with a Frenchman, that Act III takes place in a hotel somewhere, that Lopakhin is a kulak, a son of a bitch, and so on and so on... Let's forget this whole affair as soon as possible. Tell Efros that I don't want to have anything to do with him ever again.... Basta!...

[...] I've had an upset stomach and a cough for a while now. My digestive system seems to be improving, but my cough persists, and I don't know whether or not to come to Moscow. I'd love to sit in on rehearsals. I'm afraid that Anya

will speak in a tearful tone (for some reason she reminds you of Irina) and that she won't be played by a young actress. Anya never cries—not once—and nowhere is it written in the play that she speaks in a tearful tone. In Act II she has tears in her eyes, but her voice is lively and gay. Why did you say in your telegram that the play is 'teary'? Where? The only one who's tearful is Varya, and that's because she's a crybaby—that's her nature—and her tears aren't meant to make the audience feel sad. I often write 'through tears' in my stage directions, but this only indicates a character's mood, not tears literally. Furthermore, there is no cemetery in Act II.

I lead a lonely life, my diet is restricted, I cough, I get angry from time to time, I'm tired of reading. That's my life.

[...] Keep well and calm, don't be angry. I look forward to your letters. Not letter, but letters.

Yours, A. Chekhov"

(Chekhov, letter to Nemirovich-Danchencko, October 23, 1903, Yalta)

"My dear little horsey:

....If I had known that Efros's outburst would have had such a bad effect on me, I'd have never sent the play to the Art Theatre. I feel as if mud has been slung all over me.

I haven't yet received the letter that Nemirovich promised. I'm waiting for it; meanwhile Efros has spoiled my mood and I feel awful. [...]

No, I never wanted to make Lyubov Andreevna into someone subdued. Only death could subdue such a woman... It won't be difficult for you to play her. You only have to find the right tone, pick a manner of smiling and laughing, and know how to dress...

[...] So little horsey, I kiss and embrace you. Comfort me with your letters. I love you.

Your A."

(Chekhov, letter to Olga Knipper, October 25, 1903, Yalta)

"Dear Konstantin Sergeevich:

Many thanks for your letter and for the telegram. Letters are very precious to me since, first of all, I'm alone here, and secondly, I sent the play three weeks ago and received your letter only yesterday. If it hadn't been for my wife, I would have known nothing and would be imagining all kinds of things. As I was writing Lopakhin, I imagined that it was your role. If for any reason you don't like it, then take Gaev. It's true that Lopakhin is a merchant, but he's a well-meaning, decent man in every sense of the word, he conducts himself properly, he's intelligent, he's not petty, he doesn't clown around. For me this is a role that is central to the play, and one that you could play brilliantly. If you'd prefer Gaev, then let Vishnevsky play Lopakhin. He won't be an artistic Lopakhin, but on the other hand he won't be a petty one, either. Luzhsky would play him as an aloof foreigner, Leonidov would turn him into a little kulak. So when you are casting the role, bear in mind that Varya, a serious and religious young girl, is in love with Lopakhin—she would never fall in love with a kulak.

I'm longing to go to Moscow, but I don't see how I can leave here. It's getting cold, and I almost never go out. I'm not used to the outdoors, and cough all the time. It's not Moscow that I fear, but rather the journey, and the layover in Sevastopol that can last from two to eight hours, and in the most tedious company.

Write and tell me what role you've decided to play. My wife wrote that Moskvin wants to play Yepikhodov. That's fine—and the play will only profit from it. I send you my very best regards, and wish you the best. Stay well and happy. I haven't yet seen 'The Lower Depths', 'Pillars of Society' or 'Julius Caesar' and am very eager to do so.

Yours, A. Chekhov."

(Chekhov, letter to Stanislavsky, October 30, 1903, Yalta)

"Dear Vladimir Ivanovich:

Two letters from you in one day! Heartfelt thanks! No, I'm not drinking beer, the last time I had some was in July. And I'm not allowed to eat honey either, it's not good for the stomach. And now, regarding the play:

1) Anya can be played by anyone, even an unknown actress, as long as she's young and childlike, and speaks with a youthful, clear voice...

2) Varya is a more crucial role. What if Maria Petrovna

[Lilina] played it? Without her, the role will seem one-dimensional and crude, and I'd have to rewrite it, and tone it down. Tell Maria Petrovna not to worry about being type-cast—first of all, she's a talented actress, and second of all Varya isn't like Sonya or Natasha. She wears a black dress, she's nun-like, not very bright, a crybaby and so on.

3) Gaev and Lopakhin—these roles are for Konstantin Sergeevich [Stanislavsky] to chose from. If he choses Lopakhin and plays it well, the play will be a success. But if Lopakhin is colorless, played by a colorless actor, then both the part and the play will fail.

4) Pishchik: Gribunin. God forbid that the role is given to Vishnevsky.

5) Charlotta: a question mark. You can't give it to Pomyalova, of course. Muratova might be good, but she's not funny. This is Miss Knipper's role.

6) Yepikhodov: If Moskvin wants it, then so be it. He'd make a fine Yepikhodov. I had assumed that Luzhsky would play it.

7) Firs: Artyom.

8) Dunyasha: Khalyutina.

9) Yasha: If Aleksandrov, about whom you wrote, is the one who is your assistant director, then let him play Yasha. Moskvin would be a marvelous Yasha. And I don't have anything against Leonidov, either.

10) The Passerby: Gromov.

11) The Stationmaster, who reads 'The Sinner' in Act II, should be played by an actor with a deep bass voice.

Charlotta speaks proper—not broken—Russian. Sometimes she pronounces a word with a hard rather than a soft ending, or mixes up the masculine and feminine nouns, etc. Pishchik is an old Russian, crippled by gout, old age and gluttony. He's overweight and wears a long coat and boots without heels. Lopakhin wears a white vest and yellow shoes. He takes huge strides, waves his arms, and is always deep in thought. He walks purposefully, in a straight line. His hair is rather long, so he often tosses his head. When lost in thought, he strokes his beard from back to front—that is from neck to chin. Trofimov is clear, I think. Varya wears a black dress with a wide belt.

For three years I've been working on 'The Cherry Orchard', and for three years I've been telling you to engage an actress to play the role of Lyubov Andreevna. And now you're playing a one-handed game that has no hope of resolution.

I find myself in the most idiotic situation. I'm here all alone, and I don't know why. And you're wrong to say that despite all your efforts it's still 'Stanislavsky's theatre'. It's you they write about and talk about; as for Stanislavsky, they criticize his Brutus. If you leave, then I leave. Gorky is younger than we are—he's got his own life... By the way, 'national theatres' and 'national literature'—these notions are utter nonsense. It's not a matter of lowering Gogol's level to the public, but rather raising the public to his.

How I'd love to go the Hermitage, eat sturgeon and drink a bottle of wine. Once upon a time I could drink an entire bottle of champagne myself and not get drunk, and have cognac afterward and still not be affected.

[...] Why is Maria Petrovna [Lilina] intent on playing Anya? Does she think she's too aristocratic to play Varya?... Never mind, let them do whatever they want. I embrace you, be well.

Yours, A. Chekhov"

(Chekhov, letter to Nemirovich, November 2, 1903, Yalta)

"Dear Konstantin Sergeevich:

The house in the play is large and two-storied. And in Act III, they speak of a staircase going downstairs below. I must say that Act III worries me a great deal. In 'News of the Day,' Efros recounted the plot of the play, and in a recent issue confirmed it (with some insolence, let it be said), quoting my letter to Vladimir Ivanovich [Nemirovich]. According to Efros, Act III takes place 'in some hotel or other'...

The house should be large, solid and built of wood... or stone, it doesn't matter which. It is old and grand. Summer vacationers don't rent houses like that. Such houses are usually torn down, and the material is used for summer dachas. The furniture is antique, period, solid; neither wear-and-tear nor debt have touched it.

When people buy a house like that, they say: it's cheaper

and easier to build something new, rather than to renovate something old.

[...] I press your hand, and send my best regards to you and Maria Petrovna. Be well.

Yours, A. Chekhov"

(Chekhov, letter to Stanislavsky, November 5, 1903, Yalta)

"Hello, my darling, my horsey!

There's nothing new, everything's fine. I don't feel like writing, I feel like coming to Moscow, and await your permission.

... I've received letters from Nemirovich and Stanislavsky, who are evidently at a loss. You told them that I didn't like my play, and was fearful about it. Do I write so incomprehensibly, really? My only anxiety is that Simov [the designer] will draw a hotel for the scene of Act III. That mistake must be corrected... I've been writing about this all month, and all I get is a shrug of the shoulders. Obviously, they like the idea of a hotel.

Nemirovich sent an urgent telegram, asking for approval by wire on who is to play Charlotta, Anya and Varya. Three names were listed for Varya – two unknown to me, and Andreeva. It should be Andreeva.

[...] I'm feeling fairly well—except for my intestinal issues. I ought to change my routine and lead a more dissolute life. I should eat everything—mushrooms, cabbage—and drink everything, too. What do you think?

[...] And so, my poopsik, I embrace you. Get me out of here as soon as you can. Aren't you curious to see your husband in a new fur coat?

A.

P. S. Don't write to me about roast duck – don't torture me. When I arrive, I'll eat a whole one."

(Chekhov, letter to Olga Knipper, November 7, 1903, Yalta)

"Dear Konstantin Sergeevich:

Of course there can be one set for Acts III and IV—that includes both the hall and the staircase. And please don't be apologetic about the scenic design. I assure you, I'm always amazed when I sit in your theatre. It goes without saying:

whatever you do will be superb, and 100 times better than what I could have thought up.

Dunyasha and Yepikhodov stand in Lopakhin's presence, they don't sit. Lopakhin carries himself with confidence, like a gentleman, he says the familiar "you" to the servant girl, but she addresses him with the formal 'you'...

[...] If I haven't come to Moscow yet, Olga is to blame. We agreed that I'd come when she orders me to do so. I press your hand; heartfelt thanks for your letter.

Yours, A. Chekhov"

(Chekhov, letter to Stanislavsky, November 10, 1903, Yalta)

"Dear hobby horse:

...Hurry up and summon me to Moscow as soon as possible. It's clear and warm, but I don't care, I don't appreciate these delights, I need the storms and slush of Moscow. I can't live without the theatre and literature any more. Moreover, as you may know, I'm married, and I'd like to see my wife.

[...] No letter from you today. I wired you yesterday about the fur coat.... I'm afraid you're angry. But never mind, we'll make up. There's still time.

The weather is positively summer-like. Nothing is new. I'm not writing anything, I'm only waiting for your permission to start packing to come to Moscow. 'To Moscow....to Moscow'! That's not 'Three Sisters' speaking that's 'One Husband.'

I hug my little turkey hen.

Your A."

(Chekhov, letter to Olga Knipper, November 21, 1903, Yalta)

"Hello, my little Hungarian horsey:

How are you? Will you write to your husband soon?... I sit at home, listening, suffering, and cursing you. To keep me captive here in Yalta – how cruel! [...]

Konstantin Sergeevich [Stanislavsky] wants a train in Act II – he must be stopped. He also wants the sound of frogs and corncrakes. [...]

Be well , my darling... I embrace my little flea.

Your A."

(Chekhov, letter to Olga Knipper, November 23, 1903, Yalta)

"Dear Konstantin Sergeevich:

Haymaking usually takes place from the twentieth to the twenty-first of June, and during that time the corncrake doesn't cry. Frogs too are quiet at that time. Only the oriole's call is heard. There is no graveyard—there was one, a long time ago. Two or three gravestones, lying here and there, are all that remains. A bridge—that's very good. If a train can appear without any sound, then go ahead and do it. I'm not against the same scenery in Acts III and IV, except that it would advantageous to have entrances and exits in Act IV.

I'm waiting impatiently until my wife finally gives me permission to come to Moscow. I'm beginning to suspect her being sly with me...

The weather is calm, warm and gorgeous here, but when you think of Moscow and the baths, all these delights become boring and unnecessary.

I sit in my study with my eye on the telephone. Telegrams are read over the phone to me. I'm waiting for the moment when I shall finally be summoned to Moscow.

I press your hand and am grateful for your letter. Be well and successful.

Yours, A. Chekhov"

(Chekhov, letter to Stanislavsky, November 23, 1903, Yalta)

"Darling:

There has to be a dog in Act I, a small, shaggy one, so Schnapp won't do. It appears that I'm being allowed to come to Moscow in August, not earlier. My strict, severe wife, I'll do anything, I'll starve, I'll salute Nemirovich and Vishnevsky, just please allow me to come. It's awful, living in Yalta... It's time that you and everyone else understand that in Yalta I always feel worse than in Moscow. The sea was calm but now there's a storm, with waves reaching to the sky, and torrents of rain. The weather is so bad that no one can get in or out.

I'll come by sleeping car. Don't bring my coat to the train car, it will be cold, so I'll put it on in the station.

How miserly you've become! Soon you'll be putting used stamps on your letters. Why won't you wire?... I'll give you ten rubles, just don't be mean, wire me, and stop being so stingy.

[...] I embrace you, horsey, God bless you, my joy. And so I wait and wait.

Your A."

(Chekhov, letter to Olga Knipper, November 27, 1903, Yalta)

"Little horsey:

I don't know what to do or what to think any more. There seems to be an unyielding resistance to invite me to Moscow—or else they just don't want me to come. Please write and tell me honestly why this is so, so I won't waste time and can go abroad. If only you knew how dreary it is to hear the rain beating down on the roof, and how I long to see my wife. Do I really have a wife? Where is she?

I can't bear to write any more...

I embrace you.

Your A."

(Chekhov, letter to Olga Knipper, November 29, 1903, Yalta)

It was cold in January—cold and dreary. Chekhov was a prisoner indoors. He celebrated his forty-third birthday by sitting at his desk for the first time since he was diagnosed with pleurisy. But he was still an invalid. Dr. Altschuller forbade him to take walks or go to the baths. "I sit here unwashed, like a Siberian sled dog. I've even started to growl," he wrote Olga. "I'm as grubby as a galosh."[1]

As his vitality declined, his anxiety increased. How was he going to finish *The Cherry Orchard*? The play had been in his mind since the autumn of 1901, when he mentioned it to Stanislavsky as a setting for a future play. Then in 1902, after the news came that the cherry trees at Melikhovo had been chopped down, the title crystallized in his mind. During the summer of 1902 in Lyubimovka, while convalescing and fishing, the motley assortment of servants and guests on Stanislavsky's estate began to give him ideas for characters in the play.

But now, in January 1903, with his health ever deteriorating, he was unable to concentrate. He assured Olga he was working—but in fact that was only to satisfy her constant inquiries, as well as those of Nemirovich and Stanislavsky. The truth was, as he wrote to Olga in February: "I can manage to write six or seven lines a day—I couldn't do more if my life depended on it."[2]

Anxious from her constant inquiries about the play, he tried to her deflect attention away it. "Are you in a bad mood? Get over it, darling," he wrote her. "In your letter, you write that you've lost your looks. You can grow a crane's nose, for all I care, I'd still love you."[3] He entertained her with a never-ending supply of new endearments: "my hobby horse," "my Hungarian horse," "my turkey hen," "my good little dachshund," "little peasant," "little flea," "pony," "dumpling," "chicklet," etc.

Instead, he struggled to finish what was to be his very last story, "The Bride," and found that he could only write a few lines a day of that as well. His stomach was constantly upset. Visitors—Bunin, Gorky and Kuprin—tried to cheer him up, but found him dispirited and distracted. His only comfort was Schnapp, the dachshund that had been given to Olga as a gift. She hadn't wanted it, so a friend brought the dog down from Moscow. The only other good news that cheered him was that Kuba's, a fancy St. Petersburg food emporium, had opened in Yalta, so Olga didn't have to keep bringing down his favorite foods, which he could barely manage anyway. He was desperate to see Olga, desperate to come to Moscow, but the doctors forbade it.

He completed "The Bride" in March, and now there were no more excuses. He had to face finishing the play. But he continued to struggle with it. "Work on the play is not going well," he wrote Olga in March, "one of the main characters isn't fully developed yet, so I'm a little blocked."[4] Or at least that was the reason he gave her. Was there another reason for this reluctance to plunge into work on the play? Was it that he sensed that this play would be his last? His letters were filled with apologies, frustrations, longings, entreaties, all kinds of conflicting emotions. Above all, he repeatedly apologized to her for the wretched illness that kept them apart. "There's no other way, no matter hard we try to think of other alternatives," he lamented. "If you should become pregnant, on the other hand… I'd agree to anything," he wrote her, "even winter in Arkhangelsk, if only you would become a mother."[5]

The block made Chekhov more anxious than ever. Defying doctor's orders, he fled to Moscow at the end of April. There, other distractions awaited him that prevented him from working on the play—negotiating a new contract with his publisher Marx, submitting to more medical examinations, visiting the baths, and correcting proofs for his new collected works. The five flights of stairs that he had to climb to Olga's new apartment were torture. His doctors were deeply concerned—his right lung was in bad condition, and emphysema had spread to the left lung. To Chekhov's surprise, the doctors forbade him to return to Yalta.

At the same time, he and Olga were invited to a friend's estate outside Moscow near Naro-Fominskoe. Stimulated by the early summer air and the atmosphere he had been imagining in *The Cherry Orchard*, he tried to work on the play, but there were too many distractions—reports of pogroms in Kishinev, news of bankruptcy of a close friend (who ended up taking a job in a bank, material he later put in the play in the character of Gaev). He actually completed a new scene, but the pages were lost when they blew out the window during a storm. He fended off Stanislavsky's anxious letters pressuring him about the play. "My play isn't ready yet," Chekhov wrote him. "It's moving along very slowly, owing to my laziness, the marvelous weather, and the difficulty of the subject matter. As soon as it's ready, I'll write you—or better yet I'll telegram. Your role is all right so far, but I'd rather not judge it…"[6] To Nemirovich, he responded similarly, saying he was having trouble with the play but that it would be finished soon, and that he was calling it a comedy.

Working on the play, as he had done for months, in fits and starts only frustrated him more. Chekhov's restlessness returned. Defying doctors' orders, he and Olga returned to Yalta. There, Olga discouraged visitors and stood watch over him, making him write every day when he was able. But despite his and Olga's reassurances to Nemirovich and Stanislavsky that work was progressing, the latter feared that Chekhov's advancing decline in health would affect his creative process.

When Olga left Yalta in late September, Chekhov finally faced the play. After lamenting to Olga in his letters that he was finished as a writer, that he was losing heart, and that his writing was worthless, he returned to the manuscript. As an antidote to his debilitated state, he was determined to write a comedy and focused on the last act, which he wanted to be cheerful and light-hearted. It would even have farcical moments, he wrote Stanislavsky's wife.

Above all, *The Cherry Orchard*, his final play, would be a

montage of memories, culled from his past in the same way as his character Trigorin from *The Seagull* collected impressions in his notebook. The cherry trees in Act I recall those he had seen as a child in Taganrog; the selling of the estate to provide land upon which to build summer cottages is also a Taganrog memory; the breaking string was a sound he heard while fishing on the Psyol River in the summer of 1887; the chopping down of the cherry trees in Melikhovo in 1902 was a recent and vivid recollection. The characters come from prototypes whom he had met in chance encounters (a governess, a footman and a servant girl at Lyubimovka the summer before), and culled from various stories, including Trofimov from "The Bride" and Lyubov Andreevna from "A Visit to Friends."

By now, Chekhov's correspondence was almost entirely to Olga, and the letters he wrote almost daily during the months of September and October reveal a struggle to finish the play that was almost heroic. He could manage only a few lines a day, and yet he was determined. On September 27, he wrote to her that the play was finished, and that he was copying it to be sent to her at the Art Theatre. Still, it took him almost three weeks to do the copying, since he was rewriting as he went along. He wrote almost daily to Olga daily during those weeks to stave off any additional pressure from Nemirovich and Stanislavsky, and to assure her that the play would be finished. These reassurances – in tandem with his reports of weakness and coughing, as well as a lack of confidence in what he was writing—are heartbreaking. "When I send you the play you'll read it and see what it might have been had I written it under more favorable circumstances, in other words, if I were in good health," he wrote Olga, apologetically.[7]

The Cherry Orchard takes place over a summer on the Russian estate of Lyubov Andreevna, an elegant, impoverished landowner, and her brother Gaev. Lyubov Andreevna, who has been living abroad for the past five years with her lover, has returned to Russia with her young daughter Anya and her governess to face a financial crisis. The family estate must be sold to pay off their debts. Lyubov finds her childhood home just as she has left it, occupied by her brother Gaev (who spends his time playing billiards), her adopted daughter Varya (who is desperately trying to keep the household running), and Firs, the family's ancient servant and former serf, who refused to leave after the emancipation. A family friend, Lopakhin (whose father was a former serf on the estate and who is now a wealthy merchant) entreats Lyubov to sell the estate to a developer and subdivide it for summer dachas, thereby saving the family from financial ruin. But Lyubov and Gaev, intent on preserving the memories of their childhood and old way of life, cannot bear the thought of tearing down the house and the cherry orchard. Still, the inevitable happens and the estate is auctioned—to none other than Lopakhin himself, who does a drunken dance of atavistic joy, calling out to his grandfather to come up from the grave and witness that his grandson now owns the estate where he had once been a serf. The members of the household finally disburse to the sound of the cherry trees being chopped down. The old order must make way for the new.

The Cherry Orchard, Chekhov's last play, is a masterpiece in tragicomedy. The childlike naïveté of the old order provokes laughter, while ominous signs—like the strange passerby who disturbs the family's halcyon summer day—indicate that storm clouds are gathering and change is coming. Indeed, the play offers a brilliant vision of the extraordinary change in Russia that spans Chekhov's lifetime—from 1860-1904—including the emancipation of the serfs, the decline of the landed gentry, the migration of the peasant class off the estates to the towns and cities, the rise of industrialism, the formation of a new middle class, the decline of the intelligentsia, and the seeds of revolution. Always subtle, never didactic, Chekhov showed "life as it is,"[8] rather than preached it. And yet the unmistakable signs of change are there. The members of his ensemble in *The Cherry Orchard* each represented a class of Russian society in Chekhov's time—from the landed gentry (Lyubov Andreevna, Gaev, Anya, and their impoverished neighbor Pishchik), to the bourgeois class (Varya, the clerk Yepikhodov), to the serfs (Firs), to the new capitalist (Lopakhin), to the revolutionary (the student Trofimov). They represent all of Russia as Chekhov knew it, poised on the brink of change.

Chekhov also introduced two strange characters whose types had never been seen before in his plays—Charlotta, a governess of unknown origins who entertains the ensemble with magic tricks, and a passer-by, an indigent homeless man who frightens the family with pleas for money as they sit in the fields one summer afternoon. It is not known where either of these characters come from or where they are going, and this uncertainty infuses the play with an element of mysticism, as the other characters of *The Cherry Orchard* also face an unknown future. So does the strange, disquieting sound that disturbs the summer afternoon—one that no one in the ensemble can define. Chekhov's stage directions in Act II describe it as "the sound of a breaking string, dying away in the distance, a mournful sound." The characters wonder amongst themselves: Is it a heron? An owl? "Don't know," says Lopakhin, "Somewhere far away, deep in the mines, a bucket broke loose and fell… But somewhere very far away."[9]

This sound, in fact, is one that Chekhov heard one day while fishing in Babkino one summer in the 1880s. Disturbed by it, he hurried back to the Kiselyov's house to inquire, and was given the explanation that Lopakhin offers above. Like his character Trigorin, Chekhov filed the event away in his writer's notebook, to take it out decades later and use it in his final play. That sound expresses in exquisite economy and clarity the moment in the play where time stands still, where the past and future are rent asunder in one present moment. The ensemble of characters, representing every aspect of Russian life, sit on a hillside, watching the sun go down, the remains of a cemetery to one side (the past) and the indistinct view of a telegraph pole (the future) on the other. Though Chekhov mocked the symbolist movement in his play *The Seagull*, he did in fact use symbol and metaphor to great effect in his subtle, understated way (the seagull and the lotto game in *The Seagull*, the map of Africa in *Uncle Vanya*, the spinning top and the fire in *The Three Sisters*, and so on). With the sound of the breaking string, Chekhov captures the essence of his play – a Russia that is breaking with its past and facing an unknown future.

As in the three previous plays, *The Seagull*, *Uncle Vanya*, *The Three Sisters*, the plot of *The Cherry Orchard* follows the same "non-pattern." People arrive (in this case, Lyubov and Anya, returning from abroad), life happens, and people depart. Only in *The Cherry Orchard*, everyone departs, and no one is left behind – except for Firs, the symbol of the old order, who lies alone in the shuttered house, silent except for the sounds of the axe as the cherry orchard is felled. Chekhov, who scoffed at being called a symbolist, has given us one of the greatest symbols in dramatic literature, as the old order is brought crashing to the ground.

There are several other differences that distinguish *The Cherry Orchard* from its predecessors. There is no love intrigue, no gun (except Charlotta's rifle in Act II, which may or may not be loaded and provides a comedic moment)—nor is there a character of a doctor. But these are superficial details. The most significant difference is that, while life goes on in the previous three plays, in *The Cherry Orchard*, life—as his characters knew it, as his countrymen knew it, as Chekhov knew it—comes to an end.

Finally, on October 12, he reported to Olga that the copying/rewriting was finished, "positively finished," and that he'd send it off by the 14th at the latest. Olga received the manuscript only two days later, on the 16th, and as she wrote in her memoirs, crossed herself three times and brought it immediately to the Art Theatre.

Meanwhile, Chekhov waited in anxiously for a response. Five days later he received a telegram from an ecstatic Stanislavsky, who had read it immediately and wrote that he was overwhelmed, that *The Cherry Orchard* was his greatest play, and that its author was a genius. Then two days later, another telegram arrived from Stanislavsky, reporting that the company had read the play and that everyone had wept.

"Wept?!" Chekhov was dismayed. The play he had clearly subtitled a comedy was now being received as a tragedy by the director/actor whose theatre would produce it and would determine its fate. Stanislavsky's letter the next day, reiterating his conviction that *The Cherry Orchard* was indeed a tragedy, plunged Chekhov into a tailspin of anxiety that his play would be ruined. Unlike any of his previous plays, Chekhov was desperate to involve himself in the creative preparations at the Moscow Art Theatre, determined that this play (which he sensed would be his last) would come to life as he had envisioned. But how to do that while he was trapped in his "hot Siberia," his prison in Yalta? He felt increasingly anxious, irritable, and out of control over a play that mattered to him above all.

During the rest of October and November, Chekhov sent a torrent of anxious letters to Olga, Nemirovich and Stanislavsky, filled with specific instructions about every aspect of the impending production. What about the casting? What about the set? Every report Olga sent him from the rehearsal room threw him into a greater panic. Sound effects? A train in Act II? Frogs, corncrakes? Stanislavsky would ruin his play, he was convinced of it. His distress turned to fury over a petty side-farce—Efros, a leading critic, had somehow gotten word of the plot of *The Cherry Orchard* and had written about it in a publication that was syndicated all over the country. In this article, Efros mistakenly described Act III of *The Cherry Orchard* as taking place in a hotel. This minor misunderstanding infuriated Chekhov, and he began to imagine that the theatre's set designer would follow Efros's description rather than his own.

As letters flew back and forth between the playwright and the theatre, Chekhov's paranoia increased. There was only one solution—to come to Moscow, but the doctors were reluctant to allow it. Chekhov wrote almost daily, instructing Olga to buy him a fur coat and ready the apartment for his impending arrival. These requests alternated with accusations that Olga didn't really want him to come, that she was withholding "permission," and that Nemirovich and Stanislavsky wouldn't want him to sit in on rehearsals.

Looking back on the pre-production weeks of Chekhov's final play, this correspondence is invaluable, as it affords us the vision that he had for his play—and in particular, his view of the characters. During the writing of the play itself, he fretted over the casting, and sent long specific letters of instruction to Olga, Nemirovich and Stanislavsky as to his strong preferences (some of them, he insisted, were non-negotiable). In several instances, however, his ambivalence was apparent, as he fretted over certain roles and actor choices. At first he teased Olga that she should play the part of Varya, the "foolish" young ward of the estate owner, as he described her. Next, he insisted that Olga play the role of Charlotta, the eccentric governess. Finally, he conceded that she should play Lyubov Andreevna, frustrated that the theatre hadn't hired a middle-aged actress to play the role as he'd advised them to do three years ago when he had started writing the play. He remonstrated Nemirovich over this in a letter, saying that there was no one else in the company who could play the role. (Although Chekhov had imagined Lyubov as an "old woman," as he put it, once Olga originated the role at the age of thirty-five, subsequent productions would consistently cast actresses like Olga in the role who were younger than Chekhov had originally intended.)

Similarly, he vacillated over the role that Stanislavsky should play. In some letters, he indicated that he had written the role of Gaev for Stanislavsky. But as the weeks progressed, he urged that Stanislavsky should play Lopakhin because of the importance of the role and the right tone needed to play it. If not, he warned, the play would be ruined and he would be laughed off the stage. He ultimately left the choice to Stanislavsky, who, reluctant to play the role of a merchant (because of his own bourgeois origins), chose the part of the aristocratic Gaev instead. Chekhov was especially sensitive to Vanya and Anya, and in his letters he specified who should play them, as well as the qualities that the actresses should bring to the roles. Again, he would reiterate that if his warnings weren't heeded, the play would fail absolutely.

Ultimately, the ingénue role of Anya would be played by Stanislavsky's wife Lilina at the age of thirty-seven, despite Chekhov's insistence that she be played by a younger actress. (Lilina felt herself too aristocratic to play Varya.) Varya was played by an actress named Maria Andreeva. Yepikhodov was played by Moskvin so successfully that he repeated the role for decades. Meanwhile, the role Chekhov deemed most important in the play, Lopakhin, ended up being played by Leonid Leonidov, Chekhov's last choice for the role. But the stage designer Simov did indeed set *The Cherry Orchard*'s third act in the ballroom, as Chekhov had written.

By the end of November, Chekhov's letters to Olga had reached an almost desperate crescendo. On November 29, he wrote her an ultimatum. Either she give him "permission" to come to Moscow and explain why Nemirovich and Stanislavsky were reluctant to have him attend rehearsals, or else he would go abroad. "I can't bear it any more," he wrote. Then on November 29, he received a telegram from Olga in Moscow, saying that he should get Dr. Altschuller's final blessing and come.

When the doctors finally granted permission, Chekhov left on December 2. He arrived in Moscow, delighted with the new fur coat and hat that Olga had brought to the train station for him.

Chekhov spent the month of December attending rehearsals daily for *The Cherry Orchard*. According to Stanislavsky, he would sit in a corner of the rehearsal room and refuse to come to the director's table. When asked about a line interpretation, he would simply reply that he was a doctor, not a stage director, and retreat to another corner. Rehearsals were a torture for Chekhov, and his clashes with Stanislavsky intensified. The latter insisted on cutting two scenes from Act II between Charlotta and Firs. In Chekhov's original version, the act ends with Firs telling a lengthy story about an event in his youth. Stanislavsky felt that, following the tender love scene between Anya and Trofimov, the original scene would reduce the energy of the act's ending. Chekhov reluctantly permitted the scene to be cut. (Chekhov also supplied new lines in Act II to replace the cuts the censors had made in Trofimov's speech.)

Tension also persisted between them over the sound effects that Stanislavsky was fond of injecting. Stanislavky recalled Chekhov saying: "Listen!... I'll write a new play that begins like this: 'What peace and quiet… .how lovely! No birds, no dog, no cuckoos, no owls, no nightingales, no clocks, no sleigh bells, and not even a single cricket!'"[10] Above all, they disagreed on the pacing – a conflict that had persisted throughout their artistic collaboration. Chekhov insisted that Act IV be played in twelve minutes, no more, and that the tone be light. In this, his last play, he desperately wanted to "exit laughing."

After returning from a day of struggle with his director, Chekhov would climb the stairs to their flat on the third floor, breathless, only to find that Olga would be leaving to go out to the theatre or a concert. Chekhov would sit at home in the company of his faithful friend Bunin and others, waiting for her to return. (She would be out all night, returning at 4 a.m., smelling of wine and perfume.) There were some moments of pleasure, including attending a performance of Gorky's *The Lower Depths*, or hearing the news that he had been elected as chairman of the Society of Lovers of Russian Literature. Despite the tensions of the rehearsal room and his depleted state, he savored every moment of the literary and theatrical whirlwind to which he had returned after years of longing.

In addition, it would be the first time in years that he would be celebrating Christmas, New Year's Day, and his birthday in Moscow. After the cruel exile in Yalta, he had finally realized his dream: "To Moscow, to Moscow…"

"YOU ASK: 'WHAT IS LIFE?' THAT'S LIKE ASKING 'WHAT IS A CARROT?' A CARROT IS A CARROT, AND NOTHING MORE IS KNOWN ABOUT IT."

(Chekhov, letter to Olga Knipper, April 20, 1904)

1904

"Dear Fyodor Dmitrievich:

... At the first performance of 'The Cherry Orchard' on January 17, they honored me so lavishly, so warmly and indeed so unexpectedly, that I haven't yet been able to get over it.

Meanwhile, better wait till Shrovetide to come and see it. By then, the actors will have come into their own and perform 'The Cherry Orchard' with more focus and clarity than they are playing it now.

I send my greetings. Be well and happy.

Yours, A. Chekhov"

(Chekhov, letter to Batyushkov, January 19, 1904, Moscow)

"Greetings my incomparable horsey:

I'm writing to you sitting on the steamer, which will depart in about three hours. The trip has gone fine so far, all is well. Schnapp is with me; he feels very much at home, and is very agreeable. In the train, too, he behaved just as he does at home, barking at the conductors, and entertaining everyone. He was overjoyed to see me, and is now sitting on deck with his legs stretched out behind him. He's forgotten all about Moscow, evidently. So, darling horsey, I'll wait for your letters. Without them, please know that I couldn't exist. Either write me every day or divorce me—there's no middle ground.

I hear Schnapp above, barking at someone, probably some passengers. I'll go see.

...I kiss my mistress-in-charge and embrace her a million times. Write in more detail, don't spare the ink, my

dear, good, wonderful, talented little actress, God be with you. I love you very much.

Your A."

(Chekhov, letter to Olga Knipper, February 17, 1904, Sevastopol)

"My darling horsey:

It's dreary, dull and cold without you. You've spoiled me so that I'm afraid I've forgotten how to dress and undress myself. The bed is hard and cold, the rooms are freezing, outside it's zero degrees, and there's not a breath of spring. Today I spent rereading last year's mail and old newspapers, it's my only current occupation.

Schnapp is either deaf or dumb. He simply won't go outside. He runs around with the other dogs and insists on spending the night in Mother's room. He's very happy but not very bright.

[...] I haven't been to town yet, and I don't go outside. I have no wife, she's in Moscow, I'm living like a monk... Arseny has grown lazy or forgetful. Nastya cleans my clothes. I'm brushing my teeth now. I'll go to the baths in May when I come to Moscow. Meanwhile I'll plant corn on my body—at least that way I'll make a living.

[...] Write to me, or I'll give you a thrashing.... Be happy and health.

Your A."

(Chekhov, letter to Olga Knipper, February 20, 1904)

"My lovely spouse:

The sun hasn't appeared once since I've been in Yalta, i.e. since February 17. It's terribly damp, the sky is gray, and I stay in my room...

[...] 'The Cherry Orchard' is being performed three or four times in a number of cities. It's a great success, if you can believe it. Ach! If only Muratova, Leonidov [Lopakhin] and Artyom [Firs] were not performing in the Moscow production! I haven't said anything, but Artyom is positively awful.

You write that you haven't received any letters from me, even though I write to you every day. Schnapp, that devil, has made himself at home in my study,, he's lying right here with his hind legs stretched out. At night, he sleeps in Mother's room. He plays outside with the other dogs so he's always dirty....

Have you made any plans for the summer? Where shall we live? I'd like to be close to Moscow, not far from a railroad station, so we don't have to rely on a carriage or patrons or admirers. Please find a dacha, my joy, you'll come up with something. You're so clever and wise and dependable—when you're not angry, that is. I have such happy memories of our trip to Tsaritsyno and back...

And so, God be with you, my joy, my good little doggie, I miss you. I kiss and embrace my wife.

Your A."

(Chekhov letter to Olga Knipper, February 27, 1904, Yalta)

"Greetings, my krinolinchik, my glorious baby baboon:

[...] Let's do this: rent a dacha for the summer, and then if we like it, buy it in the fall or winter...

Today I heard that you are going to divorce me. Is this true? But then who will give you a beating? Whom will you sleep with in the summertime? Give it some thought first!

I'm working now, but without much result. Talk about the war interferes with my work—so do my irritable intestines. People are unlikely to be in the mood to read nowadays, because of the war...

Well, little doggie, I stroke you and pull your little tail. Be well, write to your husband more often.

A."

(Chekhov letter to Olga Knipper, March 26, 1904)

"My dear little doggie:

I've already sent you holiday greetings, so I'm writing just to say hello and send you a multitude of kisses. Stanislavsky and his wife were here last evening, and now they're sitting downstairs, drinking tea. Both are well, they're in a good mood... They like Yalta a lot...

[...] You write that I'm angry with you. But why, my own? You should be angry at me, not the other way around. God be with you, darling.

[Your brother and his fiancée] saw a performance of 'The Cherry Orchard' in March. They both said that Stanis-

lavsky performed terribly in Act IV, and that he drags it out painfully. How absolutely awful! It's an act which should take no more than twelve minutes maximum, and ours lasts forty minutes. All I can say is: Stanislavsky is destroying my play. Well, God forgive him.

... If you're happy in St. Petersburg, then I'm happy... don't pay attention to the reviews, and think about the summer...

Write to me, my little mosquito, I'm so bored without you, as well you know. I kiss you and hug you hard.

Your A."

(Chekhov, letter to Olga Knipper, March 29, 1904, Yalta)

"Hello, my dear horsey!

I received two telegrams from Nemirovich about your successes in Petersburg, and how the audience treats you like a star... For a while I've known that you're a great actress, and I hold you in high esteem, my darling, only please, I beg of you, don't catch cold, don't get overtired, sleep well. Give me your word...

Today is Sunday and I've taken some powder—heroin—and I feel pleasantly peaceful...

You've fallen out of love with me, haven't you? Confess. I love you as before and I'm even thinking of coming to see you in Petersburg. I bless my good wife, I embrace and kiss her. Be happy and well.

Your A."

(Chekhov, letter to Olga Knipper, April 4, 1904, Yalta)

"My darling little finch:

You're angry with me... but I don't remember saying a word to Masha about Tsaritsyno. In general, I leave the dacha issue to you completely. In such matters, as you know, I'm hopeless.

Why do they keep calling my play a 'drama' on the posters and in the press releases? Nemirovich and Stanislavsky do not see eye to eye with me at all on what I've written, and I'm ready to go on record saying that neither of them has ever read 'The Cherry Orchard' through carefully. Forgive me, but I assure you...

The weather here is warm, but it's chilly in the shade, and the evenings are cold. I take leisurely walks, as I'm so short of breath. There's an awful touring production of 'The Cherry Orchard' playing here in Yalta.

I can't wait to see you, my joy. I manage to live without you, the days pass, thank God, without thoughts, without desires, with only a hand a patience and pacing from one corner of the room to another. I haven't been to a bathhouse in such a long time, it seems like six years. I read all the papers, and as a result I'm turning brown.

How long will you be staying in Petersburg? Write me, please. Don't forget me. Think of the man you married from time to time. I tickle your shoulder, your little back, your neck, and kiss my darling.

Your hopeless one"

(Chekhov, letter to Olga Knipper, April 10, 1904, Yalta)

"My dearest darling:

I didn't get a letter from you yesterday, nor today either, so here I am in Yalta, lonely as a comet, feeling not particularly well. A few days ago 'The Cherry Orchard' was presented in a local theatre (without wings or dressing rooms). The mise-en-scène was that of the Moscow Art Theatre, with a vile local cast headed by someone named Daryalova... There are reviews today, tomorrow, and the day after, too. People call me on the telephone, sigh, and, even though I'm a patient here being treated here for an illness, I dream of escaping. It may sound funny, but honestly, these provincial actors are wretched.

Express trains have already started running, so I'll arrive in Moscow in the morning, my joy. I'll come as soon as I can—on May 1. I can't stay here—an upset stomach, actors, audiences, telephone calls, and the devil knows what else.

What are your houses like [in Petersburg]? Are they full? I can imagine how exhausted you all must be. Meanwhile, I sit here dreaming of going fishing and trying to figure out what I'm going to do with my catch, even though I'd fish all summer and catch one lone gudgeon, and only because of his death wish.

Write me, darling, or else I'll cry 'help'...God be with you, my joy, live, sleep soundly, dream, and remember your husband. I love you, you know, I love your letters, your acting, and your manner of walking... The only thing I don't like is how long you take over the washstand.

Your A."

(Chekhov, letter to Olga Knipper, April 15, 1904, Yalta)

"Greetings, my dear little finch bird:

No letter from you again today, but never mind, I don't lose heart. We shall see each other soon...

Come what may, we have to settle the question of the dacha in Tsaritsyno. Yes, it's damp there, but it's very close to Moscow, easily accessible, and you feel at home there, not like a visitor. We'll have to make your room as delightful and comfortable as possible, so you'll fall in love with it.

It's cool here in Yalta, and raining. My stomach is upset, and there's nothing I can do about it—either medicine or diet. [...]

I'm so short of breath! [...]

There's nothing new, everything's the same. I embrace you, my good little actress, I kiss you and tweak your little chin.

Yours, A."

(Chekhov, letter to Olga Knipper, April 17, 1904, Yalta)

"Darling doggie:

.... I'll write you one or two more letters, and then this machine will stop. I'm leaving Yalta with the greatest of pleasure; it's so dull here, there's no spring, and I'm not feeling well. Yesterday I ran to the lavatory five times, though I hadn't eaten anything in particular. I'm on a diet—and there's the cough. I haven't taken care of my teeth yet; yesterday I went into town to see the dentist, but he wasn't there... It's very dreary without a wife, but I'm afraid to take a mistress...

You ask: what is life? That's just like asking: what is a carrot? A carrot is a carrot, and nothing more is known about it. [...]

Be well, don't be sad or depressed, you'll see your

spouse soon. I embrace you and give your little leg a tug.
Your A."
(Chekhov, letter to Olga Knipper, April 20, 1904, Yalta)

"My darling, my wife:
I'm writing my last letter to you. If needs be, I'll send telegrams hereafter. I didn't feel well yesterday, but I'm better today. All I eat now is eggs and soup. It's raining, and the weather is terrible. Still, despite my health and the rain, I went to the dentist. [...]
I arrive in Moscow in the morning—the express trains have already started running. O, my blanket! O, veal cutlets! 'Sabatchka', 'sabathcka', I miss you so!
I embrace and kiss you. Behave yourself. And if you've fallen out of love with me, don't hesitate to say so.
...So Christ be with you, joy.
Your A."
(Chekhov, letter to Olga Knipper, April 22, 1904, Yalta)

(Chekhov and Olga Knipper left Moscow for Germany on June 3.)

'Dear Masha:
I'm writing to you from Berlin. I've been here a whole day now. It got very cold in Moscow after you left, there was snow, and I must have caught cold. I had aches and pain in my arms and legs, couldn't sleep, lost a lot of weight, had morphine injections, took thousands of kinds of medicine, and remember with gratitude only the heroin that Altschuller prescribed for me on one occasion. But as our departure drew nearer, I started to regain strength. My appetite returned, I began to give myself injections, and so on and so on. On Thursday I finally left the country much thinner, with emaciated legs.
The trip was fine. Here in Berlin, we're staying in a very comfortable room in the best hotel. I'm enjoying life here and haven't eaten this well and with such an appetite in a long, long time. The bread is absolutely marvelous, I've been gobbling it up, the coffee is excellent, and the dinners are beyond words. People who haven't traveled abroad

have no idea how good bread can be. On the other hand, there's no decent tea (we brought our own) and no hors d'oeuvres, but everything else is superb, and it's cheaper than in Russia. I'm gaining weight, and even took a long ride to the zoo today. So, please tell Mama and anyone else who's interested that I'm making a recovery—or that I've recovered already. My legs don't hurt, I no longer have diarrhea, I've started to gain weight, and I've begun to spend a whole day out of bed and on my feet. Tomorrow, an eminent local doctor, a gastroenterologist, will visit me. Dr. Taube wrote me about him.

Yesterday I drank some marvelous beer.

[...] The day after tomorrow we go to Badenweiler. I'll send you the address. Write if you need money, and where to send a check. I like Berlin very much, although it's cool today. I've been reading the German newspapers. The rumors that the local papers are unkind to Russians are exaggerated.

So be well and happy, and may heavenly angels watch over you. Send my regards to Mama, and tell her that all is well. I'll be back in Yalta in August....

I kiss you.

Yours, A. Chekhov

P. S. We forgot to bring the dressing gown."
(Chekhov, letter to Masha, June 6, 1904, Berlin)

"Dear Masha:

Today I received your first postcard, many thanks. I'm living [in Badenweiler] among Germans, and am already used to my room and to the routine. But there's no way I can get used to the German peace and quiet. There's not a sound, indoors or out, only at seven in the morning and at noon, when there's music in the garden... Our Russian life is far more colorful.

My health has improved, and when I walk, I no longer feel that I'm ill. I suffer less from shortness of breath, and nothing hurts. The only thing is, as a result of my illness, I'm extremely emaciated—my legs have never been so thin before. The German doctors have turned my life upside down. At seven in the morning I have tea in bed, and at seven-thirty the masseur comes and rubs me down with water, which isn't bad at all. Then I have to lie in bed a while longer, then get up at eight and drink cocoa and swallow an enormous amount of butter. At ten I'm given oatmeal. The air is fresh, it's sunny. I read newspapers. At one o'clock there's the main meal. At four o'clock, cocoa again, and at seven, supper. Before I go to bed, I drink a cup of strawberry tea, which helps me go to sleep. There's a lot of charlatanism in all this, but some of it is very good and effective – especially the oatmeal. I'll take some of it home with me.

Olga has left for Switzerland, to see a dentist in Basel. She'll be back at five. I desperately long for Italy....I'm glad that all is well with you. I'll probably spend three weeks more here, then I'll go to Italy, and to Yalta, and perhaps to the sea.

Write more often....Be well. I kiss you.

Your A."

(Chekhov, letter to Masha, June 16, 1904, Badenweiler)

"Dear Masha:

We're having a cruel heat wave, which has caught me unawares, since all I have with me is winter clothing. I'm stifling, and dream of leaving here. But where to? I thought of Como in Italy, but everyone's fleeing the heat there, too. All of Southern Europe is sweltering. I'd take a steamer from Trieste to Odessa, but I don't know if it's possible in June and July. [...]

It's so hot, enough to want to take one's clothes off. I don't know what to do. Olga has gone to Freiburg to order me a flannel suit, as there are no tailors here or shoemakers in Badenweiler...

I eat delicious food, but it doesn't matter, because my stomach is always upset. I'm not allowed to eat the local butter. Evidently, my stomach is hopeless, and there is no cure for my condition other than fasting, that means stopping to eat entirely – and 'basta'. As for my shortness of breath, the only remedy is not to move at all.

There's not one single well-dressed German woman here. What bad taste... It's depressing.

Be well and happy, send Mama, Vanya, George and Babushka my regards. Write. I kiss you and press your hand.
Your A."
(Chekhov, letter to Masha, June 28, 1904, Badenweiler)

(The letter to Masha on June 28 was the last letter he wrote.)

As the opening night of *The Cherry Orchard* drew nearer, tensions between Chekhov and Stanislavsky mounted.

There was a fundamental difference in their understanding of the play. Chekhov persisted in his view that it was a comedy. Stanislavsky held steadfast to his view that it was a tragedy—one with social commentary on the lamentable decline of the Russian landed gentry in the face of the dark forces of capitalism. Nemirovich did his best to influence the production, writing letters to the actors who were struggling with their roles, encouraging them to play the complexities of the characters. In the case of Olga, who was playing Lyubov Andreevna, he urged her to appreciate the contrasting aspects of her life - namely Paris and the cherry orchard. In keeping with Chekhov's instructions, he encouraged her to play the role with lightness and grace—making the inevitability of her decline even more poignant. In the case of Leonidov, who was playing the role of Lophakin, he encouraged him to find the complexities of the character—again in keeping with Chekhov's view and not to rely so much on actorly technique.

Then Stanislavsky had an idea. Why not schedule the official opening of *The Cherry Orchard* on Chekhov's forty-fourth birthday, January 17, to honor his twenty-five years of literary achievement? (The convoluted reason Stanislavsky gave in his memoirs centered on Chekhov's medical condition. If the production didn't go well, he reasoned, it could be blamed on the concern over the author's declining health. Others, however, interpreted it as a ploy on Stanislavsky's part to divert attention from the play and arouse pity for its author if it wasn't a success.) Whatever the true reason was, this was just the kind of public testimony that Chekhov hated. (Moreover, as he pointed out, since his first story was published in 1880, this twenty-fifth "anniversary" was a year premature.)

On opening night, January 17, the Moscow Art Theatre was packed. Rachmaninov, Gorky, Chaliapin, and the poet Andrey Bely were in attendance, and the atmosphere in the audience was electrifying. But Chekhov refused to come to the theatre, and the curtain rose on Act I without him. At the end of Act II, Stanislavsky and Nemirovich sent him an urgent message, begging him to come.

Arriving at the end of Act III, Chekhov was dragged up on the stage. Seeing his emaciated, stooped body, the audience gasped audibly. Those sounds, however, were drowned out by a tremendous ovation and dozens of long-winded speeches lasting over an hour. Chekhov was barely able to stand, and could not control his coughing. Yet he insisted on standing for the duration of the testimony honoring him. According to Stanislavsky, during one of the speeches, a professor droned on in the same manner as Gaev's speech "O venerable bookcase" from Act I of *The Cherry Orchard*, and that amused Chekhov greatly. He was showered with gifts, including with a large wreath decorated in an embroidered antique cloth that Stanislavsky had purchased especially for the occasion. Chekhov teased him, saying that it should be put in a museum, and that he'd have preferred a mousetrap instead. Indeed, his favorite gift was a fishing rod. Finally he was led off stage to lie down in a dressing room. Thereafter, he dined with the cast and was heaped with presents and more speeches.

Despite Stanislavsky's prediction, the reviews were cool. Some felt the theme (the decline of the old order) was trite; others criticized him for making light of a serious social issue. None saw it as a comedy, as he hoped.

It was only in hindsight that anyone understood the depth and the breadth of his vision. Looking back, Chekhov saw a dying Russia through the eyes of a dying man. "Good bye old life, hello new life," young Anya calls out joyously, as all the characters leave the estate, dispersing in many directions, to face the unknown. Neither the characters in the play, nor the audience, nor the critics could foresee that strikes would occur in St. Petersburg in December ten months after the play opened, and that demonstrators would gather before the Winter Palace on January 22, 1905—exactly one year and a few days after the opening of the play—to be shot down by Tsarist troops. This massacre of almost 1,000 would send waves of shock and indignation throughout Russia, provoking massive strikes in the industrial centers all over the country. "Bloody Sunday," later known as the First Russian Revolution, would be the catalyst of even greater tumultuous revolutionary change in the new century's second decade—change that would bring down the 500-year long tsarist rule in Russia (the largest country in the world) forever.

Never didactic, never overtly political, Chekhov nonetheless had a profound sense of his country and its evolution during his lifetime. The grandson of a serf, he was born a year before the emancipation of the serfs (1861), and would die a year before the first Russian Revolution (1905). The enormous change he saw during his lifetime is the final vision he wanted to convey. At the same time, he wanted to exit the stage laughing. No one heeded Trofimov, the student in *The Cherry Orchard*, who warned Anya, the last and youngest representative of the landed gentry in a Chekhov play:

"We have fallen behind, by 200 years or so, at least, we have nothing left, absolutely nothing, no clear understanding of the past, we only philosophize, complain about our boredom, or drink vodka. And it's all so clear, can't you see, that to begin a new life, to live in the present, we must first redeem our past, put an end to it, and redeem it we shall, but only with suffering, only with extraordinary, everlasting toil and suffering." (Act II, *The Cherry Orchard*)[1]

No one in the play listened to Trofimov. And why should they? He was a shabby-looking young tutor who couldn't find his galoshes, and who fell down the stairs at the family's ball. Instead, they laughed at him. No, neither the audience nor the critics took Trofimov seriously.

The lack of response to *The Cherry Orchard* made Chekhov all the more irritable. With the outbreak of the Russo-Japanese War on January 24, he acknowledged that the public understandably would have no time for a play like *The Cherry Orchard.* He tried to find distraction in the deluge of visitors to the flat, or editing manuscripts for *Russian Thought.* He even started two new stories ("The Cripple" and "Disturbing the Balance"); they were never finished. Meanwhile, true to his pattern, he was restless, and longed to escape—to the Riviera or back to the Crimea.

On February 14, he and Olga journeyed out Tsaritsyno in the countryside, to look at a dacha for the summer. In her memoirs, Olga noted that he experienced the Russian winter of his dreams, with an open sleigh ride over the deep snow in brilliant sunshine. It was a pleasure that had been denied him for seven years because of his illness.

Back in Yalta, his spirits were no better. His cough worsened, and his intestinal problems intensified. His letters to Olga in March and April grew shorter and more wistful, longing for a summer in a dacha in Tsaritsyno, speaking of a child they still hoped to have. In one letter, he wrote her how he dreamed of fishing, but remarked, ruefully, that all he'd catch would be one lone gudgeon "with a death wish."[2]

In April, Olga went on tour to St. Petersburg with *The Cherry Orchard*. The reviews there were no better than in Moscow – in fact, some were hostile. Fearing that the company would plan another testimonial, Chekhov refused to attend. He persisted in believing that Stanislavsky had ruined his play by rendering it maudlin. But Nemirovich's reassurances that the Petersburg audiences loved the play consoled him somewhat—after all, his serious career in the theatre had begun there with the disastrous premiere of *The Seagull* in 1896. Meanwhile, other productions of *The Cherry Orchard* were now being performed throughout the western part of Russia, with varying results. On April 10, Chekhov saw a performance of a local production in Yalta that, in his view, was so bad that he walked out.

Still, ideas for plays kept coming. To the actor Pavel Olenev, he spoke of a comedy in three acts that could avoid the Russian censors by being performed abroad. To Stanislavsky, he described an idea for a play involving a man, his unfaithful wife, and his wife's lover. The two men go on a polar expedition to the North Pole, and their ship is crushed in the icebergs. At the end, the men see a white vision of the woman over the snow. Apparently she had died while they were away, and her ghost has followed them. He never wrote that play. He even dreamed of volunteering as a military doctor and war correspondent in Manchuria.

Meanwhile, his health worsened, and, as usual, his anxiety and restlessness became more acute. In his letters to Olga at the end of April, he declared that he was leaving Yalta, not caring if he ever returned. His life was over in Yalta. He left on May 1, had an attack en route, and could hardly stand when he arrived in Moscow on May 3.

Understanding the seriousness of Chekhov's condition, Olga had rented a new flat with a lift. But upon his arrival, he went to bed at once with another attack of pleurisy. He suffered from fever, acute pains in arms and legs, and had difficulty breathing. Dr. Taube prescribed morphine, heroin, and opium to control the pain. When Dr. Taube proposed that Olga take Chekhov to a spa in Badenweiler, Germany, Masha knew the implication of the suggestion, and she and Olga quarreled bitterly over it. As a result, Olga kept fierce watch over him, staving off visitors including his own family members. Devastated at being excluded, Masha left Moscow for Yalta. She would never see her brother again.

On June 3, Chekhov and Olga left Moscow by train for Berlin. No one from the family was there to bid him farewell. In her memoirs, Olga recalls the peculiar smile on his face as the train pulled away from the station, and he looked out the window on a receding Russia. She surmised he must have known he was seeing it for the last time.

The couple arrived in Berlin on June 3, and installed themselves in the Hotel Savoy, the best hotel in town, according to Chekhov. Despite his constant, ever-worsening cough, Chekhov wrote to Masha of his delight in being a tourist once more (it was his and Olga's first trip together outside Russia), visiting the shops, sampling the German cuisine. They consulted a famous gastroenterologist there, who could do nothing but shrug his shoulders at Chekhov's condition.

Then they journeyed by train south to Badenweiler, a sleepy little spa town on the Western edge of the Black Forest, near Basel. There, he would be under the care of Dr. Schwörer, who had been recommended to Chekhov. In Badenweiler, his restlessness to find the proper accommodations persisted. First they stayed at Hotel Romerbad, then Villa Frederika, and then finally they found a room at the Hotel Sommer that afforded Chekhov sunlight and a view of the forest that pleased him. Dr. Schwörer, the spa physician, hovered over him, prescribing a specific diet and regimen that he recounted in detail in letters to Masha.

Chekhov soon got bored of the quiet. But his physical condition precluded him from going anywhere. He sat on balcony of Hotel Sommer watching people go by, planning trips to Trieste and Marseilles in his mind, ordering timetables and schedules.

He even sent Olga to get a white suit in Freiburg that would be proper for the local society.

A heat wave struck the Black Forest in the last days of June. On June 29, after Chekhov suffered another night of breathlessness, Dr. Schwörer administered oxygen and morphine. Olga never left Chekhov's side. On July 1, he urged her to take a walk, told jokes, made up stories to amuse her. One story he told her—about a group of spoiled American tourists who came back after a day of sightseeing to their resort, only to find that the cook had run off with one of the maids—reduced her to gales of laughter.

But the night of July 1, his condition worsened. According to Olga's memoirs, just after midnight (around 2 a.m.) on July 2, he called for a doctor—a request, according to Olga, he had never initiated before. Olga put chopped ice on his heart, but he replied: "An empty heart need no ice." Dr. Schwörer arrived, and sent for more oxygen. Then Chekhov announced to him, in German: "*Ich sterbe*" (translation: "I am dying"). According to the custom appropriate for the occasion, Dr. Schwörer ordered champagne. When the bottle arrived, Dr. Schwörer poured three glasses—one for Chekhov, one for Olga, and one for himself. After he drank his, Chekhov said: "It's been such a long time since I've tasted champagne." Then he lowered his head, turned on his left side, and stopped breathing.[3]

In her memoirs, Olga described that final night and the vigil that she kept, sitting by his side, waiting for them to come and prepare him for the journey. She wrote that there was a sudden explosive noise: "Pow!" The cork that the doctor had replaced in the champagne bottle had exploded and flown off, all on its own volition. Olga telegrammed Chekhov's immediate family of her plans to bury him in Germany, but changed her mind after the family entreated her to return him to Russia.

The arrival of Olga and Chekhov in Moscow on July 9 reads like one of his short stories. The train from Berlin, with Chekhov's coffined body, first stopped in St. Petersburg, where Suvorin met it and arranged that Chekhov's body be transferred to a refrigerated car that happened to bear the mark of "Fresh Oysters," his favorite delicacy. In Moscow, a small group including family and friends (Gorky, Chaliapin, and others) met the coffin at the train station, along with a military band. At first the family was touched by such a grand welcome—only to find out that the band had been commissioned for a general who was also arriving at the train station at the same time.

As the four-mile procession from the train station to the cemetery progressed, the crowd grew to almost 4,000. Chekhov's mother and siblings—Masha, Ivan and Mikhail—were among them. (His brother Aleksandr's train from St. Petersburg arrived late, so he missed the burial.) Chekhov was buried in the Novodevichy cemetery—the same spot where the mother of Olga, Masha and Irina was buried in *The Three Sisters*. (Life imitated art once again.) Chekhov was buried alongside his father, and on this occasion—in accordance with what he would have wanted—there were no orations.

Beginning in August following his death, and lasting several weeks, Olga wrote Chekhov a series of posthumous letters, filled with longing and remorse.[4] She wrote of her quarrel with Masha and lamented that no matter how hard she tried, they never could have gotten along, and that it was pure jealousy on Masha's part. She begged him to understand. She wrote of her profound loneliness. She wrote of her anguish in not having bore him a "little Pamphil," and begged his forgiveness. Lastly, she wrote of the theatre, not knowing if she loved it or hated it, but recognizing that now it was all she had.

Reading those letters, one recognizes an enormous sense of guilt, and speculates whether she might have been writing those letters for posterity, to set the record straight. In any event, she never remarried, never had children, and died in 1959 at the age of 91. She performed all the roles in her husband's plays that she originated at the Moscow Art Theatre until her eighties.

According to Olga's biographer,[5] after she had retired from the stage, she was given a testimonial at the Moscow Art Theatre for her ninetieth birthday. On the stage, a group of actors, dressed as officers, presented her with a spinning top, just as they did at the end of Act I in *Three Sisters*. From the box where she was sitting, her voice called out in response, loud and clear, right on cue, reciting the lines from Act I that he had written especially for her: "In a cove by the sea, a green oak stands, a golden chain wound round..."[6]

Footnotes

Act One

1860-69

[1] Aleksandr Chekhov, "Iz detskikh let A. P. Chekhova," in *Chekhov v vospominaniakh sovremennikov (Seriya Literaturnykh Memuarov)*, ed. A. K. Kotov, (Moskva: Gosudarstvennoe izdatelel'stvo khudozhestvennoj literatury, 1952), p. 3.

[2] Ibid., p. 37.

[3] Details from Chekhov's early life have been culled from the memoirs of Aleksandr Chekhov, Mikhail Chekhov, Donald Rayfield's *Anton Chekhov: A Life* and Henri Troyat's *Chekhov* (see bibliography).

[4] Chekhov, letter to Olga Knipper, February 11, 1903.

[5] Chekhov, letter to his friend Leontyev-Shcheglov, March 9, 1892.

[6] Aleksandr Chekhov, "Iz detskikh let A. P. Chekhova," op. cit., p. 37.

1870-79

[1] Chekhov, letter to Tikhonov, February 22, 1892.

[2] Chekhov, letter to Suvorin , January 7, 1889.

Act Two

1880-81

[1] Chekhov, letter to Suvorin, August 29, 1888.

[2] Mikhail Chekhov, *Vokrug Chekhova: Vstrechi I vpechatleniya,* (Moskva: Moskovsky Rabochy, 1960), pp. 97-98. (Details from Chekhov's daily life in this and succeeding chapters have been culled from his own letters, from N. I. Gitovich, *Letopis zhizni i tvorchestva A. P. Chekhova* from memoirs of his contemporaries, from Donald Rayfield's *Anton Chekhov: A Life,* Henri Troyat's *Chekhov,* op. cit., as well as other sources listed in the bibliography)

1884

[1] Chekhov to Leikin, August 23, 1884.

1885

[1] Chekhov, letter to Leikin, October 12, 1885.
[2] Chekhov, letter to Mikhail Chekhov, May 10, 1885.
[3] Chekhov, letter to Leikin, September 14, 1885.
[4] Chekhov, letter to Kiselyova, October 1, 1885.

1886

[1] Chekhov, letter to Leikin, October 25, 1885.
[2] Chekhov, "The Dramatist," in *Chekhov: The Vaudevilles*, translated by Carol Rocamora (Smith & Kraus, 1998), pp. 8-9.

1887

[1] Actually, *Ivanov* was Chekhov's third full length play. *Fatherlessness (Bezotsovshchina,* 1877) was his first, and *Platonov* (1880-81) was his second. The former manuscript was lost, and the latter was not produced in his lifetime.
[2] Chekhov, letter to Leikin, April 7, 1887.
[3] Chekhov, letter to his family, April 25, 1887.
[4] Chekhov, letter to Kiselyova, September 13, 1887.
[5] Chekhov to Korolenko, October 17, 1887.
[6] Chekhov to Suvorin, December 30, 1888.
[7] In addition to being cruel, Ivanov's behavior could also have been construed as anti-Semitic. In Chekhov's day, anti-Semitism was common, especially in the lower-middle class milieu of Taganrog. Indeed, some of Chekhov's early letters occasionally refer to a Jew as a "little yid." But neither Chekhov nor other members of his family, including his father, were anti-Semitic. Indeed, Chekhov became an outspoken defender of Alfred Dreyfus, the French army captain who fell victim to anti-Semitism in France (1898). In 1901, Chekhov married Olga Knipper, and teasingly addresses her as "my little Jewess" in his correspondence.
[8] Chekhov, letter to Aleksandr, October 10-12, 1887.
[9] Chekhov, letter to Suvorin, November 7, 1888.
[10] Chekhov, *The Seagull*, Act I, in *Chekhov: Four Plays*, translated by Carol Rocamora (Smith & Kraus, 1996), p. 42.

1888

[1] Chekhov, letter to his family, December 3, 1887.
[2] Chekhov, letter, to Polonsky, February 22, 1888.
[3] Chekhov, letter to Pleshcheev, October 17, 1888
[4] Chekhov, letter to Kiselyova, November 2, 1888.
[5] Chekhov, letter to Suvorin, November 7, 1888.
[6] Chekhov, letter to Pleshcheev, November 10, 1888.

[7] Chekhov, letter to Suvorin, December 23, 1888.
[8] Chekhov, letter to Grigorovich, October 9, 1888.
[9] Chekhov, letter to Lazarev-Gruzinsky, October 20, 1888.
[10] Chekhov, letter to Leontyev-Shcheglov, November 11, 1888.

1889

[1] Chekhov, letter to Pleshcheev, April 9, 1889.
[2] Chekhov, letter to Suvorin, April 8, 1889.
[3] Chekhov, letter to Suvorin, March 6, 1889.
[4] Idem.
[5] Chekhov, letter to Leontyev-Shcheglov, March 11,1889.
[6] Chekhov, letter to Aleksandr, August 29, 1889.
[7] Chekhov, letter to Leontyev-Shcheglov, September 1, 1889.
[8] Chekhov, letter to Suvorin, May 14, 1889.
[9] Chekhov, letter to Pleshcheev, June 26, 1889.
[10] Chekhov, letter to Suvorin, December 17, 1889.
[11] Chekhov, letter to Suvorin, December 18-23, 1889.

ACT THREE

1890

[1] Details of Chekhov's journey to Sakhalin have been culled from Gitovich, N. I., *Letopis zhizni i tvorchestva A. P. Chekhova*, from Donald Rayfield's biography *Anton Chekhov: A Life* and Henri Troyat's *Chekhov*, as well as Chekhov's own letters.
[2] Chekhov, letter to Suvorin, September 11, 1990
[3] Chekhov, letter to Suvorin, December 9, 1890.
[4] Chekhov, letter to Leontyev-Shcheglov, December 10, 1890.
[5] Chekhov, letter to Suvorin, December 17, 1890.

1891

[1] Hunyadi-Yanos (1407-1456): a powerful Hungarian general of the 15th century.
[2] Chekhov, letter to Masha, January 14, 1891.
[3] Chekhov, letter to his sister Masha, March 19, 1891.
[4] Chekhov, letter to his sister Masha, March 20, 1891.
[5] Chekhov, letter to his brother Ivan, March 24, 1891.
[6] Chekhov, letter to his family, April 21, 1891.
[7] Chekhov, letter to Suvorin, October 19, 1991.
[8] Chekhov, letter to Suvorin, November 22, 1891.
[9] Chekhov, letter to Leikin, December 2, 1891.

[10] Chekhov, letter to Suvorin, November 22, 1891.
[11] Chekhov, "A Moscow Hamlet," in *Chekhov: Vaudevilles*, translated by Carol Rocamora (Smith & Kraus, 1998), p. 177.

1892

[1] "The Medes" (a.k.a Media): an ancient Iranian kingdom, circa 700-550 B.C.
[2] "Trofim" is the name of Lika's fictitious lover that Chekhov fabricated for the purpose of teasing her.
[3] Chekhov, letter to Leontyev-Shcheglov, March 9, 1892.
[4] Chekhov, letter to Natalya Lintvaryova, April 6, 1892.
[5] Chekhov, letter to Suvorin, June 16, 1892.
[6] Chekhov, letter to Lydia Avilova, April 29, 1892.
[7] Chekhov, letter to Suvorin, October 10, 1892.
[8] Chekhov, letter to Leontyev-Shcheglov, October 24, 1892.
[9] Chekhov, letter to Suvorin, August 1, 1892.
[10] Chekhov, letter to Lydia Avilova, April 29, 1892.
[11] Chekhov, letter to Suvorin, October 18, 1892.
[12] Chekhov, letter to Suvorin, December 8, 1892.

1893

[1] Chekhov, letter to Ivan Gorbunov-Posadov, May 20, 1893.
[2] Chekhov, letter to Suvorin, April 26, 1893.
[3] Chekhov, letter to Suvorin, November 11, 1893.
[4] Chekhov, letter to Suvorin, February 13, 1893.

1894

[1] Chekhov, *The Seagull*, Act II, in *Chekhov: Four Plays*, op. cit., p. 63.
[2] Chekhov, letter to Lydia Mizinova, February 20, 1894.
[3] Chekhov, letter to Lydia Mizinova, March 27, 1894.
[4] Chekhov, letter to Leontyev-Shcheglov, July 5, 1894.
[5] Chekhov, letter to Lydia Mizinova, September 18, 1894.
[6] Chekhov, letter to Yelena Shavrova, December 11, 1894.

1895

[1] Chekhov, letter to Suvorin, November 10, 1895.
[2] Chekhov, letter to Lydia Avilova, February 15, 1895.
[3] Chekhov, letter to Suvorin, February 18, 1895.
[4] Chekhov, letter to Suvorin, May 5, 1895.
[5] Chekhov, letter to Suvorin, October 21, 1895.
[6] Chekhov, letter to Suvorin, November 10, 1895.
[7] Chekhov, letter to Yelena Shavrova, November 18, 1895.
[8] Chekhov, letter to Suvorin, December 17, 1895.

[9] Rayfield, *Anton Chekhov: A Life* (New York: Henry Holt and Company, 1997), p. 353.

[10] Chekhov, letter to Suvorin, December 13, 1895.

1896

[1] Vronsky: one of the protagonists in Tolstoy's *War and Peace.*

[2] Chekhov, letter to Lydia Mizinova, June 16, 1896.

[3] Chekhov, letter to Suvorin, October 12, 1896.

[4] Chekhov, *The Seagull*, Act III, p. 70.

[5] Lydia Avilova, *Chekhov in My Life*, p. 95.

[6] Rayfield, *Anton Chekhov: A Life*, op. cit., p. 403.

[7] Chekhov, letter to Suvorin, October 18, 1896.

[8] Chekhov, letter to his brother Mikhail, October 18, 1896.

[9] Chekhov, letter to Suvorin, October 22, 1896.

[10] Chekhov, letter to Yelena Shavrova, November 1, 1896.

[11] Chekhov, letter to Suvorin, December 14, 1896.

[12] Chekhov, *The Seagull*, Act I, in *Chekhov: Four Plays*, op. cit., p. 42.

[13] Chekhov, Ibid., Act IV, p. 85.

1897

[1] Chekhov, letter to Suvorin, January 17.

[2] Chekhov, letter to Suvorin, February 8, 1897.

[3] Chekhov, letter to Suvorin, April 7, 1897.

[4] Chekhov, letter to Lintvaryova, May 1, 1897.

[5] Chekhov, letter to Suvorin, May 2, 1897.

[6] Chekhov, letter to Suvorin, June 21, 1897.

[7] Chekhov, letter to Shavrova, October 29, 1897.

1898

[1] Chekhov, letter to Khotyaintseva, February 9, 1898.

[2] Chekhov, letter to Suvorin, February 6, 1898.

[3] Chekhov, letter to Suvorin, March 13, 1898.

[4] Chekhov, letter to Lydia Avilova, July 24-26, 1898.

[5] Chekhov, letter to Suvorin, October 8, 1898.

[6] Chekhov, letter to Iordanov, September 21, 1898.

[7] Chekhov, letter to Suvorin, October 27, 1898.

[8] Maksim Gorky, letter to Chekhov, November 21-28, 1898, in *Pis'ma, Tom I* (Moskva: Isdatel'stvo Nauka, 1997), pp. 291-292.

[9] Nemirovich-Danchenko, letter to Chekhov, December 18-21, in Vl. I. Nemirovich-Danchenko, *Tvorcheskoe nasledie, Tom, I, Pis'ma* [1879—1907] (Moskva: Izdatel'stvo

'Moskovski Khudozhestvenny teatr, 2003) pp. 246-248.

1899

[1] Maksim Gorky, "A. P. Chekhov," in *Chekhov v vospominaniakh sovremennikov*, ed. A. K. Kotov (1952), op. cit., pp. 387-388.

[2] Chekhov, letter to Lydia Avilova, February 18, 1899.

[3] Chekhov, letter to Lydia Avilova, March 23, 1899.

[4] Chekhov, letter to Orlov, March 18, 1898.

[5] Chekhov, letter to Suvorin, April 2, 1899.

[6] Stanislavsky, "A. P. Chekhov v Moskovskom khudozhestvennom teatre," in *Chekhov v vospominaniakh sovremennikov*, ed. A. K. Kotov (1952), op. cit., p. 312.

[7] Idem.

[8] Chekhov, letter to Rossolimo, October 11, 1899.

[9] Chekhov, letter to Suvorin, December 2, 1896.

[10] Chekhov, letter to Gorky, December 3, 1898.

[11] Chekhov, spoken to the writer Goroditsky, in Daniel Gilles, *Chekhov: Observer Without Illusion* (New York, Funk & Wagnalls, 1968), p. 294.

[12] Chekhov, letter to Suvorin, May 5, 1895

[13] Chekhov, letter to the editor Urusov, October 16, 1899.

[14] Chekhov, letter to Olga Knipper, September 30, 1899.

[15] Nemirovich, letter to Stanislavsky, October 10 or 17, 1899, in *Pis'ma,* op. cit., pp. 310-312.

[16] Nemirovich, letter to Chekhov, October 27, 1899, in Ibid., pp. 315-317.

[17] Olga Knippera-Chekhova, *Vospominania i stati. Perepiska s A. P. Chekhovim* (Moskva: Izdatel'stvo "Iskustvo," 1972), pp. 53-54.

[18] Chekhov, letter to Masha, November 11, 1899.

Act Four

1900

[1] Chekhov, letter to Nemirovich, March 10, 1900.

[2] Chekhov, letter to Gorky, February 15, 1900.

[3] Chekhov, letter to Menshikov, January 28, 1900.

[4] Chekhov, letter to Suvorin, March 10, 1900.

[5] Chekhov, letter to Olga Knipper, August 9, 1900.

[6] Chekhov, letter to Gorky, October 16, 1900.

[7] Chekhov, letter to Olga Knipper, September 8, 1900.

[8] Chekhov, letter to Olga Knipper, September 27, 1900.
[9] Chekhov, letter to Olga Knipper, December 21, 1900.
[10] Chekhov, letter to Nemirovich, December 19, 1900.

1901

[1] I. A. Bunin, "Chekhov," in *Chekhov v vospominaniakh sovremennikov*, ed. N. I. Gitovich (Moskva: Kydozhestvennaya Literatura, 1986), pp. 485-486.
[2] Chekhov insisted that his friend Colonel Petrov attend rehearsals of *The Three Sisters* and supervise all detail pertaining to the actors playing the military officers (costumes, comportment) for authenticity.
[3] Chekhov, letter to Olga Knipper, January 2, 1901.
[4] Chekhov, letter to Olga Knipper, January 24, 1901.
[5] Chekhov, letter to Olga Knipper, March 1, 1901.
[6] Chekhov, letter to Olga Knipper, March 7, 1901
[7] Chekhov, letter to Suvorin, November 16, 1900.
[8] Chekhov, letter to Olga Knipper, January 2, 1901.
[9] Chekhov, letter to Olga Knipper, March 16, 1901.
[10] Idem.
[11] Idem.
[12] Chekhov, letter to Olga Knipper, April 22, 1901.
[13] Chekhov, letter to Olga Knipper, November 7, 1901.
[14] Chekhov, letter to Olga Knipper, November 2, 1901.
[15] Chekhov, letter to Olga Knipper, December 30, 1901.
[16] Chekhov, letter to Olga Knipper, December 16, 1901.

1902

[1] Chekhov, letter to Lilina (Stanislavsky's wife), February 3, 1902.
[2] Olga Knipper, letter to Chekhov, March 1, 1902 in *Anton Pavlovich Chekhov: Perepiska s zhenoi* (Moskva, 2003), p. 409.
[3] Chekhov, letter to Olga Knipper, March 17, 1902.
[4] Donald Rayfield, Anton Chekhov (New York, Henry Holt and Co., 1997) pp. 556-557.
[5] Olga Knipper, letter to Anton Chekhov, April 4, 1902, in op. cit., pp. 454-455.
[6] Aleksandr Serebrov (Tikhonov), *O Chekhove,* in *Chekhov v vospominaniakh sovremennikov*, ed. A. K. Kotov (1952), op. cit. pp. 468-484.
[7] Chekhov, letter to Stanislavsky, July 18, 1902.
[8] Chekhov, letter to Olga Knipper, August 24, 1902.

[9] Chekhov, letter to Olga Knipper, August 27, 1902.
[10] Idem.
[11] Chekhov, letter to Olga Knipper, September 10, 1902.
[12] Chekhov, letter to Olga Knipper, September 22, 1902.
[13] Chekhov, letter to Olga Knipper, November 30, 1902.
[14] Chekhov, letter to Olga Knipper, December 1, 1902
[15] Chekhov, letter to Olga Knipper, December 17, 1902.
[16] Chekhov, letter to Olga Knipper, December 15, 1902.
[17] Idem.

1903

[1] Chekhov, letter to Olga Knipper, February 22, 1903.
[2] Chekhov, letter to Olga Knipper, February 5, 1903.
[3] Chekhov, letter to Olga Knipper, January 13, 1903.
[4] Chekhov, letter to Olga Knipper, March 18, 1903.
[5] Chekhov, letter to Olga Knipper, March 4, 1903.
[6] Chekhov, letter to Stanislavsky, July 28, 1903.
[7] Chekhov, letter to Olga Knipper, October 2, 1903.
[8] Chekhov, letter to Suvorin, November 25, 1892.
[9] Chekhov, *The Cherry Orchard*, in *Chekhov: Four Plays*, translated by Carol Rocamora, op. cit., p. 241.
[10] Stanislavsky, "A. P. Chekhov v Moskovskom khudozhestvennom teatre," in *Chekhov v vospominaniakh sovremennikov,* ed. A. K. Kotov (1952), op. cit., p. 344.

1904

[1] Chekhov, *The Cherry Orchard,* in *Chekhov: Four Plays*, op. cit., p. 243.
[2] Chekhov, letter to Olga Knipper, April 15, 1904.
[3] Harvey Pitcher, *Chekhov's Leading Lady* (London, John Murray, 1979), pp. 146-149.
[4] Olga Knipper, letters to Chekhov written after his death (August 19-September 11, 1904), in op. cit., pp. 774-779.
[5] Pitcher, *Chekhov's Leading Lady*, op. cit., pp. 270-271
[6] Chekhov, *The Three Sisters*, in *Chekhov: Four Plays*, translated by Carol Rocamora, op. cit., p. 149.

Bibliography

Avilova, Lydia. *Chekhov in My Life*. Translated by David Magarshack. London: Methuen, 1989.

Chekhov, Anton. *Chekhov: Four Plays*, translated by Carol Rocamora. (*The Seagull, Uncle Vanya, The Three Sisters, The Cherry Orchard*). Smith & Kraus: 1996.

Gilles, Daniel. *Chekhov: Observer Without Illusion*. New York: Funk & Wagnalls, 1967.

Gitovich, *N. I. Letopis zhizni I tvorchestva A. P. Chekhova*. Moskva: Gosudarstvennoe izdatel'stvo Khudozhestennoj Literatury, 1955

Pitcher, Harvey. *Chekhov's Leading Lady*. London: John Murray, 1979.

Rayfield, Donald. *Anton Chekhov: A Life*. New York: Henry Holt, 1997.

Simmons, Ernest J. *Chekhov: A Biography*. Chicago: The University of Chicago Press, 1962

Troyat, Henri. *Chekhov*. New York: Fawcett Colombine, 1986.

Urban, Peter, ed. *Anton Ceckhov: Sein Leben in Bildern*. Zurich: Diogenes Verlag, 1987.

The letters and plays of Anton Chekhov quoted in this book were newly translated directly from the Russian from the following source:

Chekhov, Anton Pavlovich. *Polnoye sobranie sochinenii i picem v tridtsati tomax*. Moskva: Izatelstvo 'Nauka', 1974-1983.

Excerpts from the memoirs and letters of Nemirovich-Danchenko, I. A. Bunin, Gorky, Stanislavsky, Olga Knipper, Aleksandr and Mikhail Chekhov, and others, were translated directly, from the following sources:

Bunin, I. A. "Chekhov," in *Chekhov v vospominaniakh sovremennikov* (Seriya Literaturnykh Memuarov), ed., N. I. Gitovich. Moskva: Khydozhestvennaya Literatura, 1986.

Chekhov, Anton Pavlovich. *Perepiska s zhenoj*. Moskva, Zakharavo, 2003.

Chekhov, Aleksandr Pavlovich. "Iz detskikh let A. P. Chekhova," in *Chekhov v vospominaniakh sovremennikov* (Seriya Literaturnykh Memuarov), ed. A. K. Kotov. Moskva: Gosudarstvennoe izdatelel'stvo khudozhestvennoj literatury, 1952.

Chekhov, Mikhail Pavlovich. "Anton Chekhov na kanikulakh," in *Chekhov v vospominaniakh sovremennikov* (Seriya Literaturnykh Memuarov), ed. A. K. Kotov. Moskva: Gosudarstvennoe izdatelel'stvo khudozhestvennoj literatury, 1952.

Chekhov, Mikhail Pavlovich. V*okrug Chekhova: Vstrechi i vpechatleniya.* Moscow: Moskovski Rabochi, 1960.

Gitovich, N. I. ed. *Chekhov v vospominaniakh sovremennikov* (Seriya Literaturnykh Memuarov). Moskva: Khydozhestvennaya Literatura, 1986.

Gorky, Maksim. "A. P. Chekhov," in *Chekhov v vospominaniakh sovremennikov* (Seriya Literaturnykh Memuarov), ed. A. K. Kotov. Moskva: Gosudarstvennoe izdatelel'stvo khudozhestvennoj literatury,1952.

Gorky, Maksim. *Pis'ma* (Tom I, 1888 - 1899). Moskva: Isdatel'stvo Nauka, 1997.

Knippera-Chekhova, Olga. *Vospominania i stati. Perepiska s A. P. Chekhovim.* Moskva: Izdatel'stvo "Iskustvo," 1972.

Kotov, A. K. ed. *Chekhov v vospominaniakh sovremennikov* (Seriya Literaturnykh Memuarov). Moskva: Gosudarstvennoe izdatel'stvo khydozhestvennoj literatury, 1952.

Nemirovich-Danchenko, Vladimir. "Chekhov," in *Chekhov v vospominaniakh sovremennikov* (Seriya Literaturnykh Memuarov), ed. A. K. Kotov. Moskva: Gosudarstvennoe izdatelel'stvo khudozhestvennoj literatury, 1952.

Nemirovich-Danchenko, Vladimir. *Tvorcheskoe nasledie. Tom I, Pis'ma* [1879-1907], Moskva: Isdatelstvo Moskovski khudozhestvenny teatr, 2003.

Stanislavsky, Konstantin. "A. P. Chekhov v Moskovskom khudozhestvennom teatre," in *Chekhov v vospominaniakh sovremennikov* (Seriya Literaturnykh Memuarov), ed. A. K. Kotov. Moskva: Gosudarstvennoe izdatelel'stvo khudozhestvennoj literatury, 1952.

Stanislavsky, Konstantin. *Moya Zhizn v Iskusstve*. Moskva: Iskusstvo, 1983.

Appendix: Correspondents

During his brief lifetime, Chekhov wrote over 4,000 letters to family, friends, publishers, fellow writers, mentors, and disciples. The letters included in this book are among those Chekhov wrote to frequent correspondents. Here are a few words about some of these principal *dramatis personae* (in alphabetical order):

Lydia Alekseevna Avilova (1864-1943): A married woman with three children as well as an aspiring author, Avilova wrote to Chekhov persistently for advice on her short-story writing. She fell passionately in love with Chekhov, and though he gave her no encouragement, she nurtured delusions that he returned her sentiments. Her memoir *Chekhov in My Life* was published posthumously.

Aleksandr Pavlovich Chekhov (1855-1913): The first-born of the Chekhov family (and Anton's older brother), Aleksandr was a novelist, short-story writer and essayist. His memoirs contain valuable information about Anton's childhood.

Maria Pavlovna (Masha) Chekhov (1853-1957): Chekhov's younger sister, and the only daughter of the family, Masha devoted her life to Anton and served as his secretary, archivist, deputy (in running their households), caregiver, and later, founder and curator of the Chekhov Museum in Yalta.

Maksim Alekseevich Gorky (1868-1936): Born Maksim Peshkov, the flamboyant Gorky was a playwright, novelist and political activist with Marxist-socialist views. His well-known plays include *The Lower Depths, Summerfolk* and *Enemies.* He greatly admired the later plays of Chekhov, and the two writers developed a friendship. Chekhov encouraged Gorky as a dramatist and became his mentor.

Olga Leonardovna Knipper (1868-1959): Actress and star student of Nemirovich-Danchenko, she was one of the first to be invited to join the ensemble of the newly formed Moscow Art Theatre in

1898. She married Chekhov on May 25, 1901, became the company's leading lady, and starred in all his plays at the Art Theatre. She never remarried after Chekhov's death in 1904.

Nikolai Aleksandrovich Leikin (1841-1906): Editor and publisher of the humorous journal *Fragments*, Leikin gave Anton Chekhov his first "break" as a short story writer and published over two hundred of his stories between 1882 and 1887. Chekhov wrote to Leikin frequently during that period about his development as a writer.

Ivan Leontievich Leontiev-Shcheglov (1856-1911): A contemporary of Chekhov and frequent correspondent, Leontyev-Shcheglov was a short story writer, novelist and playwright.

Lydia Stakhievna Mizinova (1870-1937): A close friend of Masha, Lydia Mizinova fell hopelessly in love with Chekhov in the early 1890s and pursued him eagerly. Frustrated by his evasiveness, she had an affair with his close friend Potapenko, bore him a child, and yet still pursued Chekhov. He borrowed significantly from their relationship for *The Seagull.*

Vladimir Ivanovich Nemirovich-Danchenko (1858-1943): A director, playwright, dramaturg, and teacher, Nemirovich-Danchenko co-founded the Moscow Art Theatre together with Stanislavsky in 1898. The company included Nemirovich's most gifted students, notably Olga Knipper. It was Nemirovich who first recognized Chekhov's gifts as a playwright and enticed him to become involved in their new theatre company.

Aleksei Nikolaevich Pleshcheev (1825-1893): An aristocratic radical, Pleshcheev was part of the Petroshevsky Circle and stood with Dostoevsky before a firing squad (Tsar Nicolas spared them and sent them to a Siberian work camp instead). A writer and poet, Pleshcheev was a mentor of Chekhov, and at the same time critical of Chekhov's work.

Konstantin Sergeevich Stanislavsky (1863-1938): An actor and theatre director from a wealthy merchant family, Stanislavsky (a.k.a. Konstantin Alekseev) founded the Moscow Art Theatre in

1898 with Vladimir Nemirovich-Danchenko. He went on to direct and act Chekhov's four final plays, and, based on this experience, developed a theory of acting that has been disseminated throughout the world by his disciples. He is widely recognized as the first modern stage director in twentieth century drama.

ALEKSEI SERGEEVICH SUVORIN (1834-1912): A wealthy newspaper and book publisher, and editor of the prestigious publication *New Times*, Suvorin became Anton Chekhov's publisher, close friend and mentor. Chekhov held Suvorin in high esteem both as a publisher and a father figure. They maintained a sizeable correspondence between 1885-1898, and Chekhov wrote the majority of his letters about his writing and the theatre to him. Their friendship was permanently ruptured over the Dreyfus affair, over which they held opposing views.

Index

This index includes names of individuals, publications, literary works, theatres, societies, select geographical locations, etc.— any titles associated with Anton Chekhov's life as a writer and a dramatist. Regarding individuals, they include family members, friends, literary figures, theatre artists, contemporaries, and other key figures who participated in (or influenced) his life as a writer and a dramatist. I have indicated occupation (e. g. actor, writer, etc.) and/or relationship to Anton Chekhov (e. g. admirer, friend, etc.). Regarding places, I have included the major ones in Chekhov's life (Taganrog, Moscow, Melikhovo, Yalta).

AUTHOR'S NOTE:

All quotations from the letters and the plays of Anton Chekhov, as well as from the letters and memoirs of others, were translated directly from the original Russian by me.

Regarding the translations of Chekhov's letters, I've remained faithful to their content, grammar and punctuation. Where I've excerpted the letters, it is indicated with "..." within a paragraph, or [...] where a paragraph or more is omitted.

Carol Rocamora
2013